America's Best Day Hikes

AMERICA'S
BEST DAY HIKES

Spectacular Single-Day Hikes Across the States

DEREK DELLINGER

THE COUNTRYMAN PRESS
A division of W. W. Norton & Company
Independent Publishers Since 1923

For information about permission to reproduce selections from this book, write to
Permissions, The Countryman Press, 500 Fifth Avenue, New York, NY 10110

For information about special discounts for bulk purchases, please contact
W. W. Norton Special Sales at specialsales@wwnorton.com or 800-233-4830

Manufacturing by ToppanLeefung
Book design by Anna Reich
Production manager: Devon Zahn

The Countryman Press
www.countrymanpress.com

A division of W. W. Norton & Company, Inc.
500 Fifth Avenue, New York, NY 10110
www.wwnorton.com

978-1-68268-265-4

10 9 8 7 6 5 4 3 2 1

To everyone who works to preserve and protect
the earth's remaining wild places.

CONTENTS

Left: A warped, moon-like landscape surrounds Mount St. Helens

A mossy path crosses near the summit of
Mount LeConte in Tennessee

INTRODUCTION

To introduce a book called "America's Best Day Hikes" is, unavoidably, to address the bold claim that you've identified America's best day hikes. Because that is a very bold claim indeed in a country as vast and varied as the United States. But let's start with this caveat: the title should not be taken too literally. As the author, I can assure you that the book you hold in your hands does not indisputably identify the 50 absolute best day hikes in the United States of America, because such a claim, taken 100 percent literally, would be slightly absurd. There are thousands of incredible hikes in America; thousands of parks and trail systems; and hundreds of thousands of miles of scenic, stunning trail. America is a beautiful and diverse country, containing hundreds of hikes that could have been covered by this book and absolutely warrant the exploration.

But most of us do not have time to explore thousands of miles of trail or hundreds of hikes. I've had the pleasure of writing two installments for Countryman's 50 Hikes series—*50 Hikes in the Upper Hudson Valley* and *50 Hikes in the Catskills*, coauthored with Matthew Cathcart—and this style of regional guide is ideal for those who live in or near that particular region or for adventurers who have the time to spend several weeks dedicated to hiking in that area. But there are so many places in America to see that on any given trip you're only likely to visit a handful of them. And after one such trip I found there really was such a thing as information overload. With only a couple days to hike, I didn't want to have to whittle down my choices from a massive list. I wanted

to know where to start—the quintessential hikes for that area that I *had* to hit while I was there.

That, essentially, is the idea behind *America's Best Day Hikes*. Think of this as a bucket list for American day hikes. The fact that a hike is on this bucket list does not mean there aren't other equally worthy hikes out there or hikes with differing merits, differing reasons they appeal. It simply means that these are hikes every hiker should experience. Most of us will only have a few days to hike while we're traveling, will only be able to hit a couple of trails. And in those areas, you'll want to know—what hikes do I *need* to do? Take Glacier National Park in Montana, which in recent years has surged in popularity. It is a huge park, and there are many miles of backcountry trail where the casual tourists do not wander. If you have a full week or two to explore Glacier, all of that time dedicated to hiking, you will want to explore that backcountry and create your own hiking route based on your own itinerary. But to start, or with only a few days to build your hiking adventures around, there are a few hikes that absolutely hit the "must experience" status. You can't, and shouldn't, visit Glacier without hiking the Highline Trail or visiting the Grinnell Glacier. These are two of the finest day hikes in all of America, and either makes for a fantastic place to start before digging deeper.

Even with this elaboration of what I mean by "Best Day Hikes," naturally, I still must explain how I came to decide on the 50 particular hikes featured in this book. The short answer boils down to lots and lots of research, and some very tough decisions. A year before I began writing the book, I started researching and compiling a list of potential day hike candidates. I sorted through hiking guides from different regions of the country, consulted hundreds of online articles making recommendations for regional and local hikes, and, finally, talked to hikers from all around the country to hear their personal favorites, their bucket list adventures. Some of these hikers were friends, family, or friends of friends, but many were simply strangers who took time out of their day to reply to an email from a random writer who found them on Instagram, and they very generously compiled a list, often with extremely thorough explanations of their recommendations. Many thanks to all of these kind people who helped me make this book happen by sharing their opinions, expertise, and experiences—a full list of their names is found in the acknowledgments section on page 323.

Still, this research resulted in quite a large list. How do you decide on only 50 hikes, spanning the whole of America? And, an even broader question: what *types* of hikes should be included? How long, how difficult, how varied? What kind of terrain and what sort of vistas or views should one focus on for any given region, considering the massive variety of the American landscape? What kind of list of best day hikes would make an adventurer who managed to cover them all feel like they've actually, relatively thoroughly, *seen* America, experienced America: The Landscape?

First, there were the practical considerations. I would have to set limitations to establish boundaries for the type of hike covered in this book, and most of these were fairly straightforward to determine. When I first conceived of the idea for this book, I naturally looked to see what similar books were already out there. Surprisingly, there were none with the specific project of covering the great American day hikes. All other similar titles tended to focus on long-distance treks: famous trails like the Appalachian Trail, the Pacific Crest Trail, or the John Muir Trail. Even the shorter hikes covered in these volumes tended to be multinight backpacking excursions. Given that I wanted this guide to focus on day hikes, this established the first and most obvious limitation: the hikes had to be short enough that the average hiker could accomplish them in a single day.

As for difficulty, I wanted this guide to be accessible to more than just the hardcore hiker, and while few of the hikes in this guide are what could universally be considered "easy," most are accessible to anyone in decent shape, with the proper patience and planning. In some cases I ruled out hikes which I determined were simply too dangerous or too far beyond the ordinary conditions of a day hike. For example, Longs Peak is one of Colorado's most popular summits to tackle and one of the quintessential hikes in Rocky Mountain National Park. However, summiting Longs Peak requires powering through 13 miles and almost 5,000 feet of elevation gain, and hikers generally begin the hike around 3 a.m. to avoid the deadly afternoon thunderstorms that reliably roll in during the summer season. The final stretch of Longs Peak is described by the park as "more of a climb than a hike," and many of the trail's most difficult sections also happen to have sheer drop-offs of several thousand feet. An average of two hikers die on Longs Peak every year.

I had to draw the line on difficulty somewhere, and so I decided that, while Longs Peak is a must-experience for a certain level of adventurer, it was the sort of trail that was beyond the purview of this book. Instead, I chose a hike up to Chasm Lake, a stunningly beautiful alpine lake nestled in a basin below the steep cliff under Long Peak's summit. Chasm Lake is a challenging day hike on its own and every bit worthy of inclusion here, with some of the best views in the park. And you don't need to have absolute confidence in your mountaineering abilities to tackle it.

After this, I realized that the hikes I selected would be featured because they fell, roughly, into one of two categories. For the most part, I wanted to focus on hikes that represented something quintessential about an area—something that captured the feeling, the views, the geology inherent to a region. For example, Mount Rainier is such a defining feature of Washington, a hike somewhere around this towering volcano was a must for this guide. Colorado's fourteeners, the balds of the southern Appalachians, or Utah's unique rock formations—all are perfect settings to experience the defining characteristics of an area via a day hike. But in some cases there are hikes that take you through a landscape that is at contrast with the rest of the world around you, a strange geological quirk in the composition of a region. Michigan's Pictured Rocks National Lakeshore and North Dakota's Theodore Roosevelt National Park scarcely resemble the rest of their respective states, and yet they are essential for this reason too. In a way, by offering such startling contrast, they come to feel just as vital in understanding the landscapes of their region.

Finally, I felt it was important to break this guide down not by state but by region. States are composed of arbitrary borders established for political and economic reasons by humankind. Geography does not give a hoot about state borders—they are made up, imagined designations. Breaking this guide down by region would allow me to pinpoint more exceptional hikes in areas with particularly memorable terrain and, most importantly, would be most true to this concept of exploring America by landscape. In this way, I could feature hikes that highlight the major geological regions of the United States and hit the important features and landmarks, regardless of where they fall along a state border.

There's truly so much more I could say about the landscapes and beauty of the American country, especially now that I've been fortunate enough to witness so much of it in person over the course of writing this book. Before even arriving at the specifics of each hike selected here, I could write whole sections on each region, each mountain range featured, the rich story of our many national parks. In the modern age, as we watch social media reshape the world around us, I think it is important to pause and celebrate the importance of learning more, experiencing more, exploring more. After all, those still curious enough to pick up an in-depth hiking guide in the age of blogs and geotags perhaps understand the value of additional information, and those bold enough to set out on a 13-mile hike over a punishing mountain summit certainly understand the value of exploring deeper—but there is always more to learn, always more to appreciate. Earth is straining under the weight of human civilization, the news seems to grow grimmer with each passing year, and perhaps there will forever be a shortage of those who come to care about preserving our wild lands. Caring for the wilderness cannot, and should not, be the job of just a few backpacking hippies.

My hope is that, in setting out to explore these constructed pathways through our great wilderness areas, in seeing both how grand and how startlingly limited they are, we can arrive at a deeper appreciation of the ways we have affected the world around us. My hope is that more of us will wish to explore those wilderness areas and come to know them better, expand them, and protect them and the world that hosts them. It is startling to observe just how many people view these few still-wild places as little more than an amusement, a ride established and gated off entirely for our enjoyment. To preserve true wilderness, we need to understand the symbiosis between ourselves and nature on a much deeper level than this. And the first step, I believe, is simply to spend more time in nature—surrounded by nature, not in a parking lot overlooking it.

In this sense, this book is a bucket list, a starting guide, in more ways than one. Whether you are an experienced backpacker or a casual weekend hiker, there will be hikes in this guide that you have not experienced, probably have never even heard of, but which are absolutely worth exploring to gain an appreciation for the richness of the American landscape. This book is meant as an introduction not in the sense that it is just for beginning hikers but in that a collection of hikes such as this can only ever be just the beginning. Start here and press on. Just as these are not the only day hikes worth visiting in America, setting out for a day hike is by no means the only way to experience our trails. Conquering an ambitious day hike often inspires an urge to do more, to see more, to feel even more connected to the untamed world. As you explore—however you experience these trails, whatever the time frame or context—consider them in relation to their greater environment. Clearly, we find the beauty of these places to be self-evident. Are we doing all we can to understand and protect the wider world and complicated ecosystems these places represent?

HOW TO USE THIS GUIDE

Imagined as a bucket list or a best of, this guide's hikes can be tackled over the course of a lifetime. Indeed, this is how I conceived of this book being used: as these hikes are scattered many hundreds or thousands of miles from one another, I envision hikers using this book as the foundation for building an ultimate bucket list of American hikes they wish to tackle. My inspiration when conceiving this guide was this: in another part of the country there's probably a hike that is especially beloved, that everyone who lives there knows about and takes for granted, but which I have never heard of simply because I live elsewhere. That hike may seem obvious to those who live in the area, but I might completely overlook that hike because I was sorting through two dozen different trail recommendations from a thousand miles away and could only pick one or two to actually visit.

When traveling, most of us may have time to accomplish several hikes in an area, and with this guide you will have a great starting point for day hikes in almost any part of the country. This guide will give you a glimpse of some of the finest sights the American landscape has to offer. Should you manage to visit every trail in this book, you will feel as if you've enjoyed a thorough tour of the full American landscape.

Here, I must note an absence that you may yourself have picked out if you've gone ahead and skimmed the table of contents: missing from the regions covered in this guide are the far-flung states of Alaska and Hawaii. Earlier, I noted that this guide will be ideal for the average traveler who may only have a few days to hike in a certain area. On the other hand, the classic regional hiking guide comes in handy when you have time to thoroughly explore a place. Few people just casually stop off in Alaska or Hawaii for a day or two—these are locations that you are likely going to visit for an extended period of time due to their remoteness. Therefore, I determined that they did not really fit within the scope or intention of this guide. In the case of Alaska, the state is so large that it could very well be its own country, and so filled with extensive wilderness areas that it could be the subject of several dozen hiking guides. Picking out a handful of day hikes in the state—likely separated from each other by hundreds of miles—seemed a foolish errand.

Which brings me to the final thing I must note

The mountains of the Pacific Northwest are home
to dramatic scenery and unpredictable weather

here: after a year of extensive research, in order to make the final call on which hikes would be included in this guide, I myself drove around the country for four months in the summer and fall of 2018. From July until mid-October, I spent nearly every day hiking, driving, and sleeping in the back of my Toyota Prius. During these four months, I hiked approximately 500 miles of trail and climbed 130,000 feet in elevation gain, or the equivalent of hiking up and down Mount Everest from sea level four and a half times. The hikes featured in this guide do make up a rough loop around the country, which can be tackled in one extended trip, as I myself did. (Of course, along the way, I also hiked many other trails which did not end up in this guide.) While I doubt that many hikers will end up using this book in this way, it is worth noting that smaller road trips can easily be planned to cover different regions—perhaps

a tour of the Pacific Northwest over the course of a week, or a loop of several Southwest states along with Colorado.

A NOTE ON LODGING AND CAMPING

While putting this book together, I spent a significant amount of time thinking about *how* people actually use a hiking guide today. I made the decision that page space was best devoted to information regarding the actual trails rather than the periphery information that you may also require while visiting these areas. I made this call with the belief that a modern travel book should not necessarily have the same focus as a travel guide written in, say, the 1970s. Today, for better or worse, the Internet dictates and guides much of our lives, and it would be foolish to

The Shortoff Mountain hike brings adventurers to the edge of North Carolina's Linville Gorge

ignore the fact that most people will turn to it as the source for most of their information. I believe it is important to consult a book for information on trails where preparation and guidance can be a matter of safety, even life or death. Educating hikers to ensure their well-being and enjoyment while out in the wilderness is the chief goal of a modern hiking guide. On the other hand, while you will still need to find someplace to sleep at night, the reality is that nearly all modern adventurers will simply turn to their phone to plan their lodging.

While I have not included information on campgrounds in most instances, I have noted, in the introductory details for each entry, whether there are campsites available along the route of the hike. Though this guide focuses on day hikes, many of these trails are excellent when enjoyed as overnights. In many areas, particularly national parks, an additional permit may be required for overnight camping.

GPS NAVIGATION TO TRAILHEADS

Another reality of the modern hiker is that most will navigate to a trailhead by typing in the name of the destination into a GPS app. While this is generally the most convenient way to reach a trail, you must be very careful with exactly *what* you type into the search bar. Many times I have thought I was pulling up to the trailhead for a hike, only to realize Google Maps had sent me to a random stretch of the road along the flank of a mountain—because I had only typed in the name of the mountain itself, and the app was simply navigating me to an arbitrary point within the vicinity of that peak, often on the exact wrong side of the mountain. To ensure you arrive at the actual trailhead and not just a random stretch of road, this guide provides "GPS shortcuts" to input

into Google Maps that will take you to the appropriate starting point for your hike.

Most wilderness areas will not have reliable cell reception, and many of the hikes in this book are in remote regions where there may not be reception for miles in any direction. To ensure you do not get lost, download maps for the area ahead of time or bring a paper road atlas for the region along on your trip.

HOW TO PREPARE FOR YOUR HIKE

When hiking in the wild, it is always better to be overprepared than caught off guard, even if it means extra time spent and extra weight carried. Effective planning could, in fact, save your life. Listed below is a set of guidelines that should aid you in your journey both on and off the trail.

Most principles of backcountry safety are based in common sense: stay on the designated trail and be extra cautious when near cliff edges or on slick rocks. Wear appropriate gear, particularly footwear, and watch the weather forecast carefully before setting out. However, there are several other steps you can take to ensure that your trip remains a safe affair.

- Leave your plans with a friend or family member. Let them know when and where you plan to hike as well as what time you expect to be finished. Establish a cutoff time a few hours after you plan to arrive home, and contact them as soon as you can upon returning from the trail. If your safety contact does not hear from you by the cutoff time, this will be a signal that they may need to seek help.

- Make a habit of looking up weather and seasonal information before you set out. It is vital that you know in advance what sort of weather conditions to expect on your hike. Particularly in the shoulder seasons—spring and autumn—the setting sun can sneak up on you, dipping behind a mountain or losing light to the tree canopy much earlier than expected. For this reason, you should always be sure you have a firm grasp of sunrise and sunset times before setting out on your hike, so you can allot plenty of time to make it back to the trailhead.

- Carry both a paper map and a downloaded digital map on your phone. While there is no replacement for a reliable paper map, compass, and a knowledge of wayfinding, there is no denying that modern technology offers a valuable resource as well. A good mapping application on your phone will allow you to determine exactly where on the trail you may be, which can be especially useful if you think you might have made a wrong turn or missed an intersection. However, digital maps and hiking apps should not be relied upon exclusively; technology is fallible and batteries can die just when you need your device the most. Simply carrying a cell phone is not a replacement for ample planning.

WHAT TO BRING ON YOUR HIKE

Many of the hikes featured in this guide are serious excursions that should not be taken lightly; therefore, you'll want to ensure you have all the equipment and clothing necessary for a safe, enjoyable hike.

BACKPACK. A comfortable backpack is a must. While not imperative, packs with hip or chest belts can increase load stability and greatly improve your balance on the trail. Whichever backpack you choose, make sure everything you plan on bringing will comfortably fit inside before you leave for the trailhead.

WATER. In general, you will want to bring about 1 liter of water for every 2 to 3 miles you plan to hike. However, this amount is just a guideline, and you will need to carry more water during hot summer months or when hiking in arid desert conditions. Never drink water directly from a stream or pond, no matter how pristine it may appear. All water must be treated before drinking to remove or kill harmful bacteria and protozoa such as *Giardia*, *E. coli*, and *Salmonella*. A number of options exist, including chemical treatments, filtration systems, or simply boiling water before you drink it. Chemical treatments such as iodine or chlorine dioxide tablets are cheap and lightweight, but they need to work for a minimum of half an hour before the water is safe to drink, and they can leave a foul taste behind. Backcountry water filters are more expensive, bulkier, and heavier, but they deliver immediate results without any impact on the flavor of the water. Many hikes may have water sources along the route, though you should not assume that you will encounter a running stream without first consulting a map—and even then, many water sources can dry up at times during the year.

FOOD. How much food you will need to pack simply depends on how strenuous your route is, as well as your metabolism. Energy and granola bars, dried fruit and nuts, candy bars, and jerky are excellent, highly portable choices that will provide your body with the necessary protein, carbohydrates, and electrolytes it needs to keep you energized and on the trail.

CLOTHING. It is important to stay prepared for any sudden weather changes by bringing along extra layers of clothing. Windy, exposed summits may require you to add layers to stay warm, while the exertion of the climb to these summits will cause you to remove layers to keep cool. The key to staying comfortable is planning for a wide variety of conditions. Choose clothing that is versatile. Wool or synthetic blends insulate well and also breathe, letting moisture evaporate quickly so that your body can regulate its temperature more naturally.

It is a good idea, even in warmer weather, to always bring a long-sleeved shirt or jacket with you. A windbreaker might enable you to extend your visit to a blustery vista, and a rain jacket or poncho will further protect you from less-than-pleasant weather conditions. Bring a hat and gloves if the weather will be cold because your hands and head radiate a significant amount of heat. Lastly, it's always a good idea to bring an extra pair of socks in case your feet become wet.

HIKING POLES. Hiking poles help tremendously in reducing wear and tear on your knees, no matter what your age or level of physical fitness might be. They are also essential in helping to keep your balance on trails with wet rocks or ice. However, on a few select trails with steep sections of climbing and rock scrambling—such as Angels Landing in Utah, Old Rag in Virginia, or the Precipice Trail in Maine—you may wish to leave the hiking poles at home. They are more likely to get in the way than to help you maintain balance.

FIRST AID KIT. Your first aid kit does not need to be extensive, but a few basic items will help alleviate any minor injuries you may sustain on your hike. You can create your own first aid kit out of things commonly found at a drugstore, such as adhesive bandages, gauze, medical tape, alcohol swabs, hand sanitizer, antibiotic ointment, tweezers, moleskin (or other blister-relief material), and over-the-counter pain medication. If you are taking any prescription medication, be sure to pack any doses you would normally take throughout the day as well.

FLASHLIGHT OR HEADLAMP. It is always wise to bring a headlamp or lightweight flashlight along on your hike, even if you're planning on finishing

Glacier's famous Highline Trail

well before dusk. You never know when an innocent error reading the trail map may delay your return to your car by several hours. In spring, fall, and winter especially, nightfall can sneak up on you. If you are forced to make your return to the trailhead in the dark, don't panic. Simply pay close attention to the trail and take extra time to orient yourself at each intersection. A decent headlamp is a relatively inexpensive investment and well worth keeping in your pack at all times.

BEAR SPRAY. Bear spray makes for an effective deterrent against bears in the unlikely case of a bear attack, but it will also work against other threats you may encounter on the trail. Be sure to educate yourself on its use beforehand, so you do not accidentally deploy your bear spray on yourself or your hiking partners.

A NOTE ON DIFFICULTY RATINGS

It is vital to note that a hike can never be given a firm, universal difficulty rating because perceived difficulty will vary between hikers based on their individual fitness and experience levels. This may seem obvious, but I consistently notice that the practice of "ranking" hikes by difficulty will pose issues for some hikers in online hiking databases. Inevitably, after only a few comments, you will encounter someone lamenting that the difficulty rating was inaccurate because they found the hike far more strenuous than expected.

It is important to understand that the difficulty rating a hike receives does not signify how difficult the hike will be for *you*, but how difficult that hike is compared to other hikes. To someone who has never hiked before and is unfamiliar with mountainous terrain, all hikes may feel strenuous—even those ranked

as easy. Before setting out, try to make an honest assessment of your own abilities and experience. A good hiking guide will attempt to offer enough context clues and parameters that you should be able to personalize the given difficulty rating and make adjustments accordingly.

In previous guides, I have relied upon the usual rankings: easy, medium, difficult, very difficult, etc. However, with this guide—given that it covers literally a country's worth of terrain and is therefore extremely varied in the types of trails featured—I have attempted to elaborate upon the usual difficulty ratings to provide guidelines with a bit more nuance. Rather than simply labeling a hike as "Very Difficult" or "Strenuous," I have attempted to briefly explain the specific challenges found along each trail, thereby adding context to what makes it more or less difficult than its peers.

WEATHER

Weather in the mountains is rarely the same as the weather in the surrounding lowland areas, and hikers should prepare to encounter a range of weather extremes when tackling high peaks. Many large mountains can generate their own weather conditions, and in many mountain chains, snow and ice can be encountered nearly all year-round. Under normal circumstances, the temperature drops by roughly 3°F for every 1,000 feet of elevation gain. This can be exacerbated even further by the strong winds often encountered on open summits. Even during the summer, always bring extra layers to stay warm once you reach an exposed vista, especially if you intend to relax there and take in the view. Before you embark on your hike, always check the weather forecast and plan to the best of your ability, but be aware that the conditions may change without warning. In the event of inclement weather or an unexpected storm breaking in the middle of your hike, be prepared to turn around if necessary.

HIGH-ALTITUDE HIKING

Altitude affects everyone differently, but many of the mountains in the American West are of high enough elevation that the altitude is very likely to affect you in some way. Some hikers may feel these effects at elevations as low as 5,000 feet, others between 8,000 and 10,000 feet, and some hikers only upon surpassing 11,000 feet. Whatever the threshold at which you begin to feel the effects of altitude, you should always plan several days to acclimate before attempting to hike up a high-elevation peak. This is especially a concern in states like Colorado, where most of the popular mountain trails begin as high as 10,000 feet and tackling a strenuous "fourteener" is an extremely popular endeavour. Even hikers in otherwise excellent shape traveling here from sea level may find their body balking at the effects of the altitude on such a hike. Some may experience headaches or nausea, or find that their energy reserves have vanished and no second wind appears to push them onward, even after rest breaks. Plan accordingly with extra time in the area to acclimate, and factor in the added difficulty to your estimated hike time.

WINTER HIKING

Covering winter hiking is difficult in a broad, national guide such as this because the challenges you will face while hiking in winter vary drastically between different regions of the country. As a general rule, I do not recommend attempting the majority of the hikes in this guide during winter unless you have prior experience with winter hiking in that region and have utmost confidence that you are prepared

The Tetons, Wyoming

Guadalupe Mountains National Park offers some of the finest hiking in Texas

for its unique challenges. Hiking in the winter can be an exciting undertaking, and outdoor winter activities are the best ways to combat seasonal depression and moderate the doldrums of short days. Even on gray, overcast winter days, an excursion outside can feel refreshing and enlivening. That being said, the risks associated with hiking are significantly intensified during the winter months. In mountainous regions and the northern stretches of the country, winter hiking requires specialized equipment and experience. Even then, hikers should not attempt to hike peaks in regions like the Rocky Mountains in winter as a casual adventure—these massive mountains can transform into a far more threatening foe, one that can easily result in death for the unprepared or unlucky adventurer. Due to the unpredictable and

varied challenges winter hiking poses, this guide assumes that you will be tackling these trails during the warmer months of the year.

For more casual cold weather adventures, you should still be sure to prepare with a checklist of all the equipment and supplies you might need during your outing. Even in early spring and fall, be sure to bring hats, gloves, and multiple layers of clothing. Regulating your body temperature is one of the greatest challenges of cold weather hiking—the exertion of the hike will cause you to heat up quickly, but once you have stopped for a break, the cold will quickly swoop back in to chill you. Without additional clothing to cover up and keep warm, excessive sweat soaking your body brings the threat of hypothermia. Additional items such as gaiters, hand warmers, and a thermos of hot chocolate or coffee will make your hike more comfortable and enjoyable. Snowshoes and poles should be used when snowy conditions are present, and crampons or similar traction devices are generally a must to provide steady footing over ice.

BEAR SAFETY

Many of the hikes in this guide fall within bear country. Black bears still thrive in most of America's forested wilderness areas, though grizzlies are significantly less common. Today, most grizzlies in North America are found in Alaska and Canada. Sadly, many subspecies of grizzly are now extinct because of humans, including the brown bear featured on the state flag of California. Only about 1,500 grizzlies are left in the lower 48 states. Of these, most live in Montana, while several hundred still make their home in the Yellowstone-Teton area of Wyoming. An estimated 70 to 100 grizzly bears live in northern and eastern Idaho, and it is thought that several dozen live in the northern Cascades of Washington, around the Canadian border.

Whenever you are hiking or camping in bear country, it is important to remember that you are sharing their home with them—you are the visitor, the interloper. While you are merely trying to enjoy a relaxing weekend, the bear is trying to survive, fighting for its existence amid the great changes humans are enacting upon its habitat. Wild animals have learned to fear humans, and most animals want a confrontation even less than you do. Always respect the creatures that call the wild their home; protect yourself, and the bears, by taking basic precautions. Most rules of bear safety boil down to a basic principle: do nothing that will unnecessarily attract the attention of bears in the first place. The vast majority of bear attacks that occur on a hiking trail happen because a hiker startled an unsuspecting bear or approached a mother bear and her cubs too closely. A surprised bear will lash out in alarm and fear, while a mother bear that has not had the chance to move her cubs to safety will fight ferociously to protect them. In all cases, the best way to avoid a confrontation with a bear is to make your presence known. Hike in groups of three to four whenever possible; the conversation of a group is usually enough to alert a bear that you're coming. Bear bells can help, though simply clacking your hiking poles together works just as well. Pay attention to the trail ahead; most bear encounters occur when rounding a blind turn, where neither party can see that the other is just down the trail. Be mindful when hiking near running water, as the sound of a loud creek can easily drown out the noise of your approach, even with a bear bell or group conversation.

Despite their fierce appearance, the average bear's diet is largely vegetarian. Bears are omnivorous, and in the wild they live off fruit, nuts, seeds, roots, insects, grasses, and carrion. Plant foods can make up as much as 90 percent of the average black bear's diet. It is important to realize that bears, while powerful and imposing creatures, are nonetheless scavengers much more than they are hunters. This is especially true of the black bears residing in the more populated regions of the country. These bears have had many years to adjust to life on the periphery of human society. Bears are extremely intelligent creatures. They will learn to associate humans with food and devise creative ways to scavenge food from mankind's waste and carelessness. Any food made available to them by lazy or unmindful humans will be happily set upon and consumed, whether in a suburb on the fringes of the bear's habitat or a heavily trafficked campground in the backwoods. If searching a certain location or repeating a certain activity results in food, a bear will attempt to re-create this scenario again in the future. Thus, food left out around a campsite, in close proximity to humans, becomes dangerous for both the bear and the humans. Likewise, if a bear encounters a human and does not acquire any food as a result of the encounter, the bear will have no reason to seek out humans again in the future. For this reason, many national parks require campers to lock their food away in either their vehicle or a specialized bear box at all times unless it is being actively cooked or eaten by the campers. In Yosemite, even storing your food in your car is not enough; bears will simply attempt to break into it. Here, anything with a discernible odor—food as well as hygienic products—must always be stored in the locked bear-proof boxes that are set up around every campsite.

If you do spot a bear, never run. Back away slowly, speaking in a low, calm voice to ensure that the bear recognizes you as a human and not a prey animal. Make sure the bear has a clear route to flee the encounter—a bear that feels trapped is likely to behave more aggressively. Do not scream or shriek. If the bear stands up on its hind legs, it is most likely just trying to get a better sense of the situation, not issuing a threat. Some bears will bluff charge as if they are going to attack but will veer off or stop at the last minute. While this situation is obviously frightening, remember that, even then, you should never run.

It is always a good idea to carry bear spray with you on your hike, especially when hiking out west. Be sure to familiarize yourself with the usage of your bear spray to avoid accidentally or incorrectly discharging it. Used improperly, you may waste your bear spray before the bear is within effective range or miss altogether. In the worst case, you may even end up immobilizing yourself with the spring, creating a far worse situation.

It is not uncommon to see a bear in many parts of the country—I saw about a dozen bears while hiking to research this book. Grizzly bears have a reputation for being far more dangerous than black bears, and while this is true in the abstract, there are also far more black bears than there are grizzlies, and thus an encounter with a black bear is far more likely. The most frightening bear encounter I have experienced thus far was in the area where I hike the most, in the Hudson Valley's Catskill Mountains. Regardless, an actual bear attack is unlikely and should not deter you from exploring America's beautiful wilderness areas. Preparedness and knowledge are always the best methods for ensuring your safety in the backwoods, and bear safety should never be taken lightly. When it comes to hiking, it is always better to be overprepared than underprepared. If a bear does engage with you, drop to the ground and lie flat on your stomach with your legs spread apart slightly. Keep your pack on to protect your back, and cover the back of your neck with your hands. Attempt to play dead until the bear ceases its attack and leaves the scene.

OTHER WILDLIFE

Bears may represent the most dramatic danger in the backwoods, but there are many other animals that you are even more likely to encounter, and most of them can be just as dangerous as a bear. Animals like mountain goats may appear cute and harmless, but it is this nonthreatening appearance that leads to many dangerous situations, as humans underestimate these animals and allow the animals to associate them with food. This intimacy is dangerous: the animals lose their fear of humans and may eventually become aggressive if they begin to see humans as nothing more than a harbinger of snacks or salt. Hikers encountering mountain goats will often get far too close to these animals for the purpose of snapping a selfie and occasionally will feed the animal or allow the creature to lick salt off of their person or their backpack. It may seem frivolous to be so concerned about letting an animal lick the sweat from your bag, but many animals desperately crave salt, which cannot easily be found in their natural habitat. Adorable though mountain goats may be, they can weigh as much (or more) than a human—and they have large, sharp spikes poking out of their skulls. Hikers have died as a result of mountain goat attacks.

Perhaps the most dangerous animals you are likely to encounter in our nation's great parks are bison and elk. Like mountain goats, these animals may not seem especially threatening, but this causes many tourists and hikers to approach much too close to these creatures, provoking them into attacking. In Yellowstone National Park, bison have injured more people than any other animal. Bison are unpredictable creatures and can run three times faster than humans. Both bison and elk are also significantly larger and heavier than you are. By far the most intimidating wildlife encounter I had while hiking to research this book was with a bison in North Dakota's Theodore Roosevelt National Park.

Rattlesnakes are a potential danger in many parts of the country. Rattlesnakes are usually not aggressive but will strike when threatened or deliberately provoked. If you encounter a rattlesnake, give it plenty of room and allow the snake to retreat. Most snakebites happen because a rattlesnake was accidentally touched by someone walking or climbing, or purposeful handling it—which, of course, you should never do.

Mountain lions—also known as pumas, cougars, or catamounts—are fierce, stealthy, and rarely seen predators. Few hikers will ever catch a glimpse of a mountain lion in their lifetime, no matter how often they hit the trails. Mountain lions generally will avoid contact with a human if at all possible, and thus the chance of being attacked by one of these shy creatures is very small.

In the small chance that you do encounter a mountain lion, make yourself appear as large as possible by opening your jacket and raising your arms. Throw stones or branches, but do not turn away from the animal. You should never run from a mountain lion. Running will trigger the animal's natural instinct to pursue fleeing prey. Pick up small children without turning away from the animal or bending over. You should never bend over or crouch down, because this will cause you to resemble a four-legged prey animal. Try to remain standing to protect your head and neck and, if the animal does attack, fight back with whatever is at hand.

No matter where you are—in the backwoods, miles from any other human, or merely on the lawn of a busy lodge inside a national park—always keep a safe distance from wildlife. Most parks dictate that you keep at least 100 feet from all wild animals, and it is good to abide by this rule at all times, on and off the trail.

TRAIL ETIQUETTE

The subject of trail etiquette is mostly concerned with preserving the serene quality of the woods for others to enjoy, both immediately and in the future. Do your best to be courteous to those sharing the trails with you. Everyone hikes at a different pace, so let others pass if they wish to go faster and yield to hikers coming downhill, especially when the trail is steep and narrow. If you are hiking in a group, try to keep your noise level low so that others may enjoy the peacefulness of the forest.

It is extremely important to remain on designated trails in order to minimize erosion and preserve the delicate flora that inhabits the mountains. Lastly, follow Leave No Trace principles and pack out anything you pack in. If you have the pack space, carry out any trash that may have been left behind by others. Never create a campfire except in an existing, designated site. It is the responsibility of everyone to ensure that the wilderness remains pristine for future generations to enjoy.

AMERICA'S BEST DAY HIKES

© The Countryman Press

1. Chain Lakes Loop
2. Burroughs Mountain Loop Trail
3. Mount Ellinor
4. Harry's Ridge
5. Tom Dick and Harry Mountain
6. Green Lakes Trail
7. Mount Scott
8. Black Butte
9. Miners Ridge and James Irvine Trail Loop
10. Sierra Buttes Lookout
11. Clouds Rest from Tenaya Lake
12. Fisher Towers
13. Peek-A-Boo Loop
14. Angels Landing
15. Humphreys Peak
16. South Kaibab Trail to Cedar Ridge
17. Alkali Flat Trail
18. Pine Tree Trail
19. Devil's Hall
20. Guadalupe Peak
21. Ice Lake Basin and Island Lake
22. High Dune and Star Dune
23. Mount Bierstadt
24. Chasm Lake
25. Dunraven Pass to Mount Washburn
26. Cascade Canyon Trail from Jenny Lake
27. Iron Creek to Sawtooth Lake
28. Grinnell Glacier Trail
29. Highline Trail
30. Blodgett Canyon Overlook
31. Elk Mountain
32. Black Elk Peak
33. Caprock Coulee Loop
34. Devil's Lake Loop
35. Chapel Trail Mosquito Falls Loop
36. Old Man's Cave
37. Whitaker Point (Hawksbill Crag)
38. Gray's Arch
39. Alum Cave and Mount LeConte
40. Carver's Gap to Grassy Ridge Bald
41. Shortoff Mountain
42. Bear Rocks to Raven Ridge
43. Old Rag
44. Ricketts Glen Falls Loop
45. Bonticou Crag and Table Rocks Loop
46. Giant Mountain
47. Mount Mansfield
48. Franconia Ridge Loop
49. Precipice Trail
50. Katahdin Knife Edge Loop

NORTHWEST

CHAIN LAKES LOOP

Washington: Mount Baker National Forest

DISTANCE: 6.5 miles

ELEVATION GAIN: 1,850 feet

TIME COMMITMENT: 4 to 5 hours

FEE: Northwest Forest Pass or Interagency Pass

DOGS: Permitted

CAMPING ALONG TRAIL: Yes

DIFFICULTY: Strenuous hike up to a saddle, followed by a difficult descent into a valley where the trail is often covered in snow through much of the summer.

Left: Mount Baker rises majestically behind the Chain Lakes

There isn't really such a thing as a definitive "best" hike for any area, of course. But when first exploring a new part of the country, there are certain hikes which are *obvious* and can't be missed because they offer such a perfect encapsulation of the natural beauty in that area. Perhaps, after this initial exploring, you will wish to find trails that offer a focus on some specific natural feature (lakes, waterfalls, looming mountain summits) or a particular kind of experience (rock scrambles, peaceful forest strolls, strenuous summiting). But to start you will want to find a hike that has a little bit of everything, a taste of what a region is like.

The Chain Lakes Loop isn't just an ideal "taste of the North Cascades" hike—it gets my vote for one of the most beautiful hikes in the country, period. Of course, northern Washington itself is a paradise for outdoor explorers and landscape photographers, with turquoise glacial lakes, craggy mountain chains rising in all directions, alpine meadows bursting with vibrant summer flowers, snow-capped volcanic peaks, and towering conifers. You'll find all of these along the 6.5 miles of the Chain Lakes Loop. The lakes themselves—Iceberg, Hayes, Arbuthnet, and Mazama— are picture-perfect, especially when viewed from Herman Saddle, looking down upon them with Mount Baker rising just behind. With an optional extra mile loop around Hayes Lake, hikers can choose to extend their hike or even make an overnight out of this adventure. Several spots for primitive camping can be found along the trail.

This loop traverses far-north terrain at high elevation; snowfields here often persist late into summer and some years may even remain year-round. When I visited in late July, I found myself descending a large, fairly steep snowfield from Herman Saddle to Galena Lake, with several more smaller but still tricky snowfields below Table Mountain. The snow added to the challenge of the hike but also the isolation: every other hiker had turned around on the saddle, and I found myself enjoying blissful sol-

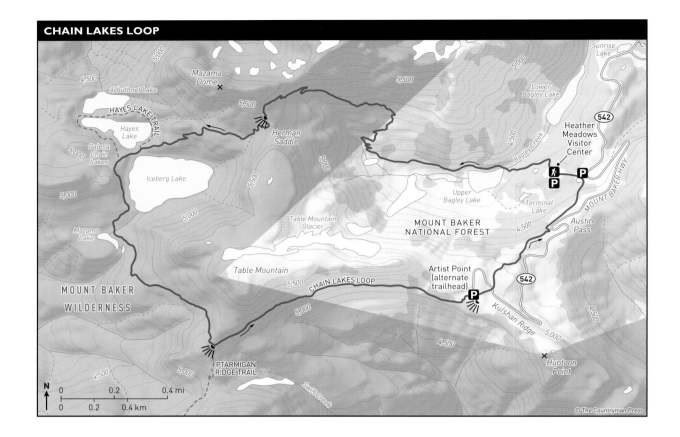

itude in one of the most scenic places I've ever visited. However, this loop is versatile in its options—another factor making it particularly ideal. By starting from the Heather Meadows parking area, one can hike up to Herman Saddle, enjoy views of the lakes, and from there choose to simply turn around and hike back down if the conditions ahead prove to be too intimidating. Since one can drive to Artist Point itself, hikers may then choose to explore this area from the Artist Point parking area rather than hiking to it and reaching it at the end of their loop.

TRAIL OVERVIEW

From the Heather Meadows Visitor Center parking area, find the trail just to the left of the path to the visitor center. Hike down over the large rock slabs, and soon you will come to an intersection. Keep left.

At 0.3 mile descend to the edge of a small lake and cross two small, stone arch bridges, then turn left. Cross a narrow section of trail across a rocky area. At 0.7 mile you will enter a boulder field. Switchback uphill, and at 1 mile you will pass a sign notifying you that you have entered the Mount Baker Wilderness.

Soon you will cross an area with several streams before the trail returns to the boulder field. At 1.5 miles you will leave the boulder field and begin hiking steadily up Herman Saddle. Soon Mount Baker will rise above the saddle before you, and its snowy summit will dominate the horizon for much of the rest of the hike.

At 2.1 miles you will reach the ridgetop. Here, you may encounter large snowfields on the slopes before you descend toward Iceberg Lake. Those without experience hiking in such conditions may wish to turn back here and retrace their steps the way they came.

Descend as the trail weaves toward the lakes, until at 2.8 miles you reach an overlook of the lake where the side trail splits to loop around Hayes Lake and Galena camps. This optional loop around Hayes Lake adds an additional mile to the hike. If not taking this loop, continue straight, and at 3.25 miles you will reach the far end of Iceberg Lake.

Continue from Iceberg Lake, and in a short distance you will hike by Lake Mazama, where there are more backcountry campsites. Soon after, you will pass a large glacial valley facing Mount Baker. Then, after a short, steep climb, you'll reach a crest with a dramatic view south toward Baker. Here, the Ptarmigan Ridge Trail splits to your right, traveling south. Keep left, following the trail that skirts the underside of Table Mountain along a steep slope. Mount Shuksan appears before you, and here the trail offers stunning views of both high mountains, one before and one behind you.

At 5.1 miles you reenter woods, and soon after, you will approach Artist Point. Cross the large parking lot and find the trail heading downhill by the bathroom facilities. The trail descends before cutting across the road once more, then across an open expanse toward rocks where cairns mark your path. Continue alongside the road until the trail brings you out to the Heather Meadows parking area.

PLANNING

This route begins from the Heather Meadows Visitor Center parking area, rather than the larger and more popular Artist Point parking area. This makes it easier to turn back after the Upper Wild Goose Trail brings

you to Herman Saddle, with views to Mount Baker and the lakes below. From this point, the trail can be very difficult, descending down to the lakes and covered in thick, slushy snowfields through much of the summer. This, of course, will vary by the year and the month, or even the week. However, it is not uncommon to encounter significant snowfields at various portions of this hike into August, and hikers are not advised to attempt this trail when there might be snow without, at minimum, hiking poles for balance and previous experience hiking in snowy conditions. Early in the summer, microspikes or snowshoes may also be necessary when hiking some portions of this trail.

GETTING THERE

The trailhead can be found on Google Maps by navigating to "Chain Lakes Trailhead" or "Heather Meadows Visitor Center." The parking area is located 1 mile up the Mount Baker Highway from the Mount Baker Ski Area.

BURROUGHS MOUNTAIN LOOP TRAIL

Washington: Mount Rainier National Park

DISTANCE: 5.2 miles

ELEVATION GAIN: 1,050 feet

TIME COMMITMENT: 3 to 4 hours

FEE: National Parks Pass or entrance fee

DOGS: Not permitted

CAMPING ALONG TRAIL: Yes

DIFFICULTY: Moderate difficulty, but with sections of steep, dizzying drop-offs that may intimidate those with a strong fear of heights.

On your way to begin the Burroughs Mountain Loop Trail, you'll encounter the first jaw-dropping viewpoint 2½ miles before you even reach the trailhead. Sunrise Point, perched on the eastern flank of Mount Rainier on the Sourdough Ridge, is aptly named—if you can manage to get here by dawn, you'll be rewarded with nearly 360-degree views of the surrounding peaks, including the looming summit of Rainier itself, seemingly close enough to touch. Of course, while Sunrise Point sits about 3,000 feet above the White River below you, Mount Rainier itself, at 14,411 feet in height, is almost another 10,000 feet higher in elevation. This staggeringly giant stratovolcano will loom over you for the entirety of your hike, but Sunrise Point makes for a good initiation to these massive views.

Continue up Sourdough Ridge and soon you will arrive at the Sunrise Day Lodge and Visitor Center parking area, where your hike begins. The parking lot here is huge but nonetheless fills up quickly; this is one of the most popular locations in the park. A number of trails begin here, but of all your options to explore the area from Sunrise, the Burroughs Mountain Loop offers perhaps the best opportunity to sample the diverse scenery on this dramatic shoulder of Rainier. Of note, the loop described here does not actually summit Burroughs Mountain but passes below the peak before looping back along the edge of a steep valley. Adventurous hikers willing to take the spur trail and scramble up Burroughs Mountain itself will find themselves on the highest maintained nonmountaineering hiking trail in the park.

The views along this moderately difficult trail include much more than just Mount Rainier: there are steep ridgeline drop-offs into sheer valleys, tranquil forests of silver fir, an alpine lake (the aptly named Frozen Lake),

Left: The Sunrise area is gorgeous at dawn

and a crest of tundra-esque alpine landscape, home to families of mountain goats. I have hiked here on several visits to the Pacific Northwest and will almost certainly return any time I'm back in the area. On my last visit, I arrived at Sunrise Point at dawn and witnessed one of the most beautiful mornings I will likely ever experience in my life. Fleeting cloud formations whipped through the valleys below and danced over mountain slopes, all illuminated by purple dawn light. On a dramatic cloudy morning, alone on the trail, slightly sleep deprived from the crucial early dawn start, the beauty of this area reached a dreamlike quality.

TRAIL OVERVIEW

From the parking area, walk past the Sunrise Day Lodge and up the pedestrian roadway. Walk up this asphalt path, and the trail will start to your right. You will soon come to an intersection; keep left. At the next intersection, shortly after, keep left once again.

A little less than half a mile onto the trail, you will come to a ridge that drops off steeply into a valley before you. The views here are quite nice, but be careful not to get too close to the edge. Soon after, at 0.7 mile, you will come to a second, similar cliff-like drop-off with more stunning views.

At 0.9 mile you will hike along an exposed rocky ridge. Soon after, you will come to Frozen Lake, where large shelves of snow and ice can be glimpsed jutting out over the blue waters of the lake well into summer. This lake serves as a water supply, and hikers should never stray off trail here.

Keep right at the intersection at 1.3 miles. Then, soon after, you will arrive at a five-way intersection. Follow the sign for the Burroughs Mountain Trail, which veers to the left.

After this you will begin to climb steeply up a rocky alpine crest. Keep an eye out—several families of mountain goats live in this area. At 2.1 miles you will reach the top of the ridge, with Rainier rising up, massive, seemingly just ahead of you. A short distance ahead, at 2.3 miles, turn left onto the Sunrise Rim Trail. The trail that turns right at this intersection is a spur trail which can be taken to the summit of Burroughs Mountain itself.

At 2.7 miles you will begin to descend into a valley, with sheer, steep drops to your right. The narrow trail hugs this precarious drop for the

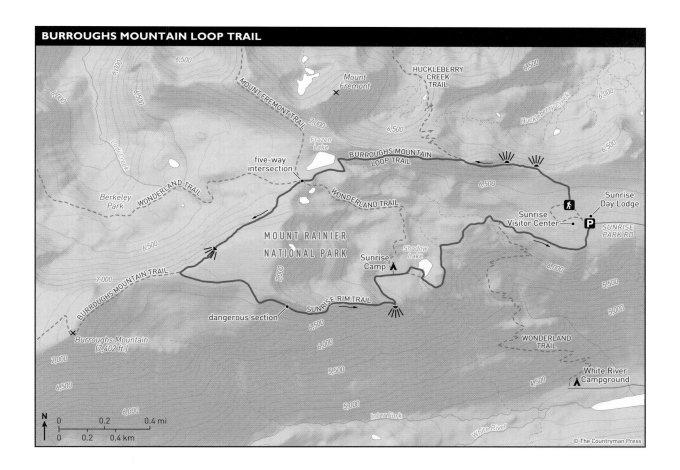

next third of a mile—this section is certainly not for those unsteady on their feet or with an extreme fear of heights, given that some sections pass spots where the earth is made up of nothing but loose shale. Needless to say, be especially cautious while hiking here.

After this dizzying section of trail levels out, continue for another third of a mile to a stone lookout terrace. From here, the trail descends toward Shadow Lake. At 3.7 miles you will come to an intersection for Sunrise Camp. Keep straight. Just after this you will pass a trail to your left, which takes a short circuit toward the edge of Shadow Lake. This side trail returns to the main trail after a short distance, where a wooden bridge crosses a stream.

At 4.2 miles the trail passes around a large meadow, and at 4.5 miles

you will traverse another wooden bridge. Just after this, stay straight on the Sunrise Rim Trail at the intersection.

At 5 miles turn left at the intersection and head toward Sunrise. Soon after, you will return to the large parking area on the opposite side of the lot from which you started.

The Sunrise Visitor Center at the Sourdough Ridge Trailhead

PLANNING

There is very little shade along some sections of this hike. Hikers should make sure to bring plenty of water, as well as sunscreen and a hat. Snow may persist on and around the trail well into summer, so hikers should research trail conditions ahead of time and bring traction devices such as microspikes if required.

The trail is very popular, as are all the trails in the Sunrise area. The Sunrise Visitor Center is open daily from early July to early September and closes for the winter. At the visitor center, you will find exhibits, guided interpretive programs, and books for sale. Across the lot, the Sunrise Day Lodge is open from early July to late September and offers food service and an extensive gift shop. However, despite the name, there is no overnight lodging at the Sunrise Day Lodge.

GETTING THERE

The trailhead can be found on Google Maps by navigating to "Sunrise Visitor Center." The parking area is located at the end of Sunrise Park Road.

MOUNT ELLINOR

Washington: Olympic National Forest

DISTANCE: 3.8 miles

ELEVATION GAIN: 2,360 feet

TIME COMMITMENT: 3 to 6 hours

FEE: Northwest Forest Pass or Interagency Pass

DOGS: Permitted

CAMPING ALONG TRAIL: No

DIFFICULTY: While the mileage is short, this only serves to compact this hike's considerable elevation gain into a very intense stretch of trail with significant exposure. Only hikers confident in their abilities should attempt this hike.

Left: Mount Ellinor offers exceptional views of Lake Cushman and southern Washington

The Olympic peninsula may not be known for the commanding volcanic peaks that dominate the rest of the Pacific Northwest, but the climb to the summit of 5,950-foot Mount Ellinor is so strenuous that you will feel like you've tackled a mountain twice its height. The experience feels like a true mountain summit as well: Ellinor's rocky crown boasts large spires and jagged ridges, with massive views down toward Lake Cushman. From the summit, you will be rewarded for your efforts with glimpses into the heart of the Olympic Range. To the northwest, Mount Olympus itself rises above the rest, unmistakable in its snow-capped beauty. Mount Washington and Mount Pershing are visible to the northeast, and on a clear day you might even glimpse Mount Baker, some hundred miles to the northeast.

To earn this mountain-summit feel, however, you'll really have to work: the trail climbs steadily for nearly the entire duration, and the last mile is a serious workout. Much of the second half of the hike chugs uphill without much in the way of shade, so hikers should be prepared with sunscreen and plenty of drinking water. With several hidden switchbacks and turns obscuring your goal, it can be hard to tell how close you are to the true summit, and thus frustrating, when the trail seems to go on and on despite its relatively short total length.

Hikers should also watch for mountain goats toward the upper reaches of the mountain. While these goats will often thoughtfully pose on rocks, making for ideal picture opportunities, you should never approach within 100 feet of wildlife. (A sign at the trailhead suggests that goats should always be distant enough that you can hold up your thumb and "cover" them from sight.) Goats and other forms of wildlife crave the salt that you produce when you sweat—which you will be doing plenty of on this hike—and will try to lick this salt off your bag and even your person. Hikers have been known to encourage this behavior in order to stage a photo, but this is not only prohibited but dangerous. Hikers often see animals like goats as cute and harmless, but even a charming mountain goat can be deadly, especially when habituated to human contact. An animal that begins to associate humans with food—or salt—can become aggressive

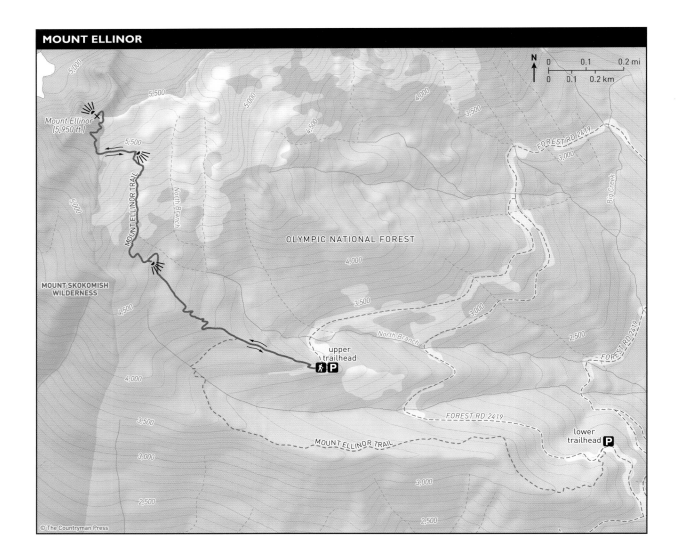

over time, and even seemingly innocent animals like goats have caused hiker deaths in the past.

TRAIL OVERVIEW

The trail immediately begins heading uphill through a grand forest of towering old-growth forest. Hike up a "spine" of earth that drops off steeply on either side of you. At 0.7 mile the trail begins to wind up wooden stairs set into the earth, and soon after you will pass a viewpoint to your left.

More viewpoints from rocky outcrops will open up as you continue, and in a short distance the trail momentarily leaves the tree cover, showcasing the best view of the hike thus far. At 1.2 miles you will begin to hike across a boulder field.

From this point, the rest of the hike is a rugged haul up a steep trail with little tree cover to offer shade. In the heat of summer, this stretch can be quite exhausting, and hikers should ensure they have plenty of water before tackling this climb.

Be on the lookout for mountain goats on your way up; they are frequently seen on the slopes below the summit.

After a long slog up a straight, steep section of the trail, you will reach a crest where the path turns sharply to the right. Several more steep switchbacks follow, with the true summit lingering tantalizingly just out of sight. Finally, at 1.7 miles, you will hike around the rocky summit. Look for a faint trail around the rocks leading to the true summit, where you will enjoy excellent views down to Lake Cushman and Hood Canal, and to the northwest, where Mount Olympus itself dominates the heart of the Olympics.

PLANNING

There are two trailheads from which you can begin your hike. If the road is dry, both trailheads can be accessed, even by low-clearance vehicles. The lower trailhead begins at 2,600 feet elevation and eases you into the hike with an easier grade. The route described in this guide begins from the upper trailhead at 3,500 feet and throws you into the hike with a climb that is steep from the onset.

A Northwest Forest Pass or Interagency Pass is required for parking at the upper trailhead, though hikers do not need one to access Mount Ellinor from the lower trailhead. The upper trailhead is the more popular of the two and, being a relatively small lot, fills quickly.

Much of this hike is exposed, and because this is an extremely strenuous climb to begin with, be sure to pack sunscreen, protective clothing, and plenty of water.

GETTING THERE

The trailhead can be found on Google Maps by navigating to "Mount Ellinor Upper Trailhead." The parking area is on Forest Road 2419, off WA-119 N, about 24 miles north of Skokomish, Washington.

HARRY'S RIDGE

Washington: Mount St. Helens
National Volcanic Monument

DISTANCE: 7.6 miles

ELEVATION GAIN: 1,450 feet

TIME COMMITMENT: 3 to 4 hours

FEE: National Park Pass or fee

DOGS: Not permitted

CAMPING ALONG TRAIL: Yes

DIFFICULTY: Moderate trail, though made more challenging on sunny, warm days by the lack of shade along the route.

Earlier in this guide I mentioned that the hikes I selected to be featured here tend to fall into two categories: hikes that seem to capture the essence of an area, and hikes that feel so distinct and singular that they simply must be experienced. The trail to Harry's Ridge, overlooking Mount St. Helens, perfectly captures how this second type of hike can still feel vital in representing a region. The devastated landscape around the volcano may resemble that of an alien planet much more than the rest of Washington State, but this is nonetheless an essential experience, a hike like no other.

Open May through October, the Johnston Ridge Observatory hosts interpretive displays, films, and talks that explain the biological, geological, and human story of Mount St. Helens. Stop in to the observatory before or after your hike to enjoy documentary films, listen to ranger talks, or purchase souvenirs. The hike to Harry's Ridge begins from the observatory itself, first setting out up one of the area's numerous small, exposed ridge lines on a paved path. While the full length of this hike nears 8 miles, there are few spots where you will be required to do any strenuous climbing, making this an ideal excursion for hikers of all skill levels. Keep in mind, however, that this terrain more closely resembles that of a desert than the rest of western Washington, as it will be many years before forests reclaim these ridges. As such, this hike is especially exposed, and the sun's rays can be quite brutal in summer. Be sure to pack sunscreen and plenty of water.

Incredible views of the blast crater begin starting from the pathways around the observatory itself and continue throughout the rest of the hike. Here, examining the slouched, truncated form of Mount St. Helens up close, one can marvel at the tremendous power behind the eruption, the staggering force required to literally blow off the top of an entire mountain. Beyond the lava dome and crater you will be able to observe the pumice plain and landslide deposits while overlooking the surround-

Left: Spirit Lake, with Mount Adams in the background

ing hillsides, still demonstrating nature's long recovery process in this stricken, ashen soil.

Harry's Ridge, the destination of your hike, was named for a local who refused to leave his homestead when the mountain was about to erupt. Note on your hike whether there is smoke rising from the crater. If you spot small wisps of smoke or steam, this is no cause for alarm. Though the eruption occurred decades ago, Helens remains restless and belches smoke from her crater periodically.

TRAIL OVERVIEW

From the observatory, take the asphalt path uphill, where a short, self-guided trail heads across the ridge. After 0.4 mile the asphalt trail turns left to head back to the parking area. Turn right onto the dirt path and hike along the ridge, with Mount St. Helens, cratered north side rising before you.

At 1.5 miles hike along a small dusty ridge, then at 1.8 miles keep left where the trail splits around the base of the next ridge. Soon after, the trail descends, and at 2.2 miles the Devil's Elbow Trail joins up to the trail from your right. Keep left, and in a short distance you will pass an intersection with the Truman Trail to your right. Stay straight.

At 2.6 miles you will reach an open area and begin to hike uphill toward the next ridge. In a little less than half a mile, you will arrive at a metal and wood bridge that crosses over a small eroded ravine.

At 3.6 miles turn right at the intersection and head up the ridge. Climb steadily for a quarter mile, and then you will arrive at Harry's Point, the crest of the ridge, with stunning views of Mount St. Helens directly ahead of you and Mount Adams to your left, across Spirit Lake. From here you can continue down the ridge for another half a mile if desired, with some additional elevation gain required when returning to Harry's Point. Otherwise, this is a good area to rest and enjoy a lunch. When you are ready to return, retrace your steps back to your car.

PLANNING

The Northwest Forest Pass and the Interagency America the Beautiful Pass are both accepted here; otherwise, you will have to pay an entrance fee.

The trail to Harry's Ridge meanders through an exposed, arid environment still warped by the volcanic blast. There is no shade on this trail,

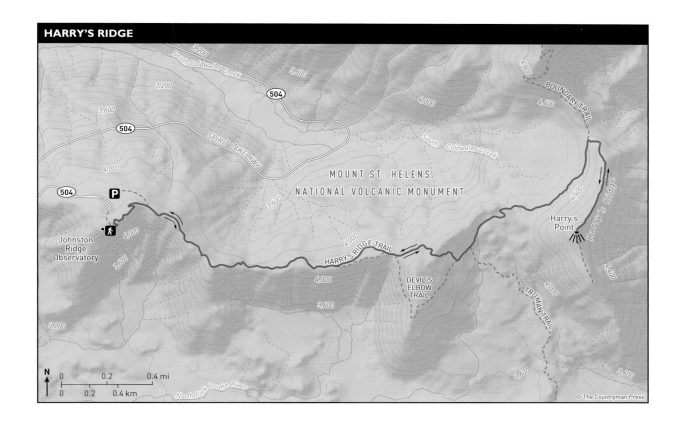

and on hot summer days an early morning or late afternoon hike is recommended. Hikers should bring plenty of water, a hat, sunglasses, and sunscreen. Water is available at the Johnston Ridge Observatory next to the trailhead.

GETTING THERE

The trailhead can be found on Google Maps by navigating to "Johnston Ridge Observatory." The parking area is located at the end of Spirit Lake Highway.

TOM DICK AND HARRY MOUNTAIN

Oregon: Mount Hood National Forest

DISTANCE: 7.8 miles

ELEVATION GAIN: 1,700 feet

TIME COMMITMENT: 4 to 5 hours

FEE: Northwest Forest Pass or Interagency Pass

DOGS: Permitted on leash

CAMPING ALONG TRAIL: Yes

DIFFICULTY: Moderate elevation gain with short sections of rocky, rugged trail.

Left: Mirror Pond is a popular spot due to its stunning framing of Mount Hood

Even with the most popular hikes, there's usually a way to dodge the crowds. Starting early is a foolproof method—trails that can feel like an amusement park in the afternoon are often completely empty for the first few hours after sunrise. But many times a trail to a popular destination simply offers more than most are willing to work for. Just west of Mount Hood's Government Camp, the busy trailhead to Mirror Lake sees many families and casual hikers setting out to spend a few hours at this beautiful lake, picnicking, swimming, and snapping photos of Mount Hood's perfect reflection in the waters of Mirror Lake. While Mirror Lake is certainly worth a visit, few hikers continue on from the lake to Tom Dick and Harry Mountain, where the views get even better.

Hiking another mile and a half from Mirror Lake, you will be rewarded with elevated views of Mount Hood from a ridge of loose rocks, a beautiful perspective of Mirror Lake nestled below and Mount Jefferson to the south. Government Camp is easily visible in the near distance, and if you look carefully you will spot Timberline Lodge on the slopes of the mountain. On a clear day, Mounts Rainier, St. Helens, and Adams may also be visible, making this one of the best viewpoints in Oregon for volcano spotting. While this viewpoint area is actually not the summit of Tom Dick and Harry Mountain, few hikers continue past this spot. Tom Dick and Harry has three distinct peaks, which together form a cirque that is now part of the Mount Hood Skibowl ski resort. The three peaks of the mountain inspired the name, referencing an old phrase used to designate any three generic persons—"any Tom, Dick, or Harry." The rocks of this ridge make for tricky footing, and hikers should be extremely careful as they explore here. Beyond the ridge, the half mile of trail to the true

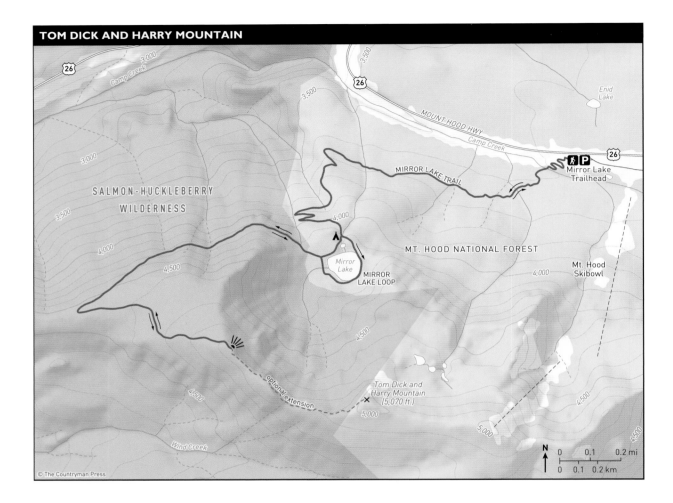

summit is rugged and rough, and for most hikers the views from the first open ridge are satisfying enough.

On the hike back down, it's recommended to add the short loop around Mirror Lake, a perfect spot for an additional rest break or a long lunch break. Several primitive campsites can be found near Mirror Lake for those looking to turn their excursion into an overnight camping trip.

TRAIL OVERVIEW

A short distance from the trailhead, the trail begins to switchback uphill. You will cross over Camp Creek at 0.25 miles, then again at 0.5 miles.

The trail heads west following a gentle incline, before intersecting with the old Mirror Pond trail, which was closed in 2018. After this, the trail will begin to climb in elevation more quickly, and soon you will tackle a series of steeper switchbacks. At the 2 mile mark, you will pass a sign indicating a designated area for primitive campsites to your right. To your left, the Mirror Lake loop trail heads into the woods. This side trail can be taken on the way up or the way down, and it adds only about half a mile to the length of your hike. The best views are found at the far side of the lake, where, as its name suggests, Mount Hood can usually be seen in a tranquil reflection off the waters of the lake.

If saving the loop for later or skipping it, stay straight, following the signs for Tom Dick and Harry. Keep right at the fork at 2.2 miles. A little less than half a mile later, the trail narrows as it crosses over a steep rock slide, with berry bushes growing tenaciously from the rocks around the trail. Look over your shoulder and you will find Mount Hood rising at your back.

At 3.2 miles you will reach a massive, igloo-shaped rock cairn indicating the sharp turn made by the trail here. The path cuts sharply to the left, and in another quarter mile, it will begin a moderate uphill climb.

At 3.8 miles you will reach an open rock ridge formed of loose scree, with open views down to Mirror Lake, Mount Hood framed perfectly behind it, and Mount Jefferson to the south. The scree here can make for difficult footing—be very careful of each step so that you don't end up with a sprained ankle. While this is not the true summit of Tom Dick and Harry Mountain, the ridge is somewhat tedious to cross and offers perhaps the best views of the hike. Most hikers simply enjoy the views from here and do not continue along the rock scramble to the summit.

PLANNING

The Northwest Forest Pass and the Interagency America the Beautiful Pass are both accepted here. This hike is extremely popular on summer weekends and the parking lot fills quickly.

GETTING THERE

The trailhead can be found on Google Maps by navigating to "Mirror Lake Trailhead." There is additional overflow parking across the street. The parking area is located off Mount Hood Highway.

GREEN LAKES TRAIL

Oregon: Deschutes National Forest

DISTANCE: 10 miles

ELEVATION GAIN: 1,200 feet

TIME COMMITMENT: 4 to 6 hours

FEE: Northwest Forest Pass, Interagency Pass, or entrance fee

DOGS: Permitted

CAMPING ALONG TRAIL: Yes

DIFFICULTY: While the mileage is on the long side, the gentle elevation gain means this is never a particularly strenuous hike, making it accessible to hikers of all skill levels.

Left: The crags of Broken Top loom over the Green Lakes

A perfect snapshot of central Oregon, the Green Lakes Trail brings you up close and personal with some of the area's most famous fixtures. You'll be hiking right up to the base of South Sister, one of Oregon's most memorable volcanoes, while directly across from this massive peak looms another, with Broken Top rising above the calm waters of the Green Lakes. On other portions of the trail, Mount Bachelor juts up behind you, a familiar constant.

The Green Lakes and waterfalls of Fall Creek would be worthy destinations all on their own, even without the mountain scenery. While these waterfalls may not be huge, there is something about the way they seem to be staged at just the right moment, perfect waymarks on your creekside route. The water is never far away as you meander through the woods, and this hike is especially peaceful; the trail itself is fairly easy, without significant elevation gain. Of course, a trail this scenic and easily accessible is going to be popular. Midday sees a large number of hikers out on the trail, but hikers who set out early in the morning or late in the afternoon will still manage to find tranquility.

While most hikes can be satisfying when done as overnights, this area is particularly ideal for camping. The sites near the lakes are especially scenic during the dawn and dusk hours, and enjoying the area during these times helps to avoid the traffic, which can be distracting during midday. Some areas simply demand to be explored in depth, and this is one that I hope to return to again for more extended adventures. The trek to Green Lakes offers a taste, a classic day hike that hits all the right marks, but one quickly senses that every mile of trail in this region offers unique rewards—and these glimpses we're allowed on our short treks are what keep us setting out to the mountains again and again.

TRAIL OVERVIEW

Shortly after the trailhead, keep right where the horse trail splits left, then cross over a wooden log bridge. Continue hiking with the stream gurgling nearby. At 0.6 mile you will approach a loud section of the stream where both the trail and stream bend to your left. Continue and enjoy the numerous waterfalls along this section of trail.

At 2 miles you will pass an intersection with the Moraine Lakes trail, which veers left.

The path to Green Lakes, with South Sister rising behind

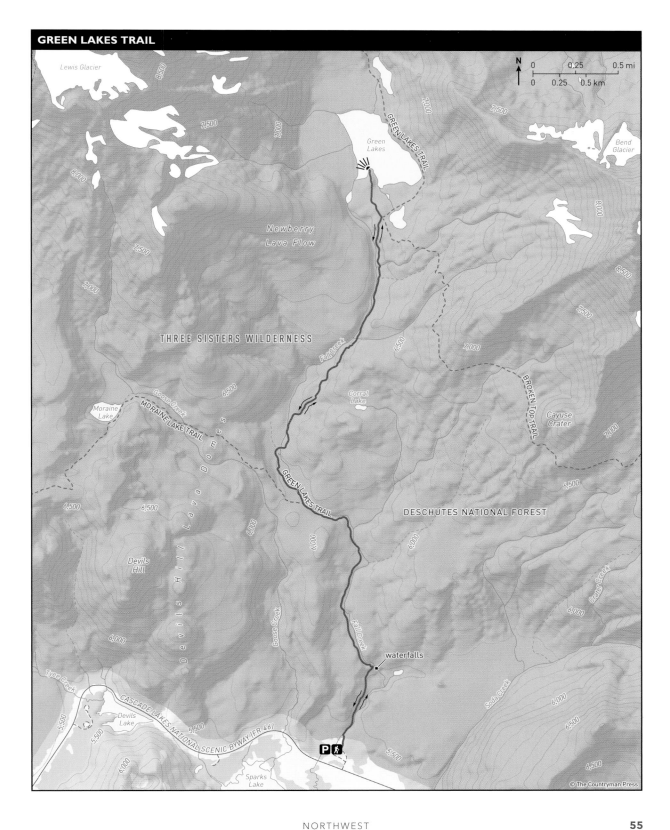

GREEN LAKES TRAIL

Lewis Glacier

Bend Glacier

GREEN LAKES TRAIL

Green Lakes

Newberry Lava Flow

THREE SISTERS WILDERNESS

Fall Creek

Corral Lake

BROKEN TOP TRAIL

Cayuse Crater

Moraine Lake

MORAINE LAKE TRAIL

Goose Creek

DESCHUTES NATIONAL FOREST

Devils Hill Lava Dome

Devils Hill

Goose Creek

Fall Creek

Crater Creek

Soda Creek

waterfalls

Tyee Creek

CASCADE LAKES NATIONAL SCENIC BYWAY (FR 46)

Devils Lake

Sparks Lake

© The Countryman Press

Left: The trail follows Fall Creek for several miles, with many scenic waterfalls along the way

At 2.9 miles cross another log bridge over the creek, which has calmed considerably after the busy waterfalls of the past few miles. At 3.6 miles the trail opens up, trees to your right, the creek to your left. Past the creek, a large rock wall rises up—actually old lava flow from the slumbering volcano before you—climbing toward the slopes of South Sister.

At 4 miles you will pass a sign indicating that you are entering the designated camping area. At 4.4 miles the trail splits. The Green Lakes Trail veers to the right, heading to the far side of the largest lake and beyond to the northernmost lake. Taking this trail will allow you to visit all three lakes but adds an additional 2 miles to the total mileage of your hike. However, you may also choose to follow this trail for a short distance, as it soon passes the north shore of small southern Green Lake.

Keeping straight at this intersection, heading uphill, will bring you to the shores of the largest of the lakes, an excellent spot for taking a rest and enjoying the views of South Sister and Broken Top.

PLANNING

This hike is extremely popular on summer weekends, and the parking lot fills quickly; however, you may park along the shoulder of the highway. The Northwest Forest Pass and the Interagency America the Beautiful Pass are accepted here; otherwise, you will have to pay a small fee for parking. A permit is required for both day and overnight hiking, available at the self-serve kiosk by the trailhead. A ranger on the trail may ask to check your permit, so be sure to fill one out before setting out on your hike.

In the spring and early winter, you should expect to encounter snowy conditions on some portions of the trail. Green Lakes is best hiked from July to October. Because the trail is near water at all times, the mosquitoes here are extremely aggressive, especially in July.

GETTING THERE

The trailhead can be found on Google Maps by navigating to "Green Lakes Trailhead." There is additional overflow parking across the street. The parking area is located off the Cascade Lakes National Scenic Byway.

MOUNT SCOTT

Oregon: Crater Lake National Park

DISTANCE: 4.2 miles

ELEVATION GAIN: 1,260 feet

TIME COMMITMENT: 2 to 3 hours

FEE: National Park Pass or entrance fee

DOGS: Not permitted

CAMPING ALONG TRAIL: No

DIFFICULTY: A moderately strenuous hike with a steady uphill climb, this hike should be accessible to most hikers who pace themselves.

The eruption of Mount Mazama, the once towering volcano and current site of Crater Lake National Park, was a staggering thing. One need only see a photo of Crater Lake—or better yet, visit in person—to imagine how a massive mountain might dissolve its own top, smothering the countryside for miles in the aftermath of its own decapitation. The remaining caldera contains the deepest freshwater body of water in the United States, with Crater Lake reaching a maximum depth of nearly 2,000 feet. Mount Mazama erupted more than 7,000 years ago, and still the pumice fields in some places are between 6 and 8 feet thick. Even 30 miles away, just the pumice fallout from the mountain would have been enough to bury any living creature unfortunate enough to be caught in the area.

The eruption of Mount Mazama was roughly 40 times the strength of the 1980 eruption of Mount St. Helens and ranks as the largest eruption in the Cascade Volcanic Arc in the past million years. The formerly 12,000-foot-tall mountain lost about a mile of height in the blast. At its former height, it would stand as Oregon's highest peak, topping Mount Hood by nearly a thousand feet. Today Mount Scott remains as the highest remnant of the once mighty peak, though merely a shard of its former self at 8,929 feet. It is commonly said that Mount Scott is the only spot within Crater Lake National Park where the average camera lens can fit the entirety of Crater Lake within its viewfinder, making it an ideal perch to truly appreciate the staggering scale of this place and the complex history of this otherworldly body of water. From the summit of Mount Scott, you'll be able to see not just Crater Lake sprawled before you but Klamath Lake, Diamond Lake, Mount Thielsen, Mount Shasta, and Mount McLoughlin as well.

The hike up is relatively simple for a peak of this elevation, with an easily followed, straightforward trail. Of course, the hike still provides a good workout, with a short but strenuous section as you ascend a series of switchbacks. At the summit, the views are enhanced by the presence of a two-story fire lookout tower. This wooden structure was

Left: Sunset over Crater Lake

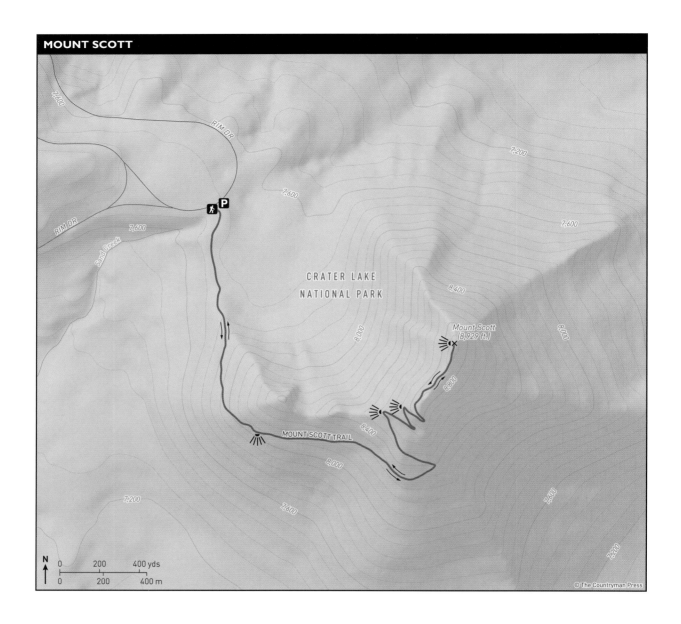

built in 1953, replacing an earlier stone lookout tower from the 1920s. While you cannot climb the tower, it makes for a scenic backdrop as you hike along the ridge and a pleasant spot to rest and picnic while enjoying the summit.

TRAIL OVERVIEW

The first quarter mile of trail is an open pumice field with a view toward the summit of Mount Scott to your left. The trail dips briefly, then begins its steady climb. Continue as the trail ascends gradually, climbing the mountain's south flank through hemlock and red fir.

At 0.7 mile the trail keeps to a rocky slope with open views to the south. At 1.4 miles you will begin hiking up switchbacks, with several good viewpoints along the way. Soon you will reach the summit ridge, where the trail levels.

Continue toward the north end of the ridge, where the fire lookout awaits you on the summit. When you are ready to return, retrace your steps back to the parking area.

PLANNING

There is little shade along some sections of this trail—be sure to come prepared with plenty of water, a hat, sunscreen, and sunglasses. The final portion of this hike is completely exposed, and the lookout tower at the top is not available to hikers for shelter. If you see a storm incoming, turn around at once. Getting caught on the exposed summit of a mountain in a storm is extremely dangerous.

GETTING THERE

The trailhead can be found on Google Maps by navigating to "Mount Scott Trailhead." The parking area is located on the eastern side of the park's Rim Drive, 15 miles from the Rim Visitor Center.

BLACK BUTTE

California: Shasta-Trinity National Forest

DISTANCE: 6.5 miles

ELEVATION GAIN: 1,850 feet

TIME COMMITMENT: 3 to 4 hours

FEE: None

DOGS: Allowed

CAMPING ALONG TRAIL: No

DIFFICULTY: A moderately strenuous hike with a steady uphill climb, this hike should be accessible to hikers who pace themselves.

Black Butte may be a straightforward hike, but not every enjoyable day hike needs to traverse miles of complicated terrain. Sometimes you just want to climb up a 6,334-foot dome looking up toward a massive stratovolcano. There's no denying that the massive profile of Mount Shasta looming over you is the highlight of this trek, but the isolated cone of Black Butte offers fantastic vistas in all directions, with views of the whole of the Eddy Range and Shasta Valley. On clear days you may be able to see all the way to Mount McLoughlin, another large stratovolcano 70 miles to the north in southern Oregon.

Black Butte is a dacite lava dome, one of several satellite cones of Mount Shasta. Black Butte was formed by eruptions from fractures on the flank of the volcano after the last major period of eruptions, around 9,000 to 10,000 years ago. Mount Shasta itself is much older, with a much more dramatic history. Almost 600,000 years ago, Mount Shasta began forming as lava flow built up its cone, until the stratovolcano had grown to a massive size, much greater than its present height. An eruption several hundred thousand years ago eventually collapsed the north side of the volcano, and the resulting landslide burst into the Shasta Valley. Today, the Shasta River has cut through what remains from this 28-mile-long flow.

The trail that this route follows was originally built as an access road for a Forest Service fire lookout at the summit; the lookout was moved to a new location in 1975. The trail is mostly exposed, and therefore it offers excellent views for nearly the entire hike.

TRAIL OVERVIEW

From the lower parking area, continue 0.6 mile up the road to the upper parking area. From the upper parking area, the rocky trail climbs at a steady rise through a forest of ponderosa pine, cedar, and Douglas fir. The trail first traverses the northern flank of the mountain and soon opens up to views of the Shasta Valley. From here you'll be able to see as far as the mountains of southern Oregon.

Left: Black Butte, though much smaller than Mount Shasta, nonetheless towers over the surrounding landscape

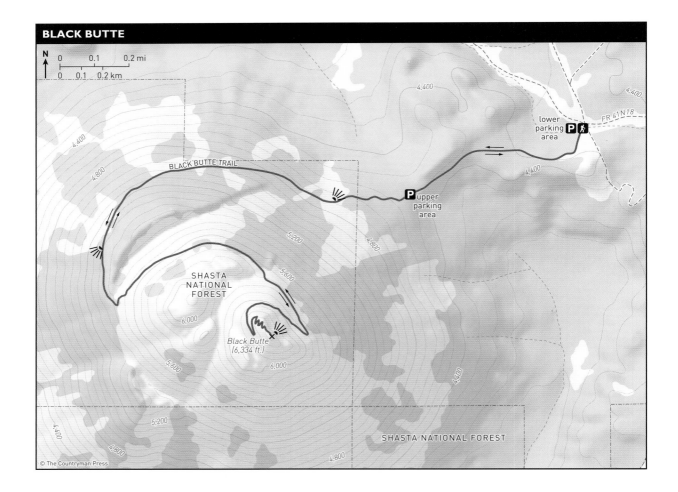

BLACK BUTTE

N
0   0.1   0.2 mi
0   0.1   0.2 km

4,400

lower
parking
area

FR 41N18

BLACK BUTTE TRAIL

4,400

4,800

4,400

upper
parking
area

5,200

4,800

SHASTA
NATIONAL
FOREST

5,600

6,000

5,600

Black Butte
(6,334 ft.)

6,000

4,400

5,200

SHASTA NATIONAL FOREST

4,400

4,800

4,800

© The Countryman Press

Around 1.6 miles from the lower trailhead, the path begins to curve south, following the curve of the mountain. You will enjoy views of the Eddy Range to the west and the Castle Crags and Trinity Divide area to the south.

About 2 miles from the lower trailhead, the trail cuts left and begins heading east over a very rocky slope of the butte. The trail here crosses above a canyon cut high into the slope of the butte. This is the most difficult section of the trail, as the path is very rocky and rugged.

At 2.6 miles you will make the final ascent to the summit via a series of short switchbacks. The final stretch, to reach the large square stone foundation of the former lookout tower, involves some rock scrambling over a narrow area.

When you are ready to return, retrace your steps back to the parking area.

PLANNING

There are two parking areas where you may begin the hike: a lower parking area mostly used by low-clearance vehicles that cannot continue along the rough road, and an upper parking area. Those using the lower parking area will have to walk 0.6 mile up the road to the upper parking area. Parking spaces are limited.

There is very little shade along this trail—pack plenty of water, a hat, sunscreen, and sunglasses. Due to the amount of exposure, heat can make this a very challenging hike on a summer afternoon. Be sure to check the weather forecast before you set out on your hike. If you see a storm incoming, turn around at once. Getting caught on an exposed section of trail in a storm is extremely dangerous.

GETTING THERE

The trailhead can be found on Google Maps by navigating to "Black Butte Trailhead." The parking area is located off Volcanic Legacy Scenic Byway, 8 miles south of Weed, California.

MINERS RIDGE AND JAMES IRVINE TRAIL LOOP

California: Prairie Creek Redwoods State Park

DISTANCE: 13 miles

ELEVATION GAIN: 1,550 feet

TIME COMMITMENT: 6 to 9 hours

FEE: None

DOGS: Not permitted

DIFFICULTY: Challenging due to the length of the trail, though with relatively little elevation gain, this hike is accessible to casual hikers who budget enough time.

Left: Redwood trees often sprout multiple trunks

Staring up at a massive redwood tree—a tree so large that you can't even *really* look at the whole thing all at once, at least not in the proximity that the lush, dense forest allows—it's stunning to think that, at one time, these awe-inspiring trees were seen as mere sources of lumber. For many decades, the now-famous redwoods of California were logged without regulation, a sad reminder of how mankind is willing to squander its natural wonders for the sake of short-term gain. In 1850, old-growth redwood forest covered more than 2 million acres of the California coast. The area initially attracted many aspiring gold miners, lured by a minor gold rush that soon fizzled. Failing to earn their fortune in mining, many of these men instead turned to harvesting lumber from the massive forests, feeding development in the West Coast's booming cities. Only in the 1920s did the work of the Save the Redwoods League finally help to establish the Prairie Creek, Del Norte Coast, and Jedediah Smith Redwoods State Parks, among others. But the Redwood National Park would not be founded for several more decades, in 1968, by which time nearly 90 percent of the original redwood trees had been logged. Today, the Redwood National and State Parks system is a fragmented combination of four parks spanning 131,983 acres of northwest California's coast—a fraction of the redwoods' original acreage in this area but nonetheless a stunning presentation of one of nature's mightiest creations.

Prairie Creek Redwoods State Park, home to the Miners Ridge and James Irvine Trail Loop, is one of the best places to visit to take in the majesty of the redwoods. While the trees are undeniably the star of the show, they are not the only attraction here. On this loop, you will hike across a scenic stretch of beach overlooked by high bluffs for a mile and a half, offering a perfect opportunity to cool off in the ocean at the halfway point of your hike.

But before the beach is Fern Canyon, a sight almost as remarkable as the redwoods themselves and certainly more singular: this short stretch of trail follows a steep-sided canyon covered from ground to top in vivid green ferns, like wallpaper come to life. Overhanging trees tower high above from the canyon rims, blocking much of the sunlight and creating the moist, shaded environment of the canyon. Strange and beautiful, Fern Canyon is a remarkable destination in itself.

At almost 13 miles, this loop isn't the easiest of day hikes, even with the moderate grade of the trail. Families with children may wish to visit portions of this trail separately as short individual excursions rather than one long loop. However, in spite of its length, the trail is never especially challenging, with relatively little elevation gain on the way. Thus even inexperienced hikers should find this loop doable, so long as they account plenty of time for the hike—consider adding an hour or two to your estimated hike time if you plan for a break to enjoy the beach along the way.

TRAIL OVERVIEW

From the visitor center, look for the trailhead by the large information signs, then follow the trail over a series of bridges through the trees. This first section of the trail is incredibly beautiful but will be the most crowded portion of the hike outside of Fern Canyon. You will pass many towering trees as you follow this easy, guided walk section of the trail. Keep left at the first intersection, following the sign, then keep left again at the next intersection. At the third intersection, turn right.

At 1 mile the Miners Ridge Trail splits left. Follow the James Irvine Trail to the right. After this junction, the path makes a short descent, following Godwood Creek. The next portion of the hike is fairly mellow as the trail meanders through the peaceful forest of giants.

At 3.4 miles keep right where the trail splits. Over the next mile and a half of trail, you will cross numerous bridges over small streams. The redwoods themselves will begin to grow sparser as you near the ocean; they are less saltwater tolerant than other tree species here.

At 4.9 miles keep right. Soon after, keep left at the bridge, following the sign for the Fern Canyon Trail. You will at once begin to descend into

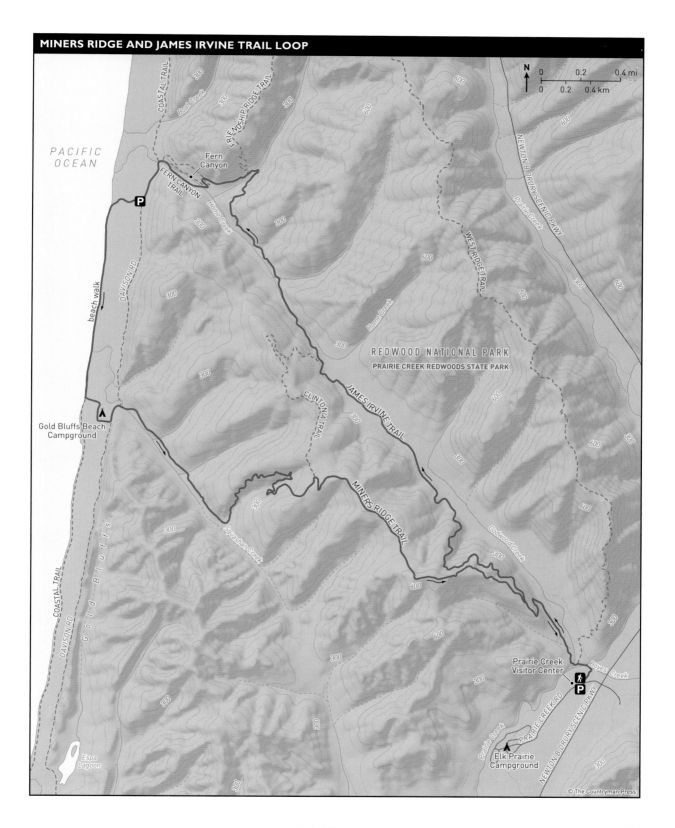

PACIFIC OCEAN

Fern Canyon

REDWOOD NATIONAL PARK

PRAIRIE CREEK REDWOODS STATE PARK

Gold Bluffs Beach Campground

Gold Bluffs

Espa Lagoon

Prairie Creek Visitor Center

Elk Prairie Campground

© The Countryman Press

the canyon. At the bottom, the trail frequently makes crossings over the shallow stream water using wooden planks. However, there will be spots where you will have no choice but to hop across rocks, through shallow trickling water.

Here at Fern Canyon, the crowds will once more reappear. While only about a half mile in length, the canyon is a stunning place where vivid green ferns cover sheer vertical walls, a corridor as scenic and hallway-like as if designed intentionally for aesthetics.

At 5.8 miles you will reach the end of Fern Canyon. Take the trail to the left. After passing the parking area for Fern Canyon you will approach Gold Bluffs Beach and the Pacific Ocean. A narrow strip of wetlands runs along the beach itself, with high bluffs overlooking the sandy shore. This is, of course, an excellent spot to break for lunch or simply enjoy a respite

A walk through Fern Canyon offers a surreal journey along walls of lush ferns and mosses

from the hiking by the crashing waves. However, keep in mind that you will have to hike for a mile and a half along the beach to reach the second leg of the hike. There is no marked trail at this point, and though it is easy enough to simply follow the path of the beach, the sand makes for much slower hiking.

At 7.5 miles you will approach the Gold Bluffs Beach Campground. At the campground, walk through the parking area and search for the dirt road by the woods. Follow the road for a short distance, then look for the trail to reenter the forest behind a barricade to the right.

Continue hiking through the woods once more. At 10.3 miles you will arrive at an intersection with the Clintonia Trail, which links the James Irvine and Miners Ridge trails at about their midway points. Turn right. At 12 miles you will return to the split where the James Irvine and Miners Ridge trails first separated, completing the loop portion of the hike. Continue for another mile, retracing your original steps back to the visitor center and the parking area.

PLANNING

At almost 13 miles, this is a long hike, and while there are no sections of strenuous climbing, a lengthy portion of the trail along the beach will slow your pace considerably—not to mention that you'll probably want to devote an hour or so to enjoying the beach itself. Make sure to give yourself plenty of time to complete this hike before nightfall.

GETTING THERE

The trailhead can be found on Google Maps by navigating to "Prairie Creek Visitor Center." The visitor center is just off Newton B. Drury Scenic Parkway.

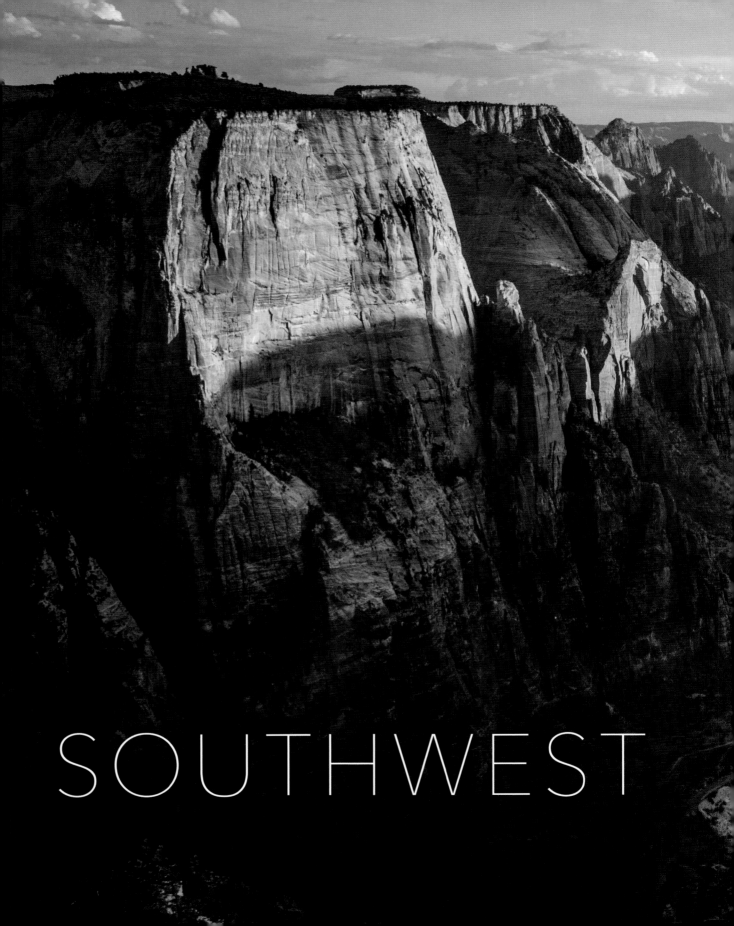

SOUTHWEST

SIERRA BUTTES LOOKOUT

California: Tahoe National Forest

DISTANCE: 4.9 miles

ELEVATION GAIN: 1,555 feet

TIME COMMITMENT: 3 to 4 hours

FEE: None

DOGS: Not permitted

CAMPING ALONG TRAIL: Yes

DIFFICULTY: While a strenuous climb, especially during the final leg to the summit, this straightforward trail should be accessible to most hikers who budget plenty of time and pace themselves.

Left: The Sierra Buttes lookout holds a commanding view of the surrounding landscape

The Sierra Buttes lookout tower is a great place for anyone wishing to challenge their vertigo. The lookout is built on a solid spire of rock rising high above the surrounding lakes and valleys—the two-story structure is of solid construction and seemingly in no danger of going anywhere. But as you scramble around the tower, with its catwalk navigating all four sides of the structure, you come to a spot where, suddenly, there is no rocky summit spire below you. There is nothing but air—for several thousand feet down. Hiking to places like this has certainly helped me tackle my healthy (though not extreme) fear of heights, but seeing nothing but air for such a tremendous distance just below your feet triggers an acute sense of alarm. Strangely, this adrenaline rush is perhaps even more immediate and all-consuming than what I've felt on hikes that are actually more challenging and likely to lead to death, like Clouds Rest in Yosemite National Park. On a dangerous narrow ridge-walk like the final stretch of the Clouds Rest trail, there's still, at least, solid rock below your feet.

I think most hikers will find themselves growing dizzy with nothing but a thin metal grate between them and this massive, sheer drop. At the top of this 8,587-foot pinnacle, you are now standing about 5,000 feet above Sierra City on one side and 2,800 feet over Sardine Lakes on the other. Far to the north, the 10,457-foot summit of Lassen Peak is visible on a clear day. All of the lookout's best vistas can, fortunately, be enjoyed without tempting fate. However, even the climb up to the lookout requires some faith; the steep metal stairs that climb the final ascent are fixed to an otherwise impassably steep rock face, and a look back down may bring that same heady feeling of vertigo. And that's after huffing and puffing to hike here in the first place—while relatively short in length, the final mile of trail offers a good workout for hikers of any skill level.

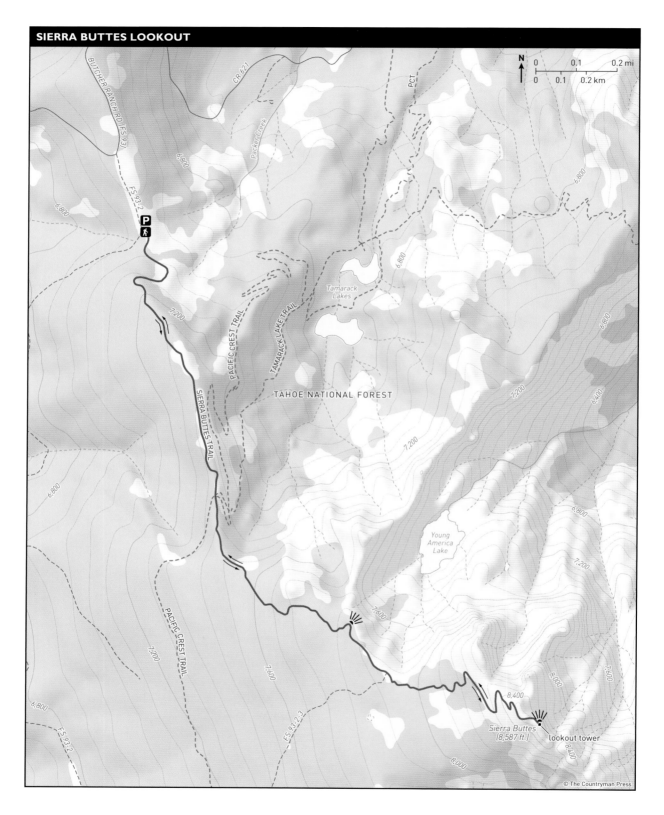

Young America Lake, with the Sardine Lakes lower in the valley

The Sierra Buttes of the Tahoe National Forest loom above the Yuba River Canyon, a remote, mountainous area home to only a few small, charming mountain towns like Sierra City and Downieville. To get to the trailhead for the Sierra Buttes lookout, you will pass through the Lakes Basin Recreation Area, also known as the Gold Lakes Basin, a popular destination for hiking, camping, and fishing. Numerous campgrounds in the area make it easy to set up here for days of outdoor recreation.

TRAIL OVERVIEW

From the parking area, the trail begins to climb almost immediately as you tackle a ridge. From the top of the ridge, the trail levels for a time as you hike through old-growth forest. Because much of this route has only

thin tree cover, you will be able to see the route ahead easily, with regular views of the lookout tower on its rocky perch. At half a mile the trail splits. Stay right. For the next mile you will hike along a rocky ridge with sparse tree cover. At 0.9 mile the trail splits to both the right and left, while also continuing straight. Stay straight.

At 1.2 miles you will begin to wind more steeply uphill through a shady, denser forest. At 1.5 miles you will hike past an area where massive rocks litter the landscape. Just after this, views open up to your left, looking down to the Sardine Lakes and, at higher elevation, Young America Lake.

At 2 miles you will climb stone steps as you appear to near the top of a ridge. However, you still have a tough climb ahead over a series of switchbacks, so don't let this deceptive sight fool you. Above, you will reach a

Below the lookout walkway is a dizzying drop to the valley below

4x4 road used to access the lookout tower above. The switchbacks here are somewhat less steep, but the lookout tower will remain frustratingly out of reach for another half mile as you trudge upward.

At 2.4 miles you will reach the base of the steep, rocky summit. Brave engineers mounted precarious-seeming metal stairs here to climb up to the lookout tower. Above the stairs you will be able to access the catwalk of the lookout via another staircase on the far side of the tower.

PLANNING

The final stretch of trail on this hike is very exposed. If you see a storm incoming, turn back at once. It is extremely dangerous to be caught on an exposed mountain summit in a storm, and the interior room of the lookout is not accessible to hikers and cannot provide shelter.

There are numerous campgrounds along Packer Lake Road on your way to the trailhead, offering many camping options. Otherwise, there are only a few small towns in the area. Far below the lookout, at the very base of the mountain, is Sierra City, a small mountain town. Twelve miles west on CA 49 is Downieville, another quirky and charming mountain town nestled in a valley. Both offer options for dining and lodging.

GETTING THERE

The trailhead can be found on Google Maps by navigating to "Sierra Buttes Fire Lookout." From Gold Lake Highway you will take Packer Lake Road west, past Packer Lake and Packer Lake Lodge. The road becomes narrow and steep as it switchbacks up to Packer Lake Saddle. From the saddle, you will turn left onto Butcher Ranch Road and drive a short distance to reach the trailhead. This final stretch of road is somewhat rough but accessible to low-clearance vehicles.

CLOUDS REST FROM TENAYA LAKE

California: Yosemite National Park

DISTANCE: 13 miles

ELEVATION GAIN: 3,170 feet

TIME COMMITMENT: 7 to 10 hours

FEE: National Park Pass or entrance fee

DOGS: Not permitted

CAMPING ALONG TRAIL: Yes

DIFFICULTY: Long and strenuous with a vertigo-inducing ridge walk at the end, this hike should only be attempted by experienced hikers confident in their abilities.

While Half Dome may get all the attention, Clouds Rest might be the single best hike in Yosemite National Park. It's certainly one of my favorite hikes, a perfect tour of challenging trails, unique landscapes, and unforgettable vistas. And the fact that it doesn't get as much attention as Half Dome helps, too: I'd rather enjoy an incredible view of Half Dome, and a dozen other incredible sights besides, than jostling for position atop Half Dome itself. At nearly 13 miles, this is a formidable day hike and is certainly worth considering as a backpacking excursion as well. However, experienced hikers will find this challenging but more than doable in a single day—and it's worth experiencing this incredible trail however you can.

The trail itself is beautiful, with several ups and downs along the way; there is one section toward the beginning that is particularly steep. The final summit to Clouds Rest brings hikers up a scenic, sparsely forested ridge with sporadic views through the trees to a narrow knife-edge of stacked granite plates. This infamous stretch of trail is not for those with a fear of heights: on either side of the path, the steeply sloped rocks dance down into nothingness, hundreds of feet to the south and thousands to the north. Exactly how challenging you will find this crossing depends on your particular fear of heights, but though it may look intimidating, the actual path is generally fairly wide, with stable footing on solid rocks the entire way. At its narrowest, you will be on ledges about 10 feet wide: plenty of room!

From Clouds Rest, you'll enjoy 360-degree views with a huge chunk of the national park sprawling out around you. You'll spot Tenaya Lake behind you, the Cathedral Spires, Mount Dana, Sentinel Dome, North Dome, Basket Dome, Mount Hoffman, Mount Lyell, and, of course, Half

Left: Clouds Rest offers an exceptional view of Half Dome

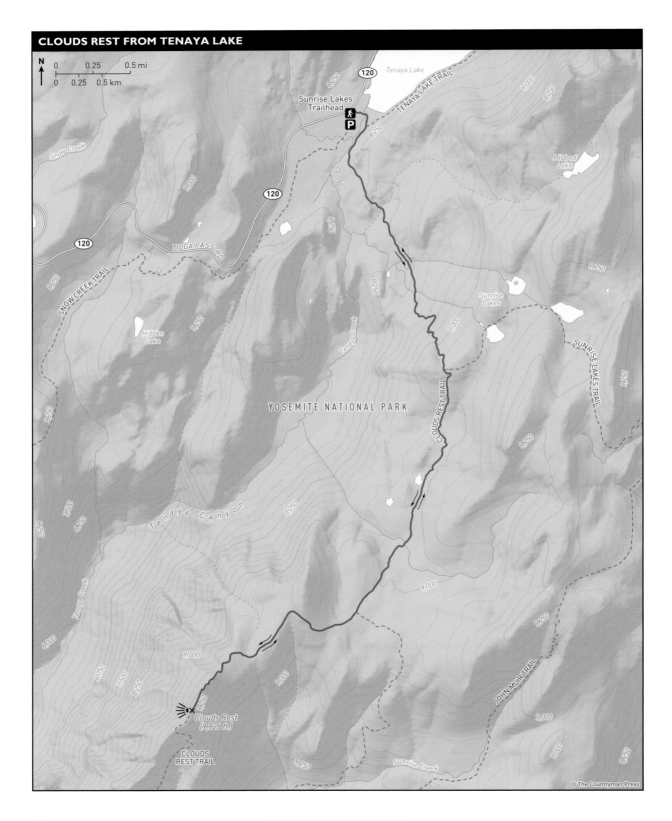

CLOUDS REST FROM TENAYA LAKE

N
0   0.25   0.5 mi
0   0.25   0.5 km

120
Tenaya Lake

Sunrise Lakes
Trailhead
P

TENAYA LAKE TRAIL

Snow Creek

120

120

TIOGA PASS RD.

SNOW CREEK TRAIL

Mildred
Lake

Sunrise
Lakes

SUNRISE LAKES TRAIL

Hidden
Lake

Tenaya Creek

YOSEMITE NATIONAL PARK

CLOUDS REST TRAIL

Tenaya Canyon

Tenaya Creek

JOHN MUIR TRAIL

Clouds Rest
[9,926 ft.]

CLOUDS
REST TRAIL

Sunrise Creek

© The Countryman Press

Dome. With good binoculars, you'll even be able to see hikers climbing up the cables to ascend Half Dome.

TRAIL OVERVIEW

From the Sunrise parking area at the west end of Tenaya Lake, cross the lake's outlet, which is fairly deep in spring but dries out completely by late summer. Several trails will split off to your left—keep right each time. Around 1.5 miles the trail will get steeper, and then steeper still as you navigate a section of rocky switchbacks. This is the most difficult stretch of trail, with most of the elevation gain of the hike stacked upon a mile of climbing.

At 2.5 miles you'll reach an intersection with the Sunrise Lakes Trail to your left. Continue straight to stay on the Clouds Rest Trail as the trail briefly heads downhill. After descending a few hundred feet you will arrive at an alpine meadow with a small pond at 3.5 miles. This is the last

The last stretch of trail to Clouds Rest follows a narrow ridge walk

AMERICA'S BEST DAY HIKES

area where you might refill your water, so plan accordingly—you will easily go through several liters of water on this hike.

You will begin to ascend once again; the climb is much gentler than before. The forest begins to thin out, with views of the surrounding distant peaks here and there. At 4.6 miles you will pass a trail to your left at an intersection marked by signs. Stay straight.

Soon you will see the ridge of Clouds Rest before you. Tackle the final climb toward the ridge, then ascend up the granite slabs to the knife-edge path. This short stretch of trail can be very intimidating for many hikers, with only about 10 feet of solid ground separating you and a sheer, steep drop.

At 6.4 miles you will reach Clouds Rest. Here you will enjoy a 360-degree view, with Tenaya Lake behind you, Tenaya Canyon to the west, Yosemite Valley below, and Half Dome rising prominently directly ahead. The Cathedral Range and Clark Range are visible to the east and south.

When you are ready to return, retrace your steps back to the trailhead.

PLANNING

With plenty of exposure, you'll want to pack sunscreen as well as bug spray for mosquitoes, which can be especially aggressive in the first few miles of trail. Earlier in the season, hikers may also encounter several water crossings that pose a notable obstacle. The first crossing, only a short distance from the trailhead, requires fording in the spring and rock hopping in early summer. However, by late summer, the water has usually dried up completely.

There are many campgrounds in Yosemite National Park, as well as yurts and lodges offering accommodations. Most of the campgrounds are available on a first-come, first-served basis and fill very quickly, even on weekdays. A few campgrounds offer online reservations but must be booked well in advance; they often fill up within minutes of their posting.

GETTING THERE

The trailhead can be found on Google Maps by navigating to "Sunrise Lakes Trailhead." The parking area is located on Tioga Pass Road, 8.4 miles west of Tuolumne Meadows Campground.

FISHER TOWERS

Utah: Castle Valley

DISTANCE: 4.6 miles

ELEVATION GAIN: 1,760 feet

TIME COMMITMENT: 3 to 4 hours

FEE: None

DOGS: Permitted

CAMPING ALONG TRAIL: No

DIFFICULTY: Rugged trail with moderate ups and downs, made challenging by the lack of shade and extreme heat in summer months.

Left: The Fisher Towers are a popular destination for climbers as well as hikers

While the crowds congregate in vast numbers at Arches National Park, visitors to the Moab area can find another stunning natural rock formation just a short drive away that few tourists are aware of. This hike below Fisher Towers is probably the best day hike in the area, an always interesting, swerving path through desert washes and gullies, under the base of staggeringly huge rock towers, and finally up to a ridge, where the towers themselves are framed dramatically against a sprawling valley, a panorama of mesas, hills, and mountains. As far as desert hikes go, it doesn't get much better than this, and even with the competition posed by Utah's varied scenery and many famous landmarks, the Fisher Towers trek remains one of my favorite hikes in all of the American Southwest.

The loftiest of the towers here—the Titan, standing around 900 feet—is the tallest freestanding natural tower in America. Composed of dark red Cutler sandstone and Moenkopi sandstone, the towers are part of a large mesa formation, having split off into huge rock fins over time and eroding into these unique, independent structures. Many of the grander towers are named: the Kingfisher in the east, and in the western section Ancient Arts, a popular rock-climbing destination with a distinct corkscrew-shaped summit. The middle fin of the mesa splits into two towers: Echo Tower and Cottontail.

During the warmer months of the year you're likely to spot climbers clinging to these sheer rock faces. The area became popular with hikers in the 1960s and was featured in the hiking guide *Fifty Classic Climbs of North America*. The corkscrew summit of Ancient Arts has become particularly popular due to its memorable shape and is often used as a filming location.

TRAIL OVERVIEW

From the parking area the trail descends briefly, then immediately picks back up as it climbs toward the mesa. Throughout the hike, you will repeat this process as you wind up and down and around the edge of several gullies.

Look for cairns to mark the way as the dirt and rock path winds toward the maze of towers, minarets, and spires. After descending from a ridge

The view southwest into the Fisher Valley

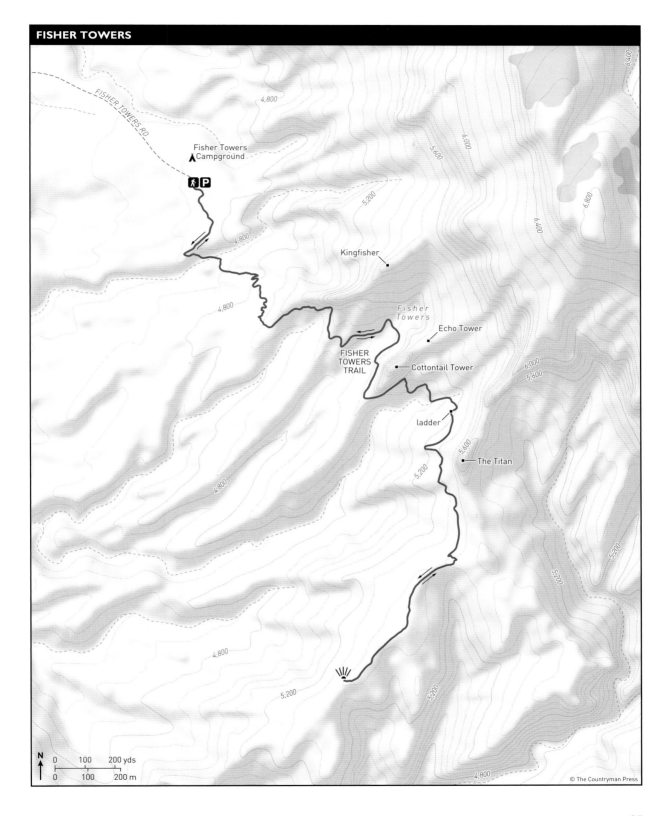

of rocks, the trail makes a sharp bend down stone stairs. At 0.3 mile you will cross the bottom of a gully.

Nearing the towers, at 0.6 mile you will hike by the base of one of the massive red giants. From here the trail is more clearly defined as it sticks to the base of the towers for some time, winding around in a series of S-curves.

At 0.8 mile you will pass a spur trail for rock climbers to the left. Stay straight. Cottontail Tower rises up before you, with Echo Tower set farther back and Kingfisher rising up closest to the parking area.

The trail makes a sharp bend as you hike around the edge of a gully, and at 1 mile you will cross a bigger gully, then climb up on the far side. At 1.3 miles a metal ladder is fixed to the rocks to help hikers descend.

At 1.5 miles you will hike around another bend as the trail skirts the tallest of the towers: the Titan. In a short distance, after a mild climb, pass through a natural "gate" in the rocks. At 2 miles you will reach the top of a ridge. There are great views to be enjoyed here, but the trail continues for another third a mile south down the ridge, with even better viewpoints to come. Continue until the trail ends at a sign at 2.3 miles. Here you will find incredible views back to the towers, which line up like the spires of a castle guarding the valley below.

When you are ready to return, retrace your steps back to the parking area.

PLANNING

This is a desert hike with almost no shade, and in the summer the heat can be very intense. If possible, this trail is best experienced in the spring or fall. In summer, an early morning or late afternoon hike is strongly recommended—hiking midday on hot summer afternoons can be dangerous. Hikers should bring plenty of water, a hat, sunglasses, and sunscreen.

While backcountry camping is not permitted along the trail, the Fisher Towers campground is located next to the trailhead, with sites available for a $15 nightly fee. However, with only five sites, it can fill up quickly on weekends. Numerous other campgrounds can be found nearby, off UT 128.

The Fisher Towers from the final viewpoint

GETTING THERE

The trailhead can be found on Google Maps by navigating to "Fisher Towers Trailhead." The parking area is located at the end of Fisher Towers Road, off UT 128.

PEEK-A-BOO LOOP

Utah: Bryce Canyon National Park

DISTANCE: 5.2 miles

ELEVATION GAIN: 1,650 feet

TIME COMMITMENT: 3 to 4 hours

FEE: National Park Pass or entrance fee

DOGS: Not permitted

CAMPING ALONG TRAIL: No

DIFFICULTY: Moderate trail until the final ascent back out of the canyon, made more challenging on summer days by the high degree of exposure on this trail.

Left: The famous hoodoos of Bryce Canyon

In a state known for its surreal landscapes, the vistas of Bryce Canyon National Park rank among the most otherworldly. First-time visitors may be surprised to find that Bryce Canyon is not really a canyon at all, but rather a chain of huge natural amphitheaters eroded off the Paunsaugunt Plateau into curiously complex natural formations. The most famous of these are hoodoos, found in various areas and myriad configurations around the American Southwest, but especially abundant in Bryce Canyon National Park. These red, white, and orange columns are formed by frost weathering and stream erosion, leaving behind formations that appear like some vast army of stone soldiers.

Summer is the busiest time of the year for most national parks, but personally I find Bryce Canyon—and other strange and surreal areas in the American Southwest—to be even more enchanting in the off-seasons or in foggy or misty weather, as often occurs during the August monsoon season. Swirling clouds and fog, or simply the contrast of snow, add to the beauty and ethereal qualities of the place. As a bonus, you'll find the park to be quieter as well, without the frantic rush of tourists clogging every viewpoint.

Regardless of the season, Peek-A-Boo Trail offers one of the best opportunities to get down into the canyon amid the hoodoos and is an ideal length, falling nicely into a Goldilocks range compared to some of the area's other hikes: this one isn't too short, but it isn't so long that it'll eat up your whole day. A short connecting trail begins at Bryce Point, where you'll already enjoy many canyon-spanning views and where tourists tend to concentrate in great numbers. From this busy spot, you'll immediately descend below the rim to connect with the Peek-A-Boo Loop, which begins only once you've reached the canyon floor. Along the way you'll enjoy views of famous Bryce landmarks like the Wall of Windows, the Three Wisemen, the Great Organ, and the Cathedral. To the

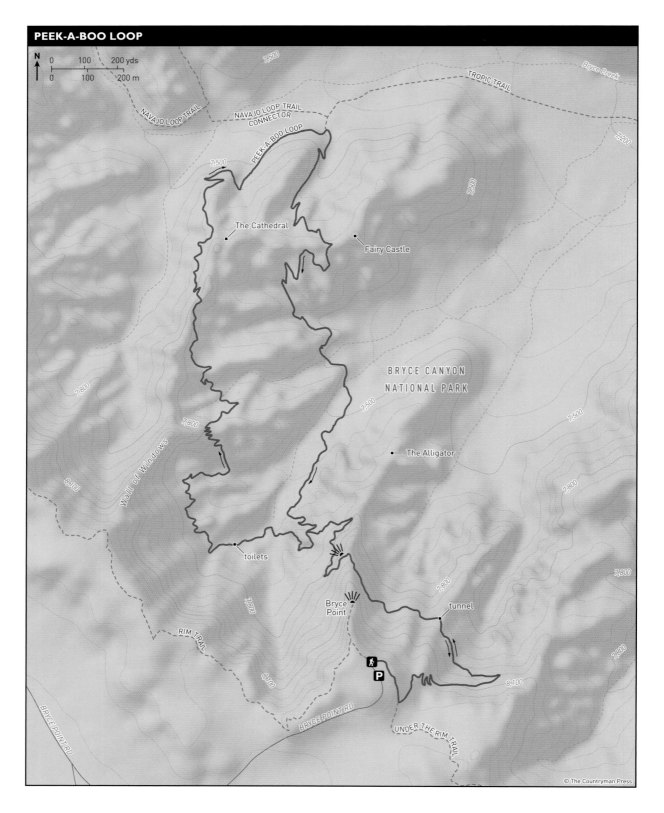

N

| 0 | 100 | 200 yds |
| 0 | 100 | 200 m |

NAVAJO LOOP TRAIL

NAVAJO LOOP TRAIL CONNECTOR

TROPIC TRAIL

Bryce Creek

7,500

7,200

7,300

PEEK-A-BOO LOOP

7,500

The Cathedral

Fairy Castle

7,500

BRYCE CANYON
NATIONAL PARK

7,500

7,800

The Alligator

7,800

Wall of Windows

8,100

7,800

toilets

7,800

7,800

Bryce
Point

tunnel

RIM TRAIL

8,100

8,100

8,100

BRYCE POINT RD

UNDER THE RIM TRAIL

BRYCE POINT RD

© The Countryman Press

east, both the Aquarius Plateau and the Kaiparowits Plateau will be visible throughout your hike. Across the Tropic Valley are the benches of Grand Staircase-Escalante National Monument.

The loop portion of this hike is shared by mule traffic, so hikers should expect to encounter these animals on the trail and be prepared to move safely out of the way.

TRAIL OVERVIEW

From the sidewalk at the north corner of the Bryce Point parking area, follow the trail around the slope descending below the parking lot. In a short distance you will reach a junction with the Under the Rim Trail. Turn left and follow the trail as it descends down a series of short switchbacks. After this the trail straightens, with white limestone cliffs towering above you and views to the north of Bryce Canyon's sprawling hoodoos and distant Boat Mesa.

At 0.6 mile you will pass through a man-made tunnel. Soon you will begin descending again to the bottom of the canyon, with views of the Wall of Windows. The view of the hoodoos is especially impressive from this point.

At 1.1 miles you will reach the beginning of the loop segment of the hike. Turn left to hike the loop in a clockwise direction. At 1.3 miles you will reach the horse corrals and pit toilets. Follow the trail down the slope, passing bristlecone and limber pines.

Heading northwest, the trail traverses a draw and begins a steep climb up switchbacks before reaching another tunnel cut into the rocks of the ridge. On the far side of the tunnel the trail cuts to the left, then climbs again up toward the ridge. After several short ascents you will be able to see the rifts and caverns of the Silent City to the north.

Follow a series of switchbacks down into another draw. At 2.9 miles you will reach an intersection with the Navajo Loop Connecting Trail, which continues straight. Make a hard cut to the right to continue on the Peek-A-Boo loop. The trail heads uphill steadily.

After another mile you will reach the end of the lollipop loop section of the hike, returning to the first section of trail. Here you will be reminded why canyon hikes can be more challenging than other hikes in surprising ways: after several miles of easy to moderate hiking, you now have to climb all the way back up to the rim of the canyon in order to return to

AMERICA'S BEST DAY HIKES

Observation Point. This return can be strenuous, but the trail should be familiar, and spectacular views still surround you whenever you need to stop and take a break.

Retrace your steps from the first leg of the hike to return to the parking area.

PLANNING

This is a desert hike with very little shade, and in the summer the heat can be intense. If possible, this trail is best experienced in the spring or fall. In summer, an early morning or late afternoon hike is strongly recommended—hiking midday on hot summer afternoons can be dangerous. Hikers should bring plenty of water, a hat, sunglasses, and sunscreen.

Canyon hikes can be very deceiving, following the inverse difficulty curve of a typical hike. Rather than immediately climbing uphill, the initial descent into the canyon is naturally easy, yet putting off the elevation gain until the very end of the hike means you have already expended a good deal of energy by the time you begin to climb. On a desert hike with little shade, the difficulty is significantly multiplied.

GETTING THERE

The trailhead can be found on Google Maps by navigating to "Peek-A-Boo Trailhead." The parking area is located at the end of Bryce Point Road, off UT 63, the main road that travels the length of the park.

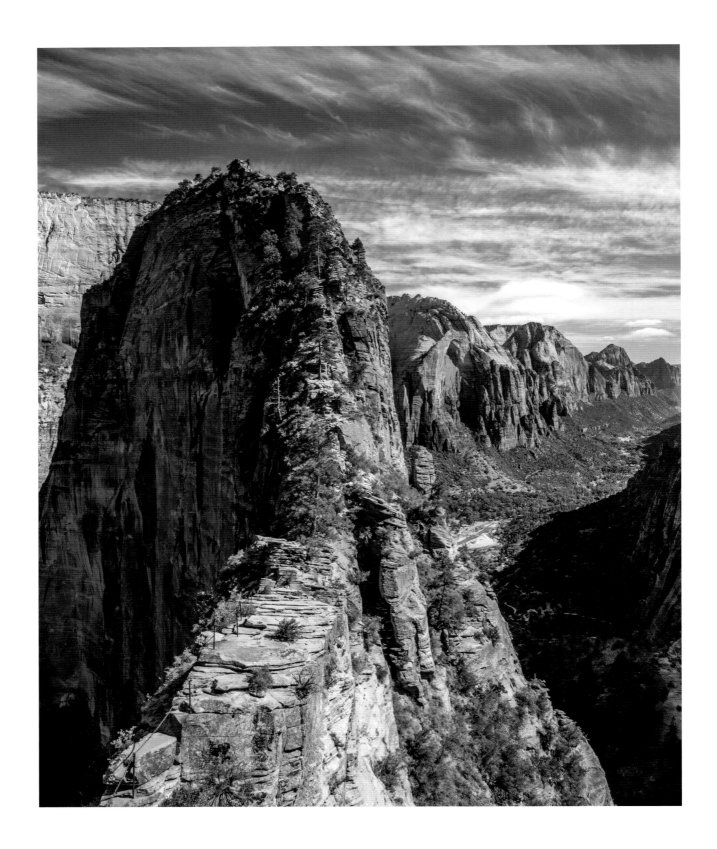

ANGELS LANDING

Utah: Zion National Park

DISTANCE: 4.8 miles

ELEVATION GAIN: 1,490 feet

TIME COMMITMENT: 4 to 5 hours

FEE: National Park Pass or entrance fee

DOGS: Not permitted

CAMPING ALONG TRAIL: No

DIFFICULTY: Final stretch of hike involves a daunting, extremely narrow knife-edge walk with steep drop-offs on either side. Not for hikers with a fear of heights.

Perhaps the ultimate appeal of hiking is that we humans, for all our ambition and accomplishments, still secretly like to feel small. Viewing the world from atop some jaw-dropping mountain vista, we enjoy a humbling experience so undeniable that it reframes our sense of self. At Angels Landing, that sense of majesty is implied right in the name: the view at the end of this challenging and potentially dangerous hike is so vast that it seems beyond the scope of our regular banal existence. As if the spot were in fact designed for the purpose of metaphor, humans attempting to reach this heavenly vision must conquer one challenge after another, culminating in a harrowing climb over a narrow rock ridge with metal chains to steer you past drops that, should you fall, would undoubtedly prove fatal.

Many mountain trails feature exposed sections with dangerous cliffs, but few hikes are known to induce vertigo quite like Angels Landing. Yet this dizzying perch is not found on the top of a mountain; in fact, it's not even the highest point in the canyon it overlooks. The path to Angels Landing skirts the top of a massive, fin-shaped protrusion of rocks jutting out into Zion Canyon, making for a trail so daunting that even many serious hikers decide to bail once they're staring down the path ahead of them. Almost any hike can prove deadly if one is careless or gets caught in bad weather, but Angels Landing poses dangers beyond those of most other hikes.

The final and most daunting obstacle of the hike is a spine of rock only a few feet wide, with a chain running along the spine to offer a scant assurance of balance. Given the crowds that still turn out for this hike, you'll be thankful for the extra aid as you're forced to pass other hikers heading the opposite direction. This is not a trail to be taken lightly, though its popularity clearly speaks to our unquenchable desire to humble ourselves before nature's grandeur. In fact, Angels Landing may be

Left: Angels Landing forces hikers to navigate a narrow spine of rock, with steep drop-offs on either side

the single most recommended hike in America, according to my research for this guide.

If you set out to tackle Angels Landing but decide to turn around before reaching the end, there's still plenty to make the hike worthwhile. Scout Lookout, a viewpoint just before the final challenging section of trail, offers fantastic views of its own. Hikers too intimidated to attempt Angels Landing at all—or anyone with a few days to spend in Zion—should head to Observation Point, just up the canyon from Angels Landing. While Observation Point may lack the memorable knife-edge climb, the trail tops out at a much higher elevation, and from the ending vista you'll actually be looking down upon Angels Landing itself, with loftier and more expansive views of the canyon. Observation Point is a challenging hike as well, simply due to the elevation gain you'll be required to climb, but it makes for a very rewarding hike without such a clear risk of death.

TRAIL SUMMARY

The trailhead is found at the bridge across the road from the Grotto Picnic Area. Hike over the bridge across the Virgin River and up the West Rim Trail. The first section of the trail is fairly easy as it follows the river. After about half a mile the trail leaves the river and crosses the canyon bottom.

After about 1 mile you will approach Refrigerator Canyon. Here, the path begins to grow steeper, tackling a series of sharp switchbacks climbing the canyon wall. This narrow canyon is very deep and shade keeps it relatively cool, even through the summer.

Soon you will reach the series of incredibly steep, short switchbacks known as Walter's Wiggles. After the wiggles, you will arrive at Scout Landing. Many hikers choose to stop and turn around at this point, given that the most dangerous and intimidating portion of the hike begins after this vista. Continuing from Scout Landing, you will tackle portions of trail where the path climbs a steep sandstone ridge, with a chain for you to hold onto and maintain your balance. You will gain about 500 feet in a relatively short distance.

After the challenging ridge traverse, you will reach Angels Landing. When you are ready to return, keep in mind that you will have to pass many hikers who are ascending to Angels Landing as you are making your way down, and at certain spots, passing others on the narrow spine of rock can be nerve-racking. Use extreme caution while descending.

ANGELS LANDING

N

0 100 200 yds
0 100 200 m

Walter's Wiggles

WEST RIM TRAIL

Scout Lookout

Refrigerator Canyon

ANGELS LANDING TRAIL

Angels Landing
[5,790 ft.]

Big Bend
shuttle stop

ZION CANYON SCENIC DR

Virgin River

The Organ

ZION NATIONAL PARK

WEST RIM TRAIL

ZION CANYON SCENIC DR

Virgin River

KAYENTA TRAIL

bridge

The Grotto
shuttle stop

GROTTO TRAIL

© The Countryman Press

Practice patience and common courtesy to ensure your safety and that of the other hikers around you.

PLANNING

Angels Landing is best hiked in either the spring or the fall. During summer you can expect to encounter both extreme heat and large crowds, making for less than ideal conditions. If you do visit in the summer months, your best bet is to plan to begin the hike as early in the day as possible. (Do not, however, attempt to hike here too late in the day—you won't want to make the descent in low light.) Angels Landing is an even more dangerous hike in the winter months, with ice or snow magnifying the hike's most dangerous qualities. Always check conditions at the visitor center before setting out, and err on the side of caution. Getting caught in a storm—or even light rain—while hiking Angels Landing would be very dangerous. If it looks as if there is bad weather setting in, turn around.

Chains have been fixed to the rock to help hikers along the narrow, potentially-dangerous ridge

Due to the popularity of this park and the limited space within the canyon, the Zion Canyon Scenic Drive is closed to traffic from April to October. To get around the canyon, visitors must use the park's free bus system. To reach Angels Landing, hikers can leave their cars at the visitor center and take the bus to the trailhead at the Grotto Picnic Area. The Grotto Trailhead is the sixth stop in Zion's main canyon. There are restrooms and picnic tables near the shuttle stop. Given that the challenging narrow sections of trail become even more daunting with other hikers edging around you, regardless of the season, your best bet will always be to start as early in the day as possible.

GETTING THERE

The trailhead must be accessed via shuttle bus (see above). The parking area can be found on Google Maps by navigating to "Zion National Park Visitor Center," located off Zion Park Boulevard. From here, take the free shuttle to the Grotto Trailhead, the sixth stop on the Zion shuttle route.

HUMPHREYS PEAK

Arizona: Kachina Peaks Wilderness

DISTANCE: 10 miles

ELEVATION GAIN: 3,350 feet

TIME COMMITMENT: 6 to 8 hours

FEE: None

DOGS: Permitted

CAMPING ALONG TRAIL: No

DIFFICULTY: Extremely strenuous, with the added challenge of high-altitude acclimation and a rough, exposed section of trail across a boulder field.

Out west it can be assumed that any state's high point will make for a true challenge of a hike. Some, like Guadalupe Peak in Texas, merely make for a strenuous hike. Others, especially in the states farther north, require actual mountaineering skills and cannot even be attempted as a day hike. Humphreys Peak, in northern Arizona, sits at a latitude where the peak is generally snow-free for most of the summer, making it a popular destination for day hikers—no ice ax or ropes required. But day hikeable though it may be, make no mistake: this one is a real ass kicker.

You may look at the elevation gain above and think: only 3,300 feet, that's not too far beyond the norm. After all, many other hikes in this guide fall in the same elevation gain range, and while 3,000 feet of gain will be a challenge anywhere, in any terrain, there's a curveball here at Humphreys Peak. Unless you happen to live in the nearby town of Flagstaff, chances are you've traveled here from somewhere that's significantly lower in elevation. The nearest major city—Phoenix, Arizona—sits at only 1,000 feet elevation. Yet the trailhead for Humphreys Peak starts you out around 10,000 feet. The summit is a few hundred feet shy of 13,000 feet. Elevation often strikes a serious blow to hikers who aren't acclimated to it, and often to those who are. I'd been hiking plenty of high-elevation peaks in the weeks before I arrived at Humphreys Peak, but I made the mistake of hiking here just 24 hours after driving over from the California coast. Despite being in excellent shape, despite having spent many recent weeks at high elevation, a few days at sea level were enough to throw me off my game. I set out to tackle Humphreys Peak with hardly a second thought as to the challenge ahead, and I soon found myself stumbling more than on any other recent hike.

An ascent of Humphrey may require up to eight hours or perhaps more for some hikers, and due to the summer storms that regularly rake across the mountain in the afternoon, you'll want to start early. You'll

Left: Humphreys Peak at sunrise

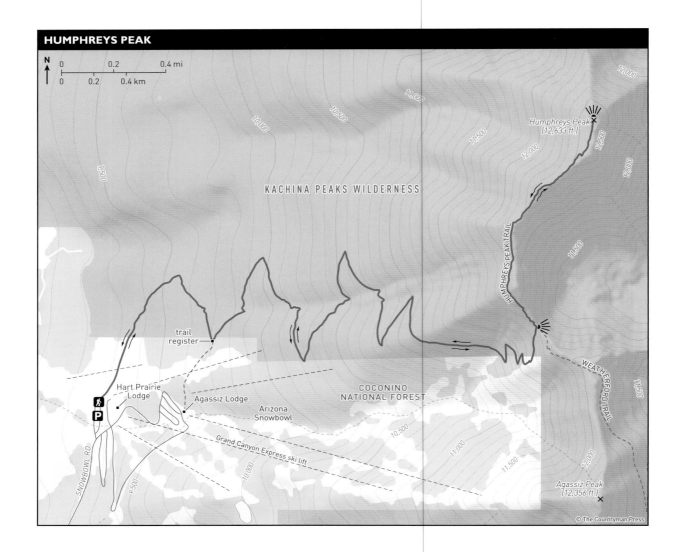

N

0   0.2   0.4 mi

0   0.2   0.4 km

KACHINA PEAKS WILDERNESS

Humphreys Peak
(12,633 ft.)

HUMPHREYS PEAK TRAIL

trail
register

Hart Prairie
Lodge

Agassiz Lodge

Arizona
Snowbowl

COCONINO
NATIONAL FOREST

WEATHERFORD TRAIL

Grand Canyon Express ski lift

SNOWBOWL RD.

Agassiz Peak
(12,356 ft.)

© The Countryman Press

find you get tired much, much more quickly than usual. Many people develop headaches and nausea above a certain altitude. Braced for the climb, the elevation, the boulder field at the summit, and the dangerous storms that must be assumed to lurk just past lunchtime, most hikers start out on their hike at sunrise at the very latest, perhaps even an hour or so before dawn.

All this isn't to scare you off from hiking Humphreys Peak, but it's certainly best to be prepared and to understand the true difficulty level of this hike. For those who do have the stamina for it, this trail is an excellent challenge. Humphreys isn't just a "hike it to brag about it" sort of feat, however. Northern Arizona is home to surprising beauty: deep miles of pine forests that appear suddenly after hours spent driving across the desert, high alpine wildflowers, and diverse wildlife. Looking out from a peak as prominent as Humphreys after scrambling above the tree line for miles to get there is always a rewarding experience. Almost anywhere, the views from a summit this high would be exceptional. But from how many other mountains will you be rewarded with views of the Grand Canyon sprawled out in the distance?

TRAIL OVERVIEW

The trail begins from the north end of the parking area. The first stretch of trail passes through a large open meadow, with views up to Humphreys Peak and Agassiz Peak to the east of Humphreys, as well as the smaller Kendrick and Sitgreaves Mountains to the west. In 0.3 mile you will enter the woods. The trail continues for more than another half mile before you finally arrive at the trail register.

The next portion of the trail, as you slowly switchback up the mountain, can feel endless. Aspens, fir, and spruce trees transition to bristlecone pines.

The trees begin to fade away around 3.8 miles in. As always, when hiking through the alpine zone of a mountain, always stay on the trail. The flora above the tree line exists in a harsh environment, weathering constant storms and wildly fluctuating temperatures, as well as human activity. This area is in fact home to a unique flower, the San Francisco Peaks groundsel, which grows only in the alpine environment of the San Francisco Peaks.

From the tree line you will be making a push to the saddle between Humphreys and Agassiz via sharper, more punishing switchbacks. The rocky terrain and high altitude make for slow going for most hikers through this stretch. You will reach the saddle just after the 4-mile mark; you are now around 11,800 feet in elevation. This is an excellent place to rest, enjoy a snack, and attempt to get a second wind. Here you can finally look out over the basin to the east, giving evidence of the San Francisco Mountains' history as a stratovolcano. When looking at this range on a map or from a plane directly above, the mountains appear to

form a rough horseshoe or U-shape. The basin to the east is the open side of the horseshoe. However, in their ancient life as a stratovolcano, these mountains were all simply one massive summit, estimated to have been around 16,000 feet high. Eruptions blasted after the cone and removed a massive chunk of the mountain's eastern flank, carving out the basin you see before you today. A similar formation, though smaller in scale, can be seen at Mount St. Helens, where the damage from the eruption is still very new on a geological time scale.

From the saddle, the trail continues to your left, heading north. After leaving the saddle, the path becomes even more difficult, as you make your way through an area of large boulders. Some moderate rock scrambling will be required from this portion of the hike on. Keep an eye out for the wooden stakes that mark the trail.

The trail continues its rocky climb over the west side of the mountain. There are several false summits obscuring your final destination, but the final mile before the summit follows a very rugged, exposed portion of trail.

The Kachina Peaks Wilderness on a hazy morning

Upon finally reaching the summit, incredible views of northern Arizona await you, including the Grand Canyon to the north.

When you are ready to return, retrace your steps back to the parking area.

PLANNING

Humphreys Peak is a strenuous high-elevation peak. If you have traveled here from a low-elevation area, it is recommended you spend a few days in the Flagstaff area before attempting to summit. Even hikers in otherwise excellent shape traveling here from sea level may find their body balking at the effects of altitude on this hike. Some may experience headaches, nausea, or find that their energy reserves have vanished and no second wind appears to push them onward, even after rest breaks. These warnings are not meant as discouragement, but merely to impress upon you the serious additional challenge that high-elevation trails pose.

Day hikers should only attempt to hike Humphreys Peak during summer and early fall. Under winter conditions the trail poses an even more serious challenge and should not be attempted by casual hikers.

As with Colorado's popular fourteeners, Humphreys Peak is the rare hike where you won't find solitude simply by starting early. On weekends you will find dozens of other hikers setting out on their hike at first light or even earlier. Due to the frequency of summer storms in the afternoon, it is best to hike very early in the day and aim to be off the mountain by early afternoon. If you are above the tree line and it looks as if a storm is imminent, turn back immediately. It is extremely dangerous to be caught on a mountain above the tree line during a storm.

GETTING THERE

The trailhead can be found on Google Maps by navigating to "Humphreys Peak Trail Parking." The parking area is located on Snowbowl Road—drive through the Snowbowl welcome gate and turn left into the large gravel parking lot. The trailhead is at the far northwestern end of the parking lot.

SOUTH KAIBAB TRAIL TO CEDAR RIDGE

Arizona: Grand Canyon National Park

DISTANCE: 3.1 miles

ELEVATION GAIN: 1,180 feet

TIME COMMITMENT: 2 to 4 hours

FEE: National Park Pass or entrance fee

DOGS: Not permitted

CAMPING ALONG TRAIL: No

DIFFICULTY: While this would be a moderate hike if not located in the Grand Canyon, any hike here in summer can be a challenge. Prepare for extreme heat and sun exposure; there is almost no shade on this trail, and there are no water sources.

Left: The South Kaibab Trail descending toward Cedar Ridge, with views of O'Neil Butte

As one of the most famous landmarks in the world, little needs be said about why you should visit the Grand Canyon. I won't attempt to wax poetic about the merits of this stunning sight—I think you probably already understand why this place would be featured in a bucket list hiking guide.

With that said, all the unique qualities of the Grand Canyon actually make it a challenging spot to enjoy the ideal day hike. For one, there's that notoriety: this is one of the most popular parks in America, and the crowds can be intense. Fortunately for hikers, however, the tourists here rarely venture beyond the rim, meaning those willing to actually leg it down into the canyon itself will not only enjoy the best views but will be able to do so free of the heaviest traffic. It is worth noting that, due to this principle, the Grand Canyon is even better when experienced via an extended backpacking trip. The farther from the rim, the fewer people you'll see, and many of the canyon's sights—including the floor of the canyon, where the Colorado River continues its grand experiment of erosion—can only be reached on a multiday trip. However, such a journey should only be undertaken by experienced backpackers, especially in the warmer months of the year.

For most, though, a day hike to Cedar Ridge via the South Kaibab Trail is the best way to experience the glory of this massive place. You'll enjoy incredible views nearly every step of the way, yet the trail is not so long that its challenges will pose an issue for most. While the mileage may seem short, keep in mind that, in summer, the extreme heat here becomes its own obstacle, and with all of the elevation gain of the hike saved for the end, the challenge of hiking back out of the canyon can sneak up on

111

you. You'll want to start very early in the day to avoid the worst of the heat, and be sure to bring plenty of water, as well as sun protection.

TRAIL OVERVIEW

The trail starts off immediately down a set of switchbacks—a good immediate reminder that whatever you hike down, you will later have to hike back up. You will drop a good amount of elevation in a short distance, quickly changing your perspective and opening up new views of the canyon. As you head down, you will find that there is very little shade on this route. Again, this is a good time to consider that while hiking back up, assuming you have begun your trip in the first half of the day, the temperature will only be higher and the workout even more strenuous. Fortunately, as you head down and enjoy the easier descent, this will be the best time to take photos.

At 0.9 mile you will reach Ooh-ahh Point. Many hikers choose to turn around here, as the next portion of trail is even more taxing. From this vista you will enjoy views to the north, east, and west.

From here you will drop several hundred feet rather quickly to the turnaround point of your hike, Cedar Ridge. In summer months, even this short next stretch of trail can require considerable effort due to rising temperatures.

You will reach Cedar Ridge at 1.5 miles, with even more impressive views now that you are fully immersed in the canyon. Many interesting geological formations surround you, including a spectacular view of O'Neil Butte. This spot, with a large open dirt area, many large rocks, and bathroom facilities, is a good place to rest and prepare yourself for the journey back up.

PLANNING

This is a desert hike with no shade, and in the summer the heat can be intense. If possible, this trail is best experienced in the spring or fall. In summer, an early morning or late afternoon hike is strongly recommended—hiking midday on hot summer afternoons can be dangerous. Hikers should bring sunscreen and protective clothing, including a hat and sunglasses. There is no water available along this route, so it is extremely important that each hiker bring plenty of water with them—at least 3 liters per person are recommended.

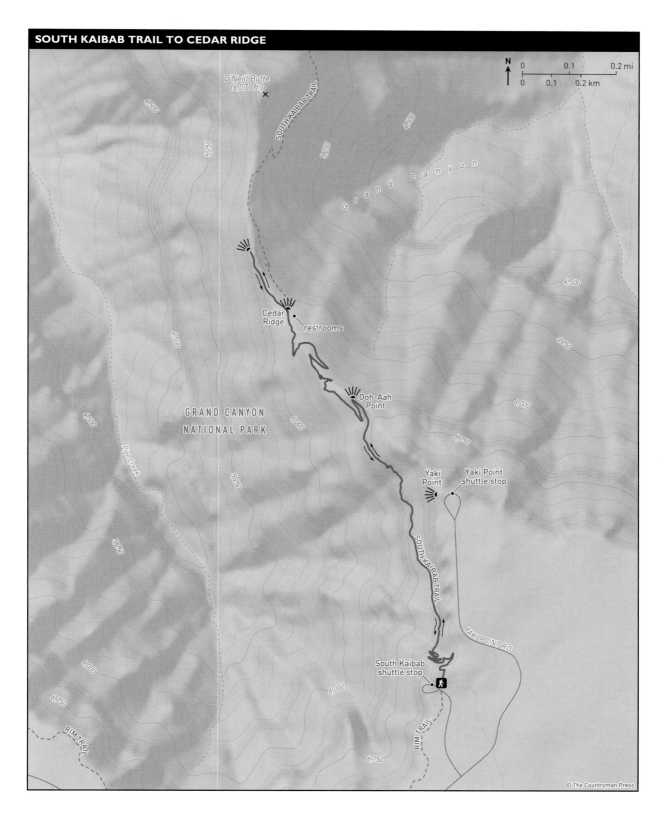

O'Neill Butte
(6,071 ft.)

SOUTH KAIBAB TRAIL

Grand Canyon

Cedar
Ridge

restrooms

Ooh-Aah
Point

GRAND CANYON
NATIONAL PARK

Pipe Creek

Yaki
Point

Yaki Point
shuttle stop

SOUTH KAIBAB TRAIL

YAKI POINT RD

South Kaibab
shuttle stop

RIM TRAIL

4,750

4,500

5,250

5,250

4,500

4,500

4,000

5,250

4,000

4,750

6,750

6,000

6,000

6,750

5,250

N
0   0.1   0.2 mi
0   0.1   0.2 km

© The Countryman Press

Canyon hikes can be very deceiving, because they follow the inverse difficulty curve of a typical hike. Rather than immediately climbing uphill, the initial descent into the canyon is naturally easy. However, putting off the elevation gain until the very end of the hike means you have already expended a good deal of energy by the time you begin to climb. On a desert hike with little shade, the difficulty is significantly multiplied.

GETTING THERE

If you are planning to visit during the South Rim's busy season—March through November—lines are long at the entrance station and parking can be difficult to find. It is recommended to park in the town of Tusayan and take the free shuttle bus into the park. A National Park Pass or entrance fee is still required.

For those visiting in the off season, or who simply prefer to leave their vehicle within the park itself, parking can be found at the Grand Canyon Visitor Center. From here, you can ride the shuttle to the trailhead—look for the Kaibab Rim Route (Orange Route) eastbound to the South Kaibab Trailhead.

ALKALI FLAT TRAIL

New Mexico: White Sands National Monument

DISTANCE: 5 miles

ELEVATION GAIN: About 700 feet*

TIME COMMITMENT: 3 to 4 hours

FEE: $5 per adult; National Park Pass also accepted

DOGS: Permitted

CAMPING ALONG TRAIL: No

DIFFICULTY: On regular terrain, this hike would be considered easy. However, given the desert environment and lack of shade, this trail can exhaust and sap your energy much faster than you might expect, posing serious dangers to hikers who are not prepared.

The Alkali Flat Trail in White Sands National Monument is almost certainly the most beautiful and surreal trail in the country located next to a missile range. While the military fighter jets roaring overhead can be occasionally distracting—the National Park Service issues somewhat disconcerting warnings about not touching any strange materials or devices found buried in the sand—these quirks do not take away from how incredible a place White Sands truly is. Here, in the Chihuahuan Desert, covering an area of 275 square miles, White Sands National Monument is part of the world's largest gypsum dune field. Framed by the San Andres Mountains to the west and the Sacramento Mountains to the east, these dunes may seem barren and lifeless, but in fact they contain a resilient water table just a short distance below the surface of the sand. This moisture allows the dune field to retain its structure and enables a surprising ecosystem of plant and animal life to endure here.

While the trails in White Sands are not quite like those you'll find in other parks, they are at least somewhat more defined than the region's other major dunes-oriented park: Great Sand Dunes National Park to the north. At White Sands the dunes are much lower in height than at Great Sand Dunes and thus somewhat easier to navigate, though many of the same desert-hiking challenges remain. Most visitors to White Sands wander around the short walking trails found just off the scenic drive: Playa, Dune Life, and the Interdune Boardwalk. However, for a true hike through these otherworldly white dunes, adventurers should attempt the Alkali Flat Trail.

Left: The White Sands are a stunning expanse of white gypsum dunes

*As this hike follows a loosely defined "trail" over ever-changing sand dunes, it is impossible to measure an exact elevation gain. You will never have to climb a dune much higher than 50 feet, though you will have to climb such dunes numerous times throughout the hike.

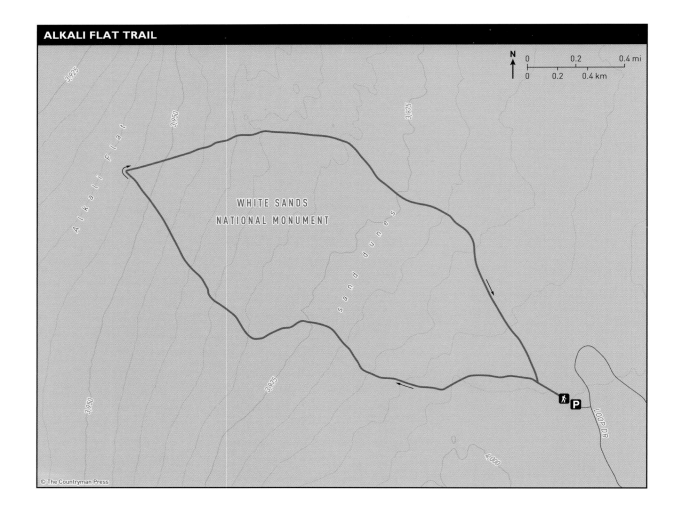

ALKALI FLAT TRAIL

N

0   0.2   0.4 mi
0   0.2   0.4 km

WHITE SANDS
NATIONAL MONUMENT

Alkali Flat

sand dunes

LOOP DR

© The Countryman Press

This 5-mile "trail" is fairly clearly marked, with posts set into the sand roughly every couple hundred yards to keep you on course. Without these posts, it would be extremely easy to become lost and disoriented. The seemingly endless landscape of pristine white sand and blue skies, so beautiful in their contrast to look at and photograph, also render navigation extremely difficult. Should you lose sight of the posts marking the trail, it would be very challenging to reorient yourself. Given the deadly heat you'll find here during the summer, it goes without saying that this is not a hike where you should take any chances—keep the trail markers in sight at all times.

The Alkali Flats lay beyond the dunes, a vast patch of flat, almost featureless desert that was once the site of an ancient lake, Lake Otero. While it may seem impossible that a desert environment like this could sustain any life, if you are lucky you may catch signs of the small creatures and tenacious plants that call White Sands their home. Earless lizards and Apache pocket mice sport light colors to blend into the backdrop of sand, making them hard to spot. Likewise, this inhospitable desert is home to kit foxes, though you aren't likely to catch a glimpse of one of these furtive creatures either; they come out at night to avoid the dangerous day heat.

Of course, this heat should be of great concern to you as well. If adventuring here in the summer, avoid hiking in the middle of the day. Early mornings are the best time to enjoy the dunes, and the hours before sunset offer some relief from the sun as well.

TRAIL OVERVIEW

From the parking area, the trail—a loosely defined route set by periodic posts in the sand—begins on firm ground between the dunes before climbing up onto the sand. There is little to orient you throughout this hike beyond the periodic marker posts. Pay extra close attention as you make your way along the loop, as this is not the hike to wander off-trail absentmindedly.

Most of the route follows the dips and contours of the dunes, with occasional steep but short climbs followed by similar descents. However, few climbs are more than 50 feet or so, as the dunes are of fairly uniform height. Along the way, keep an eye out for the occasional soap tree yucca or sumac bush.

For the first portion of the trek you will be hiking more or less straight toward the San Andres Mountains to the west. Eventually you will be able to see the end of the dune field and the empty expanse of the Alkali Flats beyond. Upon reaching the flats, there is little to see ahead of you besides the sunbaked earth, backed by the distant mountains, and a few buildings at the nearby White Sands Missile Range.

The midpoint, about a quarter mile out onto the flats, makes a hard cut back toward the dunes, sending you on the return leg of the hike. As you back into the dunes you will again be marching toward a distant mountain range rising over the sand, this time the Sacramento Mountains. Continue following the markers through the dunes until they reconnect with the route from the beginning of the hike, after which you have only a short distance to walk between the remaining dunes back to the parking area.

PLANNING

Hiking in a dune field presents all the usual challenges of desert hiking, magnified by the added challenge of having to make your way over miles of sand. However, hiking in White Sands is somewhat easier than the other sand dune hike featured in this guide, at Great Sand Dunes National Park. The dunes of White Sands are significantly lower in height, requiring far less uphill climbing, and because of the water table that remains only a short distance below the earth's surface here, the gypsum dunes are generally more moist and firm than they might be elsewhere. Nonetheless, hiking in sand is always slow going. Anticipate that it may take an hour or so longer for this hike than you might otherwise expect.

White Sands at sunset, with the San Andreas Mountains in the background

As this is an exposed desert hike, hikers should bring at least 2 to 3 liters of water per person on their hike, or more if you are hiking close to midday. It is best to hike in the early morning or toward sunset. Hiking in the middle of the day can be dangerous during summer; again, there is no shade at all on this hike and thus no opportunity for respite from the sun. Sunscreen and a hat are a must, regardless of when you set out.

Because the dunes at White Sands are of relatively uniform height, there are no real landmarks within the dune field itself, save for the regular trail posts. However, several buildings from the White Sands Missile Range are visible to the northwest throughout the hike, which should help you identify your cardinal directions. If winds pick up and begin blowing sand to the point where visibility is obscured, you should turn back immediately. If you were to lose track of the trail posts and did not have a compass, it would be extremely difficult to navigate through the dunes.

GETTING THERE

The trailhead can be found on Google Maps by navigating to "Alkali Flat Trailhead" or by navigating to White Sands National Monument and following the park road to the end of the loop (only one road in the park is open to visitors). The parking area is located just after the end of the loop, after the road has turned southwest.

PINE TREE TRAIL

New Mexico: Organ Mountains-
Desert Peaks National Monument

DISTANCE: 4 miles

ELEVATION GAIN: 1,200 feet

TIME COMMITMENT: 2 to 3 hours

FEE: $5 daily fee

DOGS: Permitted on leash

CAMPING ALONG TRAIL: Yes

DIFFICULTY: Rugged trail with
moderate grade, though made
challenging by the lack of shade
and extreme heat in summer
months.

The two New Mexico hikes featured in this book happen to perfectly capture my grounding principle for this guide: the dichotomy of quintessential and representative, or unmissable and unique. The views of nearby White Sands National Monument, even the very feeling of being there, are like nothing else you will experience in America. White Sands is unique even from other sand dune landscapes. But the Organ Mountains-Desert Peaks National Monument, home to Pine Tree Trail, offers a different sort of experience. Here, you feel, "Yes, this is what I imagined." Classic desert landscapes, with just the sort of flora and fauna you pictured in your head, are given dramatic backdrop by barren red spires jutting from a range of blistered, sun-bleached mountains. This is the sort of hike you do to experience what the New Mexico landscape, (mostly) free from the touches of civilization, feels like.

Of course, unless you have an especially good imagination, the Pine Tree Trail features beauty beyond what you pictured in your mind. Everything here simply feels a little more rugged, more dramatic. The surrounding terrain is craggy and sharp and yet it is distinct from the desert landscapes of Utah or Arizona. Much of this is due to the way this loop hike navigates the lower slopes of the rugged Organ Mountains, straddling mountain views with desert terrain. The craggy Rabbit Ears poke up into the northern sky while Sugarloaf Mountain holds the southern horizon and the Organ Needles spire directly overhead. This is not an especially challenging hike, but as it is a desert hike with little shade, hikers will have to come prepared for extreme heat if visiting here in summer. Spring and fall are the best times for an outing, though this area is quite beautiful in winter as well.

TRAIL OVERVIEW

The trail heads uphill from the parking area, past a bright yellow warning sign. The path comes to a split at 0.2 mile, where the loop portion of the hike begins. A short spur trail heads west, back toward the campground. Keep right to hike the loop in a counterclockwise direction.

Left: Organ Mountains at sunrise

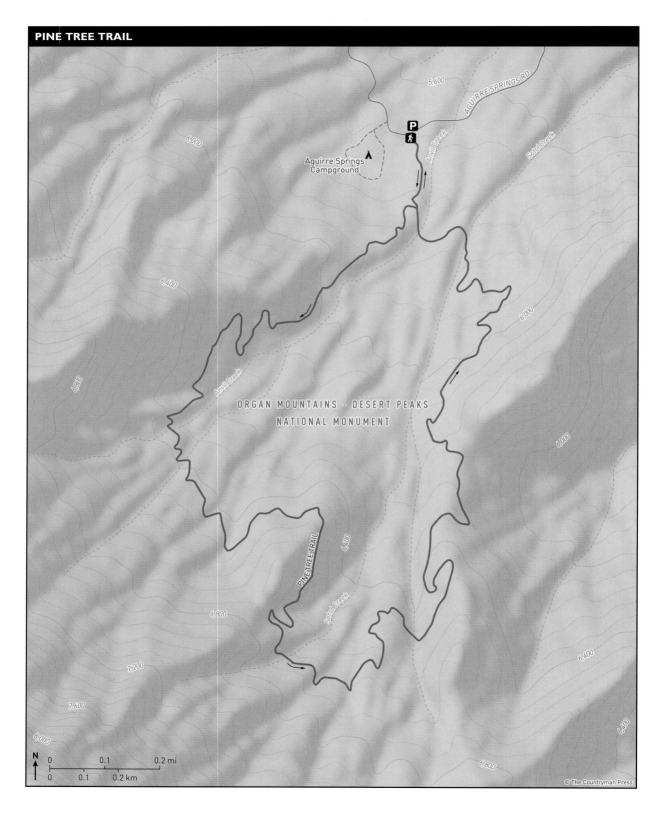

N

| 0 | | 0.1 | | 0.2 mi |
| 0 | 0.1 | | 0.2 km | |

© The Countryman Press

Hike along the bed of Anvil Creek, with a slope rising above you to your right. Heading steadily uphill, around 0.75 mile from the trailhead, the trail enters a drainage bowl that empties into Anvil Creek. Here you will pass a small pocket forest of pines. Soon the trail makes a sharp left, heading south, to navigate around the top of the bowl.

After 1.5 miles the trail begins climbing via a series of switchbacks, gaining ground to reach the top of the Sotol bowl. As you traverse this rib you will enjoy excellent views to the north, toward White Sands and the Sacramento Mountains. At the halfway point of your hike, and about midway across the bowl traverse, you will arrive at a sign marking the elevation: 6,880 feet.

The trail climbs farther toward a rib of Square Top Peak. At 2.2 miles you will veer east and begin to descend over a series of loose switchbacks. Around 2.7 miles you will hike across a col between the slope below Organ Needle and a small foothill.

The trail swerves past the foothill, curling around a ridgeline before continuing on its northbound path. At 3 miles you will pass a trail to your right, heading east. This trail would take you to the base of Sugarloaf, which is popular with climbers. Continue straight.

At 3.7 miles you will cross the bowl of Sotol Creek, and a short distance after, Anvil Creek. After this, you will return to the beginning of the loop portion of the hike. From here, you have only to turn right onto the initial trail and walk a short distance back to the parking area.

PLANNING

This is a desert hike with very little shade, and in the summer the heat can be intense. If possible, this trail is best experienced in the spring or fall. In summer, an early morning or late afternoon hike is strongly recommended—hiking midday on hot summer afternoons can be dangerous. Hikers should bring plenty of water, a hat, sunglasses, and sunscreen.

GETTING THERE

The trailhead can be found on Google Maps by navigating to "Pine Tree Loop Trail Head." The parking area is located just east of the Aguirre Spring Campground, off Aguirre Springs Road. This road is a "lollipop" road that ends at the campground before looping back; the entrance to the road can be found off US 70.

DEVIL'S HALL

Texas: Guadalupe Mountains National Park

DISTANCE: 4 miles

ELEVATION GAIN: 600 feet

TIME COMMITMENT: 2 to 3 hours

FEE: National Park Pass or entrance fee

DOGS: Not permitted

CAMPING ALONG TRAIL: No

DIFFICULTY: Moderate trail with some rock scrambling and light climbing.

The Guadalupe Mountains are a fascinating destination, not only for their epic scenery but for learning about the geological processes behind that scenery. These mountains provide one of the world's best examples of a marine fossil reef, having formed about 260 million to 270 million years ago. During this time the area was covered by a tropical ocean. Marine organisms secreted lime, helping to form a massive, 400-mile-long reef. On a hike to Guadalupe Peak, the high point of the park—and the highest point in the state of Texas—one might still find fossils from an ancient age lodged in the rocks around the summit of the mountain.

But on this trail, exploring the Pine Spring Canyon into Devil's Hall, hikers will discover an even more immersive view of this ancient geological formation. On this moderate hike—elevated beyond "easy" only due to the short portions of the trail where hikers will have to scramble around large boulders and up narrow ledges—you will trek 2 miles into the heart of one of the park's scenic, diverse canyons.

While a mile of desert hiking above the canyon offers its own beautiful sights, the real treat here is the final stretch of trail into a narrow, limestone-formed slot canyon, culminating in the namesake stretch: Devil's Hall. Around the canyon you'll even find a surprising diversity of flora. This hike is especially beautiful in autumn, as big-toothed maple trees burst with color. This is a simple hike in spite of the rugged terrain and perhaps one of easiest hikes featured in this guide. Nonetheless, it remains one of my personal favorites, both for the hidden beauty of the Guadalupe Mountains, nestled in this quiet part of western Texas, and for the way this hike demands that you focus on the trail itself, paying attention not only to the peaks above you but to the rocks that surround you.

TRAIL OVERVIEW

Just past the trailhead, you will arrive at a split. The trail to your right heads toward Hunter Peak. Turn left. Another intersection awaits you

Left: Devil's Hall features many interesting rock formations

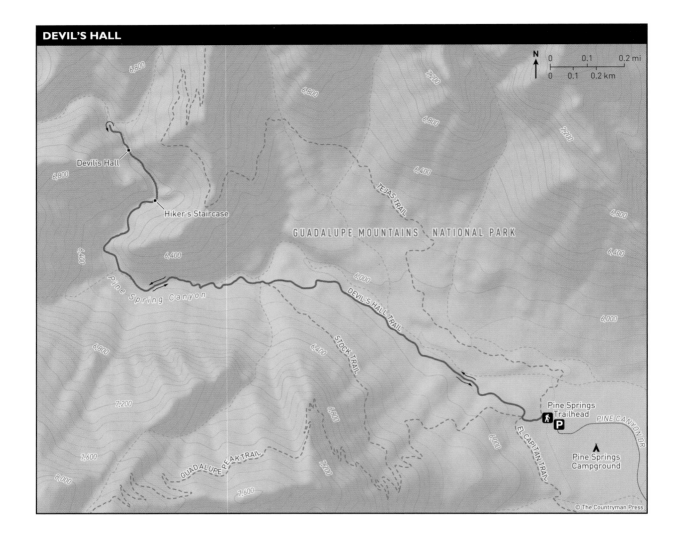

a short distance up the trail. This time, turn right, following the Devil's Hall trail, which leads directly into the canyon.

The trail has relatively little change in elevation for the next mile, making for moderate hiking. Scrub brush along the path offers a small amount of shade during this portion of the hike. At 1.1 miles the trail finally dips to enter the canyon wash.

After this, the trail traverses a rocky dry streambed riddled with large boulders of bright white rock. Footing can be difficult here, and there are portions of the trail where you will have to scramble over and between boulders. Hikers should take their time and be sure of their footing.

At 1.7 miles the terrain changes dramatically once again, shifting from a rocky wash to a narrow canyon of stratified slate. Here you will have to climb up a short, narrow staircase of ledges—appropriately called Hiker's Staircase—to continue. While only about 8 feet high, these ledges are narrow and may be unsafe to climb if the rocks are wet or icy. Just beyond the staircase lies a small, natural "bathtub" of water. Soon after this, you will reach Devil's Hall, a particularly dramatic, especially narrow portion of the canyon.

At 2 miles the canyon narrows further still. Past this point hiking is forbidden from March until August due to the sensitive wildlife habitats found here. This is the turnaround point of the trail; retrace your steps back the way you came, out from the wash to the original trail and then back to the parking area.

PLANNING

The first portion of this hike offers little shade, and in the summer the heat can be intense. An early morning or late afternoon hike is recommended on hot days. Hikers should bring plenty of water, a hat, sunglasses, and sunscreen.

The rocky sections in the latter half of this hike can be difficult and dangerous when the trail is wet or icy. There are many spots where a slip could result in serious injury. Be mindful of the weather as well: as much of this hike follows the path of a narrow canyon, flash floods can occur here quickly and would be extremely dangerous to any hikers on the trail at the time. Carefully monitor the weather. Afternoon thunderstorms are common during the summer.

GETTING THERE

The trailhead can be found on Google Maps by navigating to "Pine Springs Trailhead." The parking area is located next to the Pine Springs Campground, just up the road from the visitor center. The park entrance is off US 62.

GUADALUPE PEAK

Texas: Guadalupe Mountains National Park

DISTANCE: 8.6 miles

ELEVATION GAIN: 3,010 feet

TIME COMMITMENT: 5 to 7 hours

FEE: National Park Pass or entrance fee

DOGS: Not permitted

CAMPING ALONG TRAIL: Yes, with permit

DIFFICULTY: This is a strenuous trail with significant elevation gain and minimal shade.

Left: Hunter Peak, from the trail up Guadalupe Mountain

State high points are always an especially alluring challenge for a certain breed of hiker, but few of them actually make for ideal day hikes. In some cases the challenge is too great: out west, in the land of ultra-rugged, snow-capped peaks, few state high points are even accessible to the casual hiker. Then there is the opposite extreme: many state high points are only notable for that designation alone but might be found on a flat high prairie, off a random street in a suburb, or simply on a hill that, in other states, would simply be just another hill. Guadalupe Mountain, on the other hand, has all the poise and grandeur one might hope for from a state like Texas, a state known for its scale. Not only does it do its state proud, but it is simply a superb day hike all around. Indeed, while I have only tackled about half of the state high points in the country, I'm ready to go ahead and say that Guadalupe Peak is almost certainly one of the best that you can accomplish as a day hike.

Of course, Texas is not especially known for mountains, and it may be hard for those who have never visited the area to visualize what this hike might be like. It is not, as you may think, a ramble up a rocky mound in the middle of the desert. The terrain in the Guadalupe Mountains National Park is diverse, dramatic, and incredibly beautiful, a world unto itself amid the more typical desert landscape that surrounds it. While Guadalupe Peak makes for a strenuous day hike, at 8,749 feet it is not so difficult a hike as to be inaccessible to casual hikers. In fact, it's just the right amount of challenge to feel like an accomplishment, with the views and stunning scenery to make it plenty worthwhile on its own merits.

One of the most fascinating aspects of this trail to me is the way it essentially inverts the typical mountain climbing experience. Usually, the higher you go, the less vegetation you'll find. If the mountain

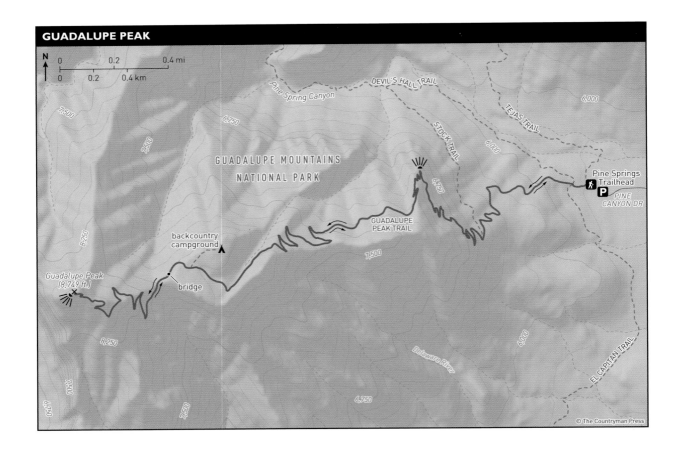

you're climbing is big enough to rise above the tree line, you will eventually find yourself hiking out of the trees into a harsh subalpine or even arctic-like landscape. Because this trail begins in the desert and ends in a cooler, moister environment, this usual experience is flipped. When hiking up Guadalupe Peak, you will instead find life thriving the higher you go: a beautiful forest of pine trees and fir doesn't make its appearance until you're 2 miles away from the summit. Of course, the more traditional desert portions of this hike offer their own sort of beauty too. You'll pass through desert shrubbery like yucca, prickly pear, snakeweed, and pickleweed; deer can often be seen amid this low shrubbery toward the beginning of the hike.

TRAIL OVERVIEW

Just past the trailhead, you will arrive at a split. The trail to your right heads toward Hunter Peak. Turn left. Another intersection awaits you a short distance up the trail. Once again, keep left. The trail heading right would take you to Devil's Hall.

After about half a mile the trail begins switchbacking uphill, gaining elevation much more steadily. At 0.8 mile you will pass another trail to your right, which again connects to the Devil's Hall trail.

The Guadalupe Mountains experience dramatic shifts in weather during the late summer monsoon season

Most of the elevation gain of the hike is tackled in these first few miles, so keep this in mind if it feels like the mountain is throwing everything it's got at you right from the beginning. While the climbing is fairly steep during this section, the views also get better and better with each turn. At 1.6 miles, after a switchback around a ridge, the trail opens up to fresh new views, including Guadalupe Peak and its false summits. At 2 miles, or around 7,300 feet elevation, you will find that you have hiked high enough to enter a new ecosystem where trees still thrive around the north-facing slope. Here you will find pinion pine, ponderosa pine, Douglas fir, and southwestern white pine adapted to the shady, cooler slopes high above the desert below.

At 3 miles you will pass a spur trail to the right that leads to a backcountry camping area. A short distance ahead, cross over a bridge as the trail cuts around a shoulder of the mountain. From here the trail switchbacks sharply as it gains ground toward the peak.

You will reach the summit at 4.3 miles. Here there is ample space to sit and relax and enjoy the seemingly endless views of the Texas landscape around you. South of you is El Capitan, which, from this perspective, has a distinct mitten-like shape.

When you are ready to return, retrace your steps down the trail to the parking area.

PLANNING

The first portion of this hike offers little shade, and in the summer the heat can be intense. An early morning or late afternoon hike is recommended on hot days. Hikers should bring plenty of water, a hat, sunglasses, and sunscreen.

Check the weather before setting out on your hike. During the summer, to avoid both midday heat and afternoon thunderstorms, plan to start your hike early in the day. Afternoon thunderstorms are common in the summer and can roll in suddenly. Lightning storms are extremely dangerous at high elevations above the tree line. If you see a storm developing, turn back at once. Guadalupe Peak is also known for its severe winds, especially in the winter and spring months. During winter, winds at the peak can exceed 80 mph.

While generally not a danger to hikers, rattlesnakes live in this area. If you encounter a rattlesnake on your hike, give it plenty of space.

Right: Beyond Guadalupe Mountain, the landscape drops off quickly into the desert landscape usually associated with Texas

GETTING THERE

The trailhead can be found on Google Maps by navigating to "Pine Springs Trailhead." The parking area is located next to the Pine Springs Campground, just up the road from the visitor center. The park entrance is off US 62.

MOUNTAIN

ICE LAKE BASIN AND ISLAND LAKE

Colorado: San Juan National Forest

DISTANCE: 7.7 miles

ELEVATION GAIN: 2,650 feet

TIME COMMITMENT: 4 to 6 hours

FEE: None

DOGS: Permitted on leash

CAMPING ALONG TRAIL: Yes

DIFFICULTY: A strenuous, steady climb uphill is made even more difficult by the high elevation of this hike.

Standing at Ice Lake, startled by the incredible vibrancy of the waters, a thought occurred to me: why is it so fascinating to see a lake this blue? All in all, this was one of the finest hikes I've ever done: world-class mountain scenery, and a huge variety of it, plus perfect late afternoon weather on the day I was out. And yet the deep, almost neon blue of Ice Lake was truly startling to witness in person, demanding my attention for several minutes. Water is generally known for being blue, yet when we see water *this* blue, it flips some switch in our brain, triggering amazement. It is such a simple sight—water, with the vibrancy dial turned up a few notches—but this is one of the many sights that make Ice Lake Basin among the finest hiking destinations in Colorado. And Colorado is certainly not wanting for fantastic hiking destinations.

While the main—or at least initial—impression of Ice Lake may be made by its blueness, there is much else to behold on this tremendous trail. There are the other nearby alpine lakes, for starters. While many hikers choose to turn around at Ice Lake itself, visiting only this one lake, this route includes a short loop to Island Lake, an even higher elevation lake nestled just above Ice Lake. A visit to Island Lake not only enhances the views of the hike without significant additional effort but allows hikers to complete a lollipop loop around the basin, adding only about three-quarters of a mile to the total mileage. For another additional mile and a half—or as a destination to replace Island Lake, after visiting Ice Lake—one can also hike up to Fuller Lake. Like Island Lake, this third alpine lake is nestled just a few hundred feet in elevation above Ice Lake and is relatively easy to access from the lake basin.

Before reaching any of the lakes at all, however, hikers will be treated to tranquil woods along a creek, hidden waterfalls, alpine meadows burst-

Left: Vermillion Peak and Golden Horn behind Ice Lake

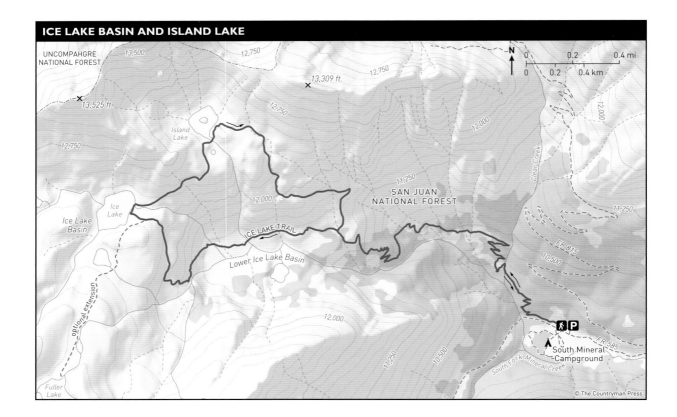

ICE LAKE BASIN AND ISLAND LAKE

ing with wildflowers, and the huge open basin below the lakes, home to several backcountry camping sites that make this an ideal overnight location as well as a great place for a day hike. Upon reaching the lower basin, you'll find stunning views of Fuller, Vermillion Peak, Golden Horn, and Pilot Knob.

Of course the real treat is the lakes themselves: the alpine terrain here is delicate, the views are nearly overwhelming, and the lake is as vivid as any you'll find anywhere in the United States. While other areas like Glacier and the Pacific Northwest may get all their attention for their bright turquoise lakes, it turns out they've got nothing on Colorado. This is truly a special place: be careful in the alpine tundra, as these ecosystems are very fragile and easily damaged. Please leave this scenic spot as beautiful and healthy as when you found it.

TRAIL OVERVIEW

The trail heads west from the parking area, soon nearing and following the path of Clear Creek. At 0.6 mile you will cross over the stream using a bridge of makeshift logs. Shortly after, cross through an open meadow. At 1.2 miles you will pass a rockslide area.

At 1.7 miles the trail again approaches the creek. From a small spur to the left of the trail, at the turn of a switchback, you will be able to glimpse a small waterfall not far from the trail. Soon, as you approach the basin, the grade becomes easier. At 2.2 miles a small, easily missed side trail heads uphill, toward Island Lake. This will be the trail you return on, completing a partial loop, if you choose to hike to Island Lake.

You will arrive at the basin below the alpine lakes at 2.4 miles. Peaks now tower above you on almost all sides, with the ridge guarding the lakes directly before you. As you hike through the basin, you will pass many backcountry campsites, which make this an excellent place for an overnight excursion.

At 2.8 miles you will begin to hike steeply uphill toward the ridgetop. While you may feel that you *surely* must be close, after reaching the basin, you have nearly another mile of steep climbing after starting upslope again from the basin. You will crest the ridge at 3.5 miles and reach Lower Ice Lake at 3.7 miles.

At Lower Ice Lake, many hikers choose to turn around and retrace

Ice Lake, from the trail to Island Lake

their steps back to the trailhead. However, there are two relatively easy extensions you can add on to your hike from here, and if you have time I highly recommend you attempt at least one of them. A trail runs southwest from Ice Lake to Fuller Lake; however, this option is only available as a there-and-back extension, which adds a little more than a mile and a half to your total distance. The second optional extension is to Island Lake, which is recommended, as it creates the potential for a lollipop loop back to the beginning of the basin below Ice Lake.

From Ice Lake, the trail to Island Lake heads northeast, up and around a slope. In about a third of a mile, you will reach Island Lake, where a small rock island gives the body of water its name. Heading around the lake, look for the trail down by the east edge. This trail is not as commonly used as the main route and thus may be faint in places, but it is never difficult to follow. As you descend, be mindful of the loose rocks and soil that can easily slide out beneath you.

At 5.5 miles you will rejoin the main trail at the far east edge of the basin. You are now just a little more than 2 miles from the trailhead. Turn left onto the main trail and retrace your steps back to the parking area.

PLANNING

Island Lake is a strenuous high-elevation hike. If you have traveled here from a low-elevation area, it is recommended that you spend a few days in the area before attempting to hike. Even for fit, experienced hikers, altitude can quickly rob you of your strength, as well as bring on headaches and nausea. This would be a challenging trail at any elevation, but the difficulties are enhanced significantly by the high altitude.

The final portion of this hike is above the tree line, and there is no shelter from either sun or weather. Bring sunscreen, protective clothing, and, as always, plenty of water. If it appears that a storm is incoming, turn back immediately. It is extremely dangerous to be caught on a mountain above the tree line during a storm.

GETTING THERE

The trailhead can be found on Google Maps by navigating to "Ice Lakes Trailhead." The parking area is next to South Mineral Campground, on Forest Road 585, 4.3 miles west of US 550.

HIGH DUNE AND STAR DUNE

Colorado: Great Sand Dunes National Park

DISTANCE: 5 miles

ELEVATION GAIN: 800 feet

TIME COMMITMENT: 3 to 4 hours

FEE: National Park Pass or entrance fee

DOGS: Not permitted

CAMPING ALONG TRAIL: Yes

DIFFICULTY: Hiking in dunes is unlike any other kind of hike, and even experienced hikers will find their speed greatly reduced. Hiking through sand is very challenging, and exposure to the sun adds significant difficulty.

Left: The Sangre de Cristo Mountains rise dramatically behind the Great Sand Dunes

There are few other places in North America offering anything like the scenery of Great Sand Dunes National Park: huge mountains of sand backed by actual huge mountains, snow-capped and all the more dramatic for the contrasting scenery. Nearly any spot within the dune field offers picture-perfect views, but because the terrain here is so challenging to traverse, few hikers ever venture beyond High Dune to the true high point of the dune field, Star Dune. At approximately 750 feet, Star Dune is the highest sand dune in North America, though from the parking area it is actually High Dune that you will see towering and prominent before you.

As there is no actual trail leading to High Dune, or any other dune in the dune field, this hike poses the added adventure of navigating through an open and unusual landscape. There are, of course, many challenges you will face here that you will not encounter on a more typical hike, further elaborated upon in the Planning section but serious enough to note here as well. Because there is no trail of any kind through the dunes, you will have to rely upon your own instincts to navigate. However, because of the clear landmarks visible throughout the hike, doing so is not terribly difficult if there is good visibility. Because you will be hiking through the dune field for the entire duration of this hike, there is no shade available, and the temperature of the sand may rise as high as 150°F. Prepare to hike through extreme heat during summer months—hiking very early or late in the day is strongly recommended to avoid the worst of the afternoon sun. This is also an excellent destination for the cooler months of the year, when the dynamic scenery is further contrasted by highlights of snow.

The sand that forms the dunes mostly originates in the San Juan Mountains, some 65 miles to the west. In the flatter stretch of ground around Medano Creek, however, you may notice that the sand is rougher and mixed with small stones. This rougher sand and sediment comes from the Sangre de Cristo Mountains, which rise just to the east of the dunes and provide a scenic backdrop as you hike. It is estimated that the dunes are around 440,000 years old, forming where an ancient lake once sat. How could features like sand dunes, so prone to restructuring and reshaping in the wind, survive for nearly half a million years? In fact, it is the wind itself that formed and still maintains the dune field, after an anomaly of geography and wind patterns trapped so much sand at the foot of the mountains. Prevailing winds from the southwest and storm winds blowing over the mountain passes from the east and northeast keep the dunes relatively stable at the foot of the Sangre de Cristo, while Sand Creek to the northwest of the dunes and Medano Creek to the southeast further shape the perimeter of the dune field.

TRAIL OVERVIEW

Unlike any other hike in this guide—even the Alkali Flats Trail in White Sands National Monument, which also takes you questing through a maze of sand dunes—there is no trail whatsoever to High Dune in Great Sand Dunes National Park. While the Alkali Flats Trail is a marked, unchanging route indicated by markers set into the sand, the High Dune Trail offers no markers at all. The dunes themselves are constantly changing, and therefore there is no recommended, established path to the top of High Dune. You will simply have to pick a course and make your own way.

However, as long as visibility is good—and you should not attempt to hike in the dunes if it is not—finding your way to High Dune is not difficult. While not actually the highest dune in the dune field, High Dune is the highest dune visible from the parking area and will be a prominent landmark throughout your hike.

From the parking area you will first have to walk across the wide and shallow Medano Creek to reach the dunes. The creek typically flows strongest from late May to early June. However, after July the water is usually very low, and in some years the creek will have dried up entirely. Make your way toward High Dune, sticking to ridges and high points on the dunes building up to it. This will help shelter you from the worst of the wind, which typically whips up and over the ridges, blasting sand several feet off the ground at high speed. From atop a ridge, your upper body will usually be spared from this sand blasting and you should be able to

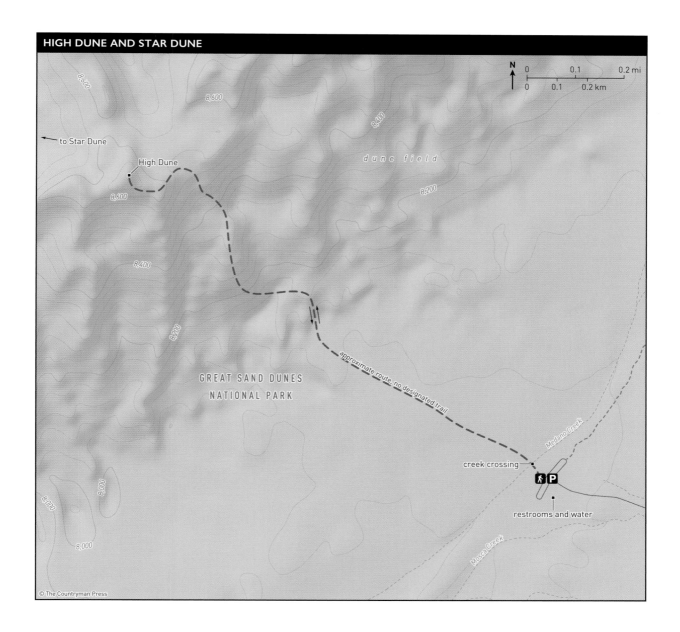

maintain a clear view of your surroundings, making navigating toward High Dune easier.

From High Dune, Star Dune is visible to the northwest. Most hikers go no farther than High Dune, making Star Dune a satisfying trek, offering plenty of solitude if you have the energy and time to do so. Overnight

AMERICA'S BEST DAY HIKES

Left: Hikers must tackle steep hills of shifting sand to reach High Dune

camping is allowed in the dune field, and given the effort of reaching these high dunes, an extended trip through the dunes can be a unique and gratifying way to escape from the crowds.

PLANNING

Hiking in dunes poses all the usual challenges of desert hiking, magnified by the additional challenge of having to make your way over miles of sand. The dunes of Great Sand Dunes National Park are high and constantly shifting as they're buffeted by strong winds. Getting caught in these winds can mean that a blizzard of sand is blasted into your exposed skin. Even on calm days, hiking up a dune is a strenuous feat because the sand constantly shifts beneath your feet, slowing your pace to a crawl.

As this is an exposed desert hike, hikers should bring at least 2 to 3 liters of water per person, and perhaps more if you anticipate being out in the dunes more than three hours during the hottest portions of the day. It is best to hike in the early morning or toward sunset. Hiking in the middle of the day can be dangerous during summer, because, again, there is no shade at all on this hike and thus no opportunity for respite from the sun. Sunscreen and a hat are a must, regardless of when you set out on your hike.

If winds pick up and begin blowing sand to the point where visibility is obscured, you should turn back immediately. If you were to lose track of the trail posts and did not have a compass on your person, it would be extremely difficult to navigate through the dunes.

GETTING THERE

The trailhead can be found on Google Maps by navigating to "Great Sand Dunes Parking." The park entrance is on CO 150.

MOUNT BIERSTADT

Colorado: Pike National Forest

DISTANCE: 7.4 miles

ELEVATION GAIN: 2,850 feet

TIME COMMITMENT: 5 to 7 hours

FEE: None

DOGS: Permitted

CAMPING ALONG TRAIL: No

DIFFICULTY: Extremely strenuous, with the added challenge of high-altitude acclimation and a rugged, exposed trail with no shade or shelter from the elements.

Left: The peaks of the Rockies are often frosted in snow as early as the beginning of September

Colorado may have alpine lakes just as beautiful as any in the Pacific Northwest or Montana—as evidenced by the Ice Lake Basin hike—but inevitably this great state will always be known for its fourteeners: mountains above 14,000 feet in height. And for good reason: while most other nearby states are absent of any fourteeners entirely, Colorado is home to 53 such behemoth mountains. It is strange to think about so many of these peaks in this one state, when only a few other states have any fourteeners at all. California and Washington are home to the few others that lie in the continental United States, and while Alaska can claim the uniquely massive Denali, the highest point in all of North America, it is nonetheless home to only about half as many fourteeners as Colorado.

These fourteeners are understandably the focus for many hikers who visit the state, but hiking such high mountains demands special considerations. With nearly 3,000 feet of elevation gain, summiting Mount Bierstadt would be a strenuous undertaking under any conditions. But hiking at such high elevation requires acclimation: this should certainly not be the first hike you attempt after arriving in Colorado, and even spending several days in the "mile-high" city of Denver will not truly prepare you for hiking to 14,000 feet. Camping for at least one night beforehand near the trailhead, which starts from a high mountain pass, will help far more than simply driving straight here from Denver. But for many, even several days of acclimation might not be enough to ward off high elevation's subtle obstacles. Some hikers develop lingering headaches at this elevation, and almost all will find their energy sapped more quickly than normal as they push up the mountain. Here, 3,000 feet of elevation gain may feel like twice the challenge it would on another, lower mountain.

Besides the sheer challenge of the hike, this trail poses a few other hazards. The final scramble to the summit involves a rock scramble that

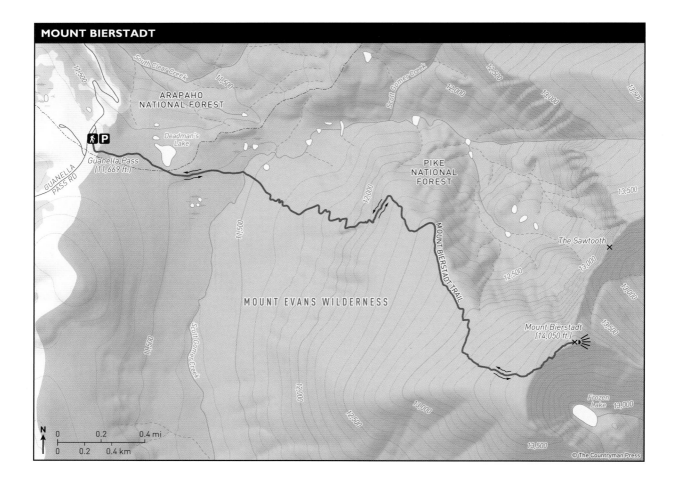

is short but arrives just when you'll be most sapped of energy. And since even the beginning of the hike will find you at high elevation, there is essentially zero shade along the trail, as you'll be hiking above the tree line. But that's not all! Oh, no. There are also the regular afternoon thunderstorms to consider, a reliable fixture of Colorado's fourteeners. During the short summer hiking season, assume that a thunderstorm will roll in sometime after noon, regardless of the weather down off the mountains. Always check the forecast for the mountain you'll be climbing itself—not the forecast for a town or city nearby.

Finally, there are the crowds. In spite of all these challenges, tackling a fourteener is a popular quest among hikers in Colorado, and Mount Bierstadt is not only one of the easier fourteeners to summit but also relatively accessible from Denver via car-friendly paved roads. On most trails, one might simply start early to avoid the crowds. Here, starting early is assumed, and necessary, to stay safe. On weekdays, you can still avoid the crowds, but on weekends you'll be hiking with company. Plan to be at the trailhead by sunrise at the latest, but an hour before sunrise is better still.

All that said, hiking a fourteener is an excellent challenge for any fit, prepared hiker, and Mount Bierstadt is an excellent summit to start with. No mountain should be approached without preparation and planning, and this hike, while popular, is an excellent test of your abilities, especially should you wish to attempt a more dangerous climb elsewhere. Hikers perish on Colorado's fourteeners every year, often simply due to overestimating their abilities or underestimating the challenge of the mountain before them. Bierstadt offers an enjoyable trail with excellent views: at the summit, you'll be face-to-face with neighboring Mount Evans, where America's highest paved road allows nonhikers to make a very different sort of ascent up a fourteener. Many other peaks can be seen, including Front Range fourteeners like Torreys Peak and Grays Peak. And if you're lucky, you may catch sight of the summit's resident caretakers, a family of mountain goats. Marvel that such creatures can make their living in such a place, under such harsh conditions, as you struggle to catch your own breath.

TRAIL OVERVIEW

The trail begins past the restrooms, heading toward Deadman's Lake. The first mile of trail is relatively flat and easy, easing you into the hike with several boardwalks over streams, meandering through subalpine brush. At 0.4 mile you will pass Deadman's Lake and descend slightly toward Scott Gomer Creek.

At 0.8 mile you will cross Scott Gomer Creek. Earlier in the season this crossing may involve wading through high water, with no possible way to cross without getting wet. Later in the summer and in early fall, however, the crossing can be made by rock hopping.

After this the trail begins to climb steadily. You will soon be hiking through delicate alpine tundra, so be sure to stay on the trail to avoid harming this fragile ecosystem.

At 2 miles the trail climbs to a bench and a large cairn. A brief, mostly level section of trail follows before making another strenuous push uphill, tackling the mountain over a series of switchbacks before climbing to the mountain's southwest shoulder. At about 3.4 miles you will reach a saddle below the peak of the mountain. Here, if you are lucky, you may catch sight of the mountain goats that live in this area.

From this point the trail makes a direct assault up Bierstadt to the summit. Only a short distance remains between you and the summit; however, this stretch of trail is composed of a steep uphill rock scramble. The path is unclear in many spots because the boulder field changes frequently, and it is easy to find yourself "off trail." However, even if the path is unclear, push uphill and be mindful of your footing.

Soon, the way to the summit becomes obvious. There, the peak of Bierstadt will reward you with fantastic views of Mount Evans and the sawtooth ridge connecting it directly to Bierstadt. To the west you will be able to see Mount Wilcox, Argentine Peak, Decatur Mountain, Grays Peak, and Torreys Peak. Abyss Lake and Frozen Lake gleam in their basins just below you. While there is ample space at the summit to break for lunch, it is often very windy here, and on busy weekends choice perches to sit fill quickly.

When you are ready to return, retrace your steps back to the parking area.

PLANNING

Mount Bierstadt is an extremely strenuous high-elevation peak. While its challenges have already been elaborated upon in this guide, these warnings should be taken very seriously. If you have traveled here from a low-elevation area, it is recommended that you spend a day or two above at least 8,000 feet before attempting to summit. Even hikers in otherwise excellent shape traveling here from sea level may find their body balking at the effects of the altitude on this hike. Some may experience headaches or nausea, or find that their energy reserves have vanished and no second wind appears to push them onward, even after rest breaks.

Day hikers should only attempt Mount Bierstadt during summer and early fall. Under winter conditions the trail poses an even more serious challenge and should not be attempted by casual hikers. Fall storms can roll in seemingly out of nowhere, and above-tree-line trails such as this become very deadly and difficult to navigate in whiteout conditions.

While an enjoyable hike in many ways, this is not a hike to be done in pursuit of solitude. This is a very popular trail, and many hikers start

Frozen Lake is nestled below the col of Mount Bierstadt

several hours before sunrise. It is best to be off the mountain by afternoon due to the frequency of summer storms, so try to gauge how much time you will need for your hike and plan accordingly. With no shelter or shade, you do not want to be caught on this mountain in a storm. If it looks as if a storm is imminent, turn back immediately.

GETTING THERE

The trailhead can be found on Google Maps by navigating to "Guanella Pass Trailhead." The parking area is located on Guanella Pass Road, 11 miles south of the town of Georgetown. The parking area fills quickly on weekends, often before sunrise.

CHASM LAKE

Colorado: Rocky Mountains National Park

DISTANCE: 9 miles

ELEVATION GAIN: 2,600 feet

TIME COMMITMENT: 5 to 7 hours

FEE: National Park Pass or entrance fee

DOGS: Not permitted on leash

CAMPING ALONG TRAIL: Yes

DIFFICULTY: A strenuous, steady climb uphill is made even more difficult by the high elevation of this hike.

Left: Chasm Lake

Chasm Lake has the sort of payoff that would make this hike a bucket list destination no matter where it was located, but in some ways this route is almost as much about the hike you aren't doing as the one you are. Chasm Lake is located just below the summit of Longs Peak, the high point of Rocky Mountain National Park and one of the most challenging fourteeners to hike in Colorado, with some sections that are closer to technical climbs than to hikes. Longs Peak, popular though it remains, has a deadly record: an average of two hikers die attempting to climb Longs Peak each year.

While Longs Peak itself may be a more technical and demanding challenge, beyond the purview of this book, hikers will find that the route to Chasm Lake, nestled below the summit, is just as satisfying. Indeed, there is a thought among some naturalist writers—a view that I happen to agree with—that the best vistas are often not found from the obvious high point, looking out at the world sprawled around you, but from ideal vantage points looking up at a mountain summit itself. By this thought, we should cherish the valley every bit as much as the peak. After all, is not the sight of that dramatic looming summit not inherently more dramatic than the many miles of distant, hazy land and smaller summits that surround it?

The sheer east-facing wall of Longs Peak, known as the "Diamond," rises more than 2,400 feet above Chasm Lake, making this one of the most dramatic alpine lakes in Rocky Mountain National Park and a solid rebuttal to the notion that one must tackle the highest peak to enjoy the best views. The hike itself is exceptional, at first making its way along creeks and brooks, passing from a rich forest into subalpine krummholz, over a boulder field, along a gorge, and offering vantages of gorgeous waterfalls as well as several alpine pools and lakes. Both Chasm Lake and Longs Peak are very popular hikes, understandably so—they offer some of the best views in one of the nation's premier national parks. Much of the final stretch of this hike is above the tree line and therefore dangerously exposed in the event of inclement weather, so be sure to plan and prepare thoroughly before your excursion.

TRAIL OVERVIEW

The trail begins past the Longs Peak Ranger Station, climbing steadily through a forest of lodgepole pine, fir, and spruce. At 0.5 mile you will come to an intersection with the Eugenia Mine Trail. Continue straight. At 1.2 miles you will pass a side trail that heads to the Goblins Forest Campground, a backcountry campsite.

At 1.7 miles the trail crosses the Larkspur Creek and begins switchbacking uphill. Shortly after, you will cross a bridge over Alpine Brook.

Around 2.2 miles you will leave the forest behind and enter the subalpine zone. With only small groves of twisted trees—known as krummholz—to block your view in this section, you will enjoy your first views of Longs Peak, as well as Mount Meeker and Mount Lady Washington.

At 2.6 miles the Battle Mountain Trail splits right. Turn left. At 3.4 miles you will arrive at the Chasm Lake Trail junction. The Longs Peak Trail, to the right, takes climbers to the summit of Longs Peak. Turn left. Just beyond the intersection, there is an outhouse with perhaps one of the best views you will ever experience from a public toilet.

The Chasm Lake Trail heads southwest along the wall of a deep gorge. Peacock Pool and Columbine Falls are visible ahead of you, while Chasm Lake is still hidden. After skirting the wall of the gorge, you will reach the alpine basin below Chasm Lake. From here the trail climbs up the steep shelf to the basin containing Alpine Lake. The rocks here are often slick, and hikers should be careful as they tackle this final obstacle.

You will arrive at Chasm Lake at 4.5 miles. Chasm Lake fills in a deep cirque at the base of Mount Lady Washington and Longs Peak. Mount Lady Washington is visible to the north, or to your right as you face the lake. Longs Peak rises above the lake to the west.

When you are ready to return, retrace your steps back to the parking area.

PLANNING

Chasm Lake is a strenuous high-elevation hike. If you have traveled here from a low-elevation area, it is recommended that you spend a few days in the area before attempting this hike. Even for fit, experienced hikers, altitude can quickly rob you of your strength, as well as bringing on headaches and nausea. This would be a challenging trail at any elevation, but the difficulties are enhanced significantly by the high altitude.

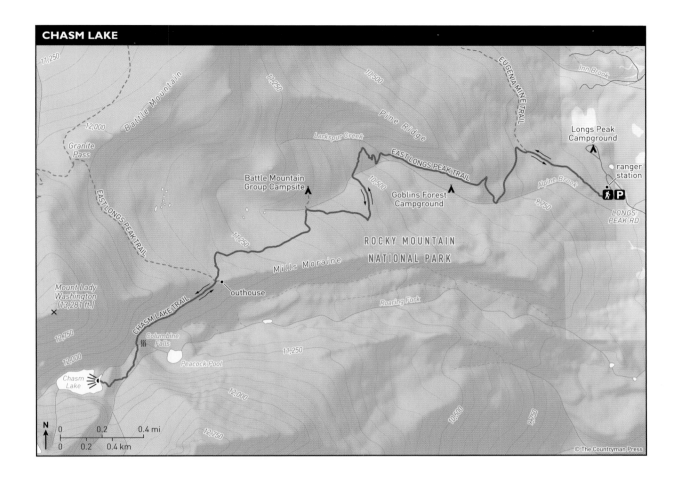

The final portion of this hike is above the tree line, and there is no shelter from either sun or weather. Bring sunscreen, protective clothing, and, as always, plenty of water. If it appears that a storm is incoming, turn back immediately. It is extremely dangerous to be caught on a mountain above the tree line during a storm.

GETTING THERE

The trailhead can be found on Google Maps by navigating to "Longs Peak Ranger Station." The parking area is off Longs Peak Road, accessed from CO 7, about 11 miles south of Estes Park, Colorado.

DUNRAVEN PASS TO MOUNT WASHBURN

Wyoming: Yellowstone National Park

DISTANCE: 6.8 miles

ELEVATION GAIN: 1,400 feet

TIME COMMITMENT: 4 to 5 hours

FEE: National Park Pass or entrance fee

DOGS: Not permitted

CAMPING ALONG TRAIL: No

DIFFICULTY: A strenuous, steady climb uphill is made even more difficult by the high elevation of this hike. However, a broad and easily navigated trail makes this hike accessible to all hikers who budget enough time and pace themselves.

Left: Mountain goats frequent the summit of Mount Washburn

Fire lookout towers aren't uncommon on the higher peaks of this nation's parks, but few of those fire towers are still actually staffed and used for their intended purpose. Mount Washburn is one of the exceptions: inside the tower, amid informative panels for tourists and the expected viewing platform, there are signs warning you not to attempt to enter the upper floor, as it is a private residence. Here, a ranger stationed alone for the summer spends morning to evening in a one-room cabin atop the tower, watching for signs of distant fires. An incredible and unique job, to be sure, with a whiff of the romantic about it—at least for those of us who already ascend mountains searching for solitude. While the crowds that gather in the bottom portion of the tower would no doubt grow distracting, I couldn't help but think that such a job might be my ideal. Why spend some of the time on top of a mountain when you could spend *all* of the time on top of a mountain?

Of course, there are many other, more important reasons why I've singled out Mount Washburn as the most memorable hike in Yellowstone National Park, a park with seemingly endless natural fascinations. While this trail is busy and you are unlikely to find yourself alone for more than short stretches of time, the crowds are not nearly so extreme as at many of the park's other, easier attractions, and even these drop off quickly as you ascend the mountain. Only a fraction of the hikers who set out up Mount Washburn seem determined enough to make it to the summit. Those who don't make it are missing out; as the views from the top are truly spectacular, but the views are not the only attraction. You may find yourself with some nonhuman company

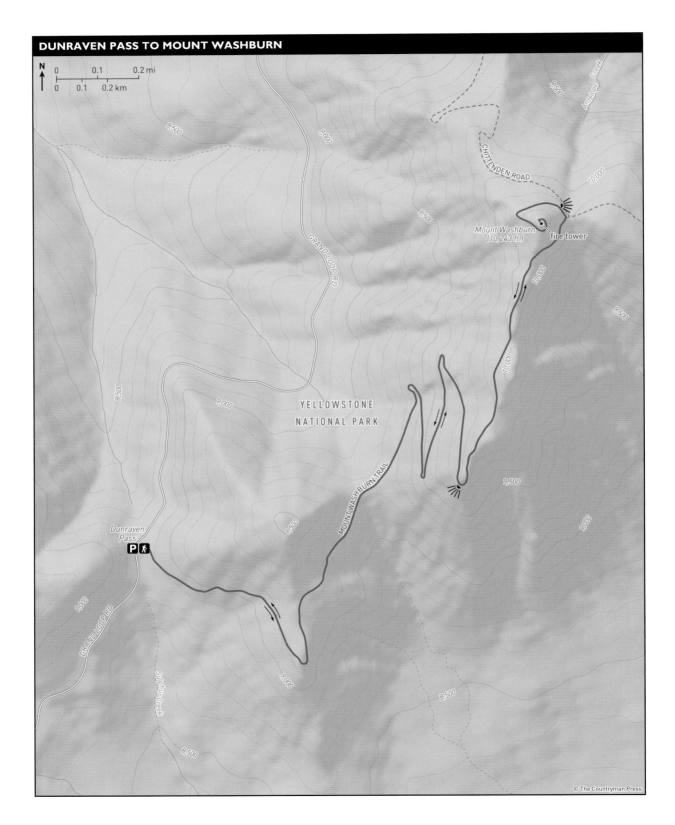

below the peak: families of goats live near the summit. A fairly reliable sight, these goats are not pets and should not be approached closely or touched, but they seem comfortable enough with the presence of humans that getting photos of them scrambling around the mountain is a trivial matter.

While Mount Washburn is not the highest peak in Yellowstone—that honor goes to Eagle Peak, a much less accessible and significantly more difficult mountain to climb—the views along the way really are unrivaled. They begin almost at once, with a mountain meadow dropping off steeply below the trail, flowers adding a vibrant splash of color in summer. Soon more views open up to the south and east, where the Grand Canyon of Yellowstone cuts apart the horizon—a massive, intimidating jag in the earth. On a clear day you'll even be able to see the sharp teeth of the Grand Tetons cutting into the sky 75 miles to the south.

The lookout tower atop Mount Washburn

TRAIL OVERVIEW

The trail starts uphill at once, an early indicator of the sort of grade you'll face for the vast majority of the hike. Almost at once, a valley will open up to your right, with Yellowstone's Grand Canyon visible in the distance. Colorful mountain flowers grow all around in the summer.

The trail climbs steadily for 0.6 mile before briefly leveling as it heads around a bend. The summit is visible ahead, with the Grand Canyon still to your right. Soon the steady uphill grade resumes.

At 1.4 miles you will reach the first of a series of switchbacks—the second bends at 1.7 and the third at 2.1 miles. Here you will be able to enjoy views to the west side of the park.

At 2.5 miles the final switchback offers another view of the tower on the summit before the trail swings around a rocky, open area. At 3 miles, hike along a wooden fence and the remains of the asphalt road that once ran to the summit. At 3.3 miles you will come to a col, with massive views

The Grand Canyon of Yellowstone cuts through the landscape below Mount Washburn

back down into the valley toward the canyon and equally impressive glimpses to the northwest. Around this area you will likely encounter the goats that live just below the summit—respect these creatures as the wild animals they are.

At 3.5 miles you will arrive at the summit and fire tower. When you are ready to return, retrace your steps back down to the parking area.

PLANNING

Summer and early fall are the recommended times to hike Mount Washburn. Snow may persist on the mountain well into summer, and hikers wishing to make their way up the mountain in June may need to consult a ranger to see what conditions are like at the top. Deep snow may persist on the path until the end of June or even early July.

Hikers should, as always, pay close attention to the weather forecast for the day and attempt their hike on another day if it appears that a storm is imminent. Nonetheless, even after careful monitoring of the forecast, storms may roll in out of nowhere. Always carry appropriate gear and assume that there is at least some chance you will get caught in a storm. Mount Washburn has the advantage of a secure lookout tower up top, which is well protected against lightning. Hikers close to the tower when a storm sweeps in should plan on riding out the storm from the safety of the tower.

GETTING THERE

The trailhead can be found on Google Maps by navigating to "Dunraven Pass." The parking area is located on Grand Loop Road, 5 miles north of Canyon Village.

CASCADE CANYON TRAIL FROM JENNY LAKE

Wyoming: Grand Tetons National Park

DISTANCE: 9 miles

ELEVATION GAIN: 1,100 feet

TIME COMMITMENT: 5 to 7 hours

FEE: Ferry ride fee; check online for current rates

DOGS: Permitted on leash

CAMPING ALONG TRAIL: Yes

DIFFICULTY: Relatively strenuous, with steep section at start and rugged rocky trail through canyon.

Left: Cascade Canyon provides almost nonstop mountain views

In some regions it's nearly impossible to pick a single, obvious "must-visit" hike. The geography is simply too vast, the trails too sprawling; a dozen summits and paths call out, each in its own unique way. While the Grand Tetons of Wyoming boast all these qualities, it is nonetheless easy to pick out the Cascade Canyon Trail as one all visitors should explore. Cascade Canyon is a popular hike in every way, to be sure, though there are ways to dodge the crowds. For one—as is often the case on a hike with an easily accessible and obvious attraction a short distance down the trail—most visitors turn around only about a mile into the hike. Few press on to reach the end of the canyon, but here, in this narrow valley nestled below the greatest of the area's peaks, you will experience the true grandeur of the Tetons up close.

The park began an extensive project in 2014 to rehabilitate overused trails and make improvements to popular viewing areas. The two spots that were the focus of this project—Hidden Falls and Inspiration Point—are the ultimate destination for most hikers who set out from Jenny Lake, and both of these scenic spots are found within a mile of the lake. By some estimates, fewer than a third of hikers who set out on this hike continue past Inspiration Point—meaning they miss out on 8 miles of gorgeous canyon views.

To reach the trailhead for this hike, visitors have the option of cutting out several miles of trail and taking a ferry ride across Jenny Lake. If you don't take the ferry, you'll be hiking an additional 2.8 miles (each way) around the edge of the lake. The ferry makes for an enjoyable ride, but it also means you'll be starting out on your hike at the same time as many others, and thus you'll have to make haste from the starting line if you wish to get ahead of the crowds. Personally, I enjoy simply skipping the boat ride and hiking around the lake.

From either starting point this hike is a simple there-and-back, though the network of trails extends far beyond the turnaround point, continuing into the heart of the park. While the Cascade Canyon Trail eventually forks, with a trail heading northwest to Lake Solitude and another veering southwest around the western flank of the Tetons, this fork will serve as the end point of your hike. Most of the elevation gain is tackled in the first mile, so, conveniently, the crowds will die off just after you've gotten all the hard work out of the way. You can expect to see wildlife here, including moose and bears, but as always, keep a safe distance from any animals you spot. Huckleberry bushes in the area are extra appealing to bears when they're in season, so you'll want to be extremely vigilant and mindful of bear safety practices.

TRAIL OVERVIEW

Hikers who are not taking the ferry across the lake will begin from the parking area by the visitor center and take the trail by the boat dock as it heads west, across the southern end of the lake. At 0.8 mile you will reach a split in the trail. The trail to the right takes a lower route along the lake, staying close to the shore. The trail to the left cuts higher up the bank, farther from the lake. Occasionally one of these trails may be closed for rehabilitation, but both will bring you to the boat dock and the main trailhead. Continue for 2.5 miles, until you reach the Cascade Canyon Trail by the boat dock. Skipping the ferry and hiking around the lake adds 5.6 miles round-trip to the mileage given in the stats for this hike.

For hikers taking the ferry across the lake, the trail begins by the boat dock, climbing through stately conifers. After crossing Cascade Canyon Creek, you will pass the Valley Trail, which serves as the western section of a loop around Jenny Lake. After about a half mile you will pass an intersection with a horse trail. Continue straight. Shortly after, you will pass the side trail leading to Hidden Falls to your left. Take this side trail to visit this beautiful, nearly 200-foot-tall waterfall.

From here, the trail climbs up a steep and rocky trail. As you approach Inspiration Point, you will cross a section of trail that follows a steep, rugged ledge. Practice extra caution here, especially if the trail may be wet.

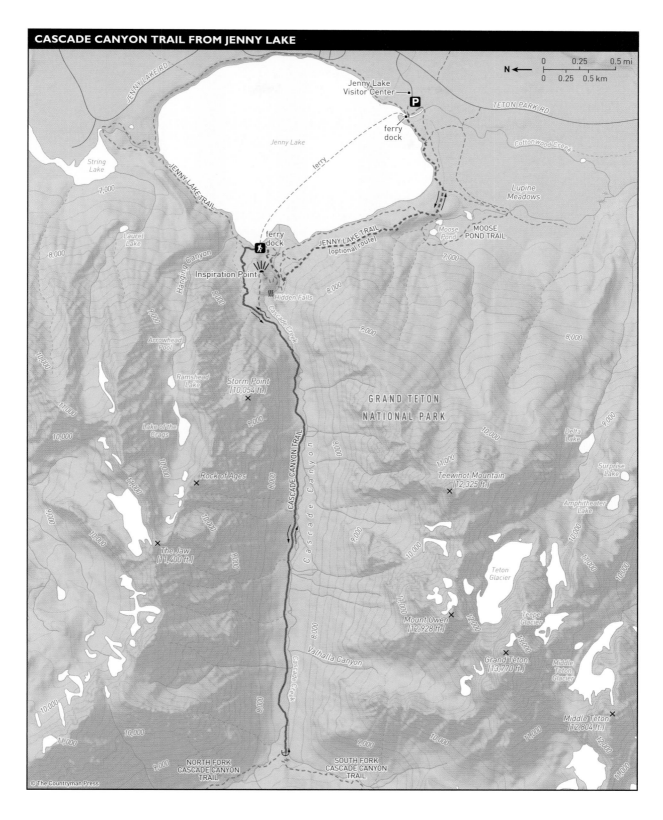

Just over a mile from the trailhead at the boat dock, you will arrive at Inspiration Point, where you will enjoy fantastic views of Jenny Lake below you and the Gros Ventre Mountains to the east. From here the trail continues west into the canyon. The most rugged and steep section of the trail is now behind you.

The trail will now follow Cascade Canyon Creek for the remainder of the hike. As there are many huckleberry, thimbleberry, and raspberry bushes throughout the canyon, you will have to be extra mindful of bears in this area. The creek can easily drown out the sound of your approach, and it's never a good idea to catch a bear by surprise. Make lots of noise, especially when approaching blind bends in the trail, and if possible, travel in groups of three or more (here is where the popularity of this trail might not be such a bad thing). It is always a good idea to carry bear spray on any hike where there is a chance of bear encounters.

At just under 2 miles, you will reach a large boulder field at the southern slope of Storm Point. Mount Owen, the second-highest mountain in Grand Teton National Park at 12,928 feet, will be visible to the south, with dramatic views of its craggy summit looming over the canyon. Around 2.6 miles you will pass a series of small ponds. Soon, more mountain views will open up around you, with Table Mountain and The Wigwams visible to the west.

At 5 miles you will come to the fork in the trail—your turning-around point.

PLANNING

If you plan to take the ferry to the trailhead to start the hike, make sure to consult the ferry schedule before arriving. As of 2018—depending on "water, weather, and trail conditions"—the ferry schedule is as follows:

May 15 through June 7, 10 a.m. to 4 p.m.

June 8 through September 3, 7 a.m. to 7 p.m.

September 4 through September 30, 10 a.m. to 4 p.m.

While most of the elevation gain in this hike is tackled in the first mile, keep in mind that temperatures in the canyon will continue to drop as you climb. Snow at the higher elevations may persist into summer, and if you are planning to hike here in the spring, you will likely need snow gear. Expect to encounter a range of temperatures and conditions, especially in the spring and the fall—the temperatures at the start of the hike, by Jenny Lake, can be as much as 20 degrees warmer than those higher up in the canyon. For this reason, it is not uncommon for rain by the lake to transform into snow higher up.

Bears are very active in this area, and all hikers should carry bear spray with them and hike in groups of three or more if possible. Make noise as you hike, especially in the canyon, where the sound of running water can cover up the sound of your approach. Most bear attacks occur simply because the bear was taken by surprise, so use extra caution while rounding blind turns.

GETTING THERE

The trailhead can be found on Google Maps by navigating to "Jenny Lake Visitor Center" or "Jenny Lake Trailhead." The parking area is located on Teton Park Road, 7 miles north of the park's southern entrance outside the town of Moose. The parking area, though large, fills very quickly on weekends.

Jenny Lake

IRON CREEK TO SAWTOOTH LAKE

Idaho: Sawtooth National Forest

DISTANCE: 10 miles

ELEVATION GAIN: 1,850 feet

TIME COMMITMENT: 5 to 6 hours

FEE: Permit required from self-serve kiosk along trail; no fee

DOGS: Permitted on leash

CAMPING ALONG TRAIL: Yes, with permit

DIFFICULTY: Strenuous and fairly long; intermediate hikers should allot extra time and account for plenty of rest breaks.

Left: Alpine Lake, nestled below Alpine Peak

When it comes to outdoor scenery, Idaho may be America's best-kept secret. Some corners of the state are treeless and seemingly empty—drive to the Sawtooth Wilderness from the east, and you'll go for so long without seeing a relic of civilization that you might begin to glance nervously down at your gas tank indicator and wish you'd topped off the tank one last time. Indeed, you shouldn't count on even finding a McDonald's for lunch out on a road trip here, but even the emptiness of eastern Idaho has its charm. Grasslands slowly rise into brownish-red stumps of hills, and then suddenly you will find yourself amid the Lost River Range, where Mount Borah, the highest peak in the state, presides over the lonely landscape. Eventually you'll be driving through the rugged canyons carved out by the Salmon River and surrounded by resilient greenery once again. Finally, from the west, the mountains of the Sawtooth Wilderness rise before you, and their craggy forested slopes simply demand exploration.

Though lesser in height than the Lost River Range, the Sawtooths are more, well, *mountainy*. Like the Tetons to the east, these rocky summits have that shapely quality we seem to look for in our peaks: the perfect angles, triangular peaks, the patches of snow clinging in just the right spots through summer, the sprawling forest at their base. They are postcard-perfect mountains, nestled in a beautiful sprawl of rugged wilderness dotted with alpine lakes and meadows. Yet outside of Idaho, hardly anyone seems to know this place is here.

Of course, with Boise only a few hours' drive away, the most popular hikes in the Sawtooth Mountains still see a good amount of traffic on weekends. You won't always experience total solitude here—but you easily could if you sought it. Many day hikes in this area could be extended

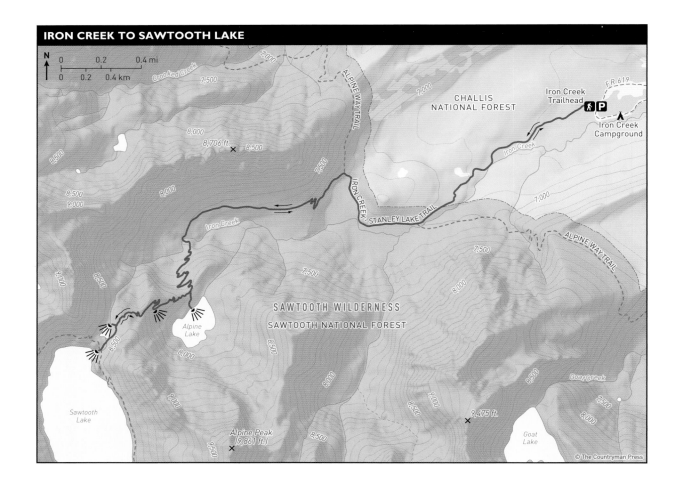

IRON CREEK TO SAWTOOTH LAKE

into backpacking trips, questing farther into the Sawtooth Wilderness, where one will likely see only a few other humans over the course of several days. In fact, while the Iron Creek to Sawtooth Lake hike is easily doable as a day hike, hikers with the gear for an overnight trek may wish to consider camping up top, by Sawtooth Lake.

TRAIL OVERVIEW

The trail begins alongside Iron Creek, gurgling downhill to your left. There will be little elevation change for this first segment of the trail, and at 1.2 miles you will enter the Sawtooth Wilderness, well marked by a sign.

Soon after, you will pass an intersection where the Alpine Way Trail cuts to your left. Stay straight toward Sawtooth Lake. At 1.8 miles the trail begins climbing uphill. Very soon after, you will reach a clearing and another intersection. Turn left at the sign, continuing uphill.

At 2.2 miles you will begin to switchback uphill. Soon you will be hiking a steep slope above a mountain meadow, then, at 3 miles, you will reenter the woods.

Soon you will find yourself near Iron Creek once more, and this time you will have to manage several creek crossings before again heading up a series of steep switchbacks. After climbing steadily, you will reach an intersection for a small spur trail heading downhill to Alpine Lake at 3.8 miles. This spur trail offers an up-close view of the lake, but more views—and better views—will arrive as you continue to ascend toward Sawtooth Lake. The views along this final stretch—following yet more switchbacks—are stunning, looking down to Alpine Lake and Alpine Peak behind it, and back north toward a spiny ridge of massive stone protrusions.

At 4.8 miles you will arrive at a small pond that precedes Sawtooth Lake. Continue around the left side of the pond, and very shortly you will arrive at Sawtooth Lake itself. Here you will find a number of potential

Sawtooth Lake

AMERICA'S BEST DAY HIKES

campsites for those wishing to turn this into an overnight expedition and many spots from which to enjoy a view of the lake. The trail continues around the east edge of the lake if you wish to push forward and find new perspectives, while another trail splits off on the north end of the lake and heads west.

When you are ready to return, retrace your steps down the trail and back to the parking area.

PLANNING

As with any mountainous area, especially at the higher elevations of the west, there are many additional dangers posed by inclement weather, ice, and snow. Keep an eye on the forecast. In the spring, early summer, and late fall, it is best to search for trail reports online—or talk to park rangers—to get an idea of what trail conditions are like. Snow persists late into the season at high elevations, and snow may still cover portions of the trail here well into July. Only very experienced hikers with the appropriate gear should attempt this hike in winter.

There is no fee for access to the trailhead, though you will have to fill out a permit once entering the Sawtooth Wilderness from a self-serve kiosk found about a mile into the hike. While there is no fee, you may be fined if you are found hiking in the Sawtooth Wilderness without having filled out a permit form, and rangers can regularly be found working on the trail.

GETTING THERE

The trailhead can be found on Google Maps by navigating to "Iron Creek Trailhead." The parking area is located at the end of Forest Road 619, approximately 3 miles off ID 21.

GRINNELL GLACIER TRAIL

Montana: Glacier National Park

DISTANCE: 10.5 miles

ELEVATION GAIN: 1,840 feet

TIME COMMITMENT: 5 to 7 hours

FEE: National Park Pass or entrance fee

DOGS: Not permitted

CAMPING ALONG TRAIL: No

DIFFICULTY: Strenuous but manageable grade; challenges may arise with trail conditions at higher elevations.

Left: Angel Wing looms above you for much of the hike

Glacier National Park is undoubtedly one of the most beautiful pieces of America you will ever encounter. With its turquoise lakes and arrowhead-like mountain peaks, it's distinct from any other park in the United States. Like many of the world's most curious geological formations, these distinct summits and scenic valleys are a remnant of ice ages past, evidence of the powerful force of massive glaciers sculpting the land. Of course, a place as memorable as Glacier—especially one designated as a National Park—does not escape attention. Glacier National Park has recently begun to beat Yellowstone for attendance numbers, which would be an astonishing feat on its own but is especially significant when one considers that Glacier has only one main road through the park and offers a much shorter season due to its northern location and mountainous terrain. Going-to-the-Sun Road, the main avenue through the park, is often not cleared of snow until late June and generally closes for the season again in September. This concentrated season, plus the unique beauty found here, means that the experience of driving through Glacier can often be a stressful one, with traffic resembling a trip through New York City more than a quiet backwoods getaway. Hikers should plan accordingly. The trails are similarly busy, and the Grinnell Glacier hike—while located off the more remote Many Glacier campground, one of the few major campgrounds not situated along Going-to-the-Sun Road—is among the most popular in the park.

Once you set out on this hike, however, there is no question that this is a can't-miss, bucket list–worthy trek; its popularity is completely understandable. The views along several alpine lakes—including the brilliantly colored Grinnell Lake—are absolutely stunning, with the massive form of Mount Gould dominating the horizon for much of this trail's length. Mile by mile, this hike has some of the most stunning views I've ever experienced, one right after another. And there is one benefit from the popularity of this trail: although grizzlies are known to hop onto the trails in this area (a shortcut through rough terrain for humans works just as well for a traveling bear), there is safety in numbers. It is always recommended that you hike in groups of three or more when wandering through bear country, so solo hikers and couples should consider hiking close to, or joining with, another group. However, the mere presence of other humans nearby does not mean you should let your guard down, as a bear might still wander across

The trail to Grinnell Glacier skirts several lakes, including Lake Josephine

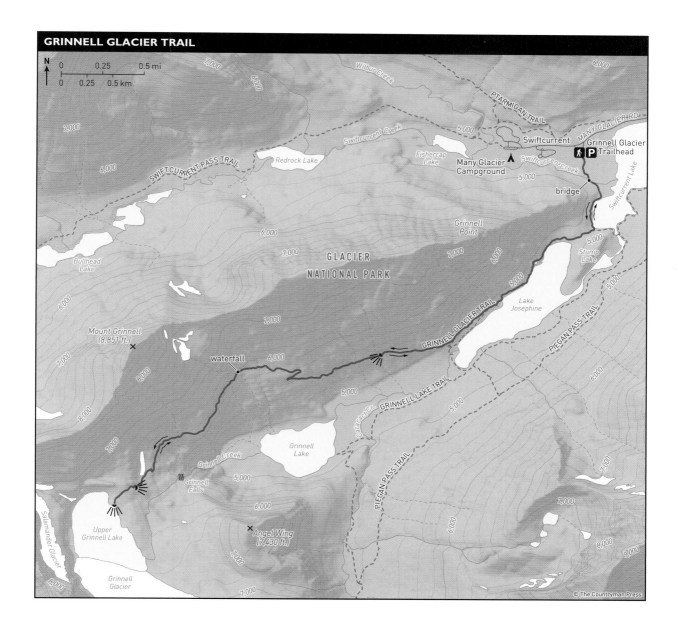

a popular trail at any time. You should never assume that your group is a guarantee that you *won't* see a bear—it is merely a helpful deterrent, because a group of humans chatting and making noise will alert a nearby bear that you are headed its way.

The Grinnell Glacier itself is a bit of a relic, one that future generations

sadly will not be able to enjoy in the same way, as the glacier is rapidly shrinking and will most likely disappear within the next few decades. In 1850, at the end of the Little Ice Age, Grinnell Glacier was measured at 710 acres, including the area of the Salamander Glacier, a shelf glacier that at that time was attached to Grinnell but is now separate. Between 1966 and 2005, however, Grinnell Glacier lost almost 40 percent of its acreage. By some projections, all the glaciers in the park will be gone within the next few decades.

Grinnell Lake from the trail to Grinnell Glacier

TRAIL OVERVIEW

The trail begins at the south end of the parking area. Cross a wooden bridge over Swiftcurrent Creek, and in a short distance you will begin hiking around the southwestern edge of Swiftcurrent Lake. Soon, as you skirt the edge of the lake, you will glimpse the massive flat-fronted profile of Mount Gould, with Angel Wing rising, rounded and smaller, before it.

At 0.7 mile keep right at the intersection, marked by a sign, and pass the end of Swiftcurrent Lake. Soon after, at 0.9 mile, keep right once again at the next fork as you begin to hike around the edge of Lake Josephine. The trail to the left descends downhill toward the lake. Be extremely vigilant for wildlife here—if you are lucky, you may spot a moose in the lake below, but grizzlies have also been known to use the Grinnell Glacier Trail around this area. Be sure to make noise so that any wildlife knows you are approaching, and keep bear spray at the ready.

At 1.8 miles keep right at the fork. Soon you will pass the end of Lake Josephine, and the trail will begin to head more steeply uphill. Below you the Cataract Creek winds between Swiftcurrent Lake and Lake Josephine. Around 2.5 miles you will begin to enjoy great views of Grinnell Lake, a glistening turquoise-blue alpine lake, from an exposed ridge. The trail here is somewhat narrower, with steep drop-offs to the side, so families with children should be extra cautious.

As the trail continues to climb, you will pass through alpine meadows with beautiful wildflowers, and soon you will spot several small waterfalls ahead, tumbling from the cliffs of Mount Grinnell to your right. At 3.8 miles you will pass below a waterfall and approach a section of the trail that hugs the cliff face. Snow often persists in this area well into July, so be prepared to navigate treacherous snow bridges here. Early in the season, the trail is often closed beyond this point, and hikers will have to stop here to enjoy views of the glaciers and lakes from this nonetheless magnificent vantage. Keep an eye out for bighorn sheep and goats in this area as well, as they are often seen resting in the meadows above the trail.

At 4.6 miles the trail begins to climb a series of steep switchbacks through a glacial moraine riddled with boulders. From here you'll be able to enjoy a stunning view back down into the valley, with Grinnell Lake and Lake Josephine below you and Sherburne Lake far off in the distance.

At 5 miles you will arrive at the Grinnell Glacier overlook, with dramatic views of the glacier, which spanned about 700 acres a century ago but is rapidly shrinking with each passing year. The 9,553-foot summit of Mount Gould towers above you, and just below its summit you may spot Gem Glacier, the smallest named glacier in the park.

When you are ready to return, descend the way you came and retrace your steps back to the parking area.

PLANNING

Glacier National Park is an extremely popular park that has only a narrow season in which visiting is practical. Going-to-the-Sun Road is generally only open from late June to September. As such, the park sees an intense rush of tourism in July and August. Only a few campsites in the park offer advance reservations, and most are first-come, first-served. Campgrounds fill up very early in the day. There is little difference in traffic between a Monday and a Friday in the park—assume that all of the major campgrounds will be full by late morning. The Many Glacier Campground is just down the road from the trailhead; all other campgrounds are a significant distance away, because this section of the park is relatively isolated from the main corridor. The Many Glacier Lodge offers an alternative to camping for those who wish to stay in the comfort of a full-service hotel.

Snow often persists at higher elevations in the park well into the summer, and hikers attempting the Grinnell Glacier Trail in June and July will most likely encounter snow bridges and potentially difficult snow crossings. Hiking poles can help a great deal with keeping your balance in slick, slippery spots. Traction devices are also recommended early or late in the season when ice may be present.

Hikers often spot mountain goats, marmots, moose, and sometimes, of course, grizzlies along this trail. As a reminder, always stay at least 100 feet from wildlife in the park, as it is extremely dangerous for any large animal to become accustomed to humans, and especially for these animals to associate humans with food. Collecting flowers and picking plants is prohibited in the park, and hikers should always stay on designated trails to avoid trampling and harming the fragile ecosystems found in mountain climates.

GETTING THERE

The trailhead can be found on Google Maps by navigating to "Grinnell Glacier Trailhead." The parking area is located just past the Many Glacier Hotel road. This trailhead is not located along Going-to-the-Sun Road—Many Glacier has its own entrance into the park off US 89 in the town of Babb.

HIGHLINE TRAIL

Montana: Glacier National Park

DISTANCE: 11.8 miles

ELEVATION GAIN: 1,950 feet

TIME COMMITMENT: 6 to 9 hours

FEE: National Park Pass or entrance fee

DOGS: Not permitted

CAMPING ALONG TRAIL: Yes, with permit

DIFFICULTY: While a long hike, the Highline Trail does not have any especially strenuous sections and should be accessible to all hikers who budget plenty of time.

Left: A steep trail winds upslope to the ridge separating the Highline Trail from the Grinnell Glacier

Among Glacier National Park's most obvious geographical landmarks, its valleys may not stand out as prominently as its stunningly colored turquoise lakes or its arrowhead-shaped mountain peaks. Like those features, the dramatic U-shaped valleys of Glacier were formed by the glacial action of past ice ages and help to create the park's distinct, memorable landscapes—particularly noticeable along the busy Going-to-the-Sun Road and the Highline Trail, which follows the contours of the road at a slightly higher elevation for much of its length.

Because the Highline Trail traces the U-bends of sheer glacial valleys, the grade on either side of the trail is generally extremely steep. During the first mile of the hike, a handrail made of hoseline is set into the rock cliff that forms the trail, giving hikers with an extreme fear of heights something to hold on to. As the Highline Trail is extremely popular, there will be many instances where you will have to pass other hikers traveling the opposite direction, forcing one party to take the outside, cliff-edge route. However, nothing on the Highline Trail approaches the level of dizzying heights of knife-edge hikes like Utah's Angels Landing. There are ample spots where it is easy to pass other hikers without tottering over the edge of a cliff. I myself have a fairly standard fear of heights, and I had no trouble at all with this stretch of trail.

The characteristic U-shape of Glacier's valleys, with extremely steep sides and flat or rounded bottoms, is formed when a glacier moves down a slope, scouring out a valley in its path. Valleys in other parts of the country that were formed by rivers are usually V-shaped, and thus more severe; Glacier's U-valleys give the landscape a unique, wavy appearance. Besides providing hikers with an eye-opening vantage of these glacial valleys, the Highline Trail takes hikers past a number of notable Glacier landmarks. Going-to-the-Sun Road and the Highline Trail cut into a portion of what is known as the Garden Wall, named for the abundance of flowering plants and shrubs that grow here in the summer. Part of this area is also referred to as the Weeping Wall for the many waterfalls that spring from the rocks and cascade past the road below. For the

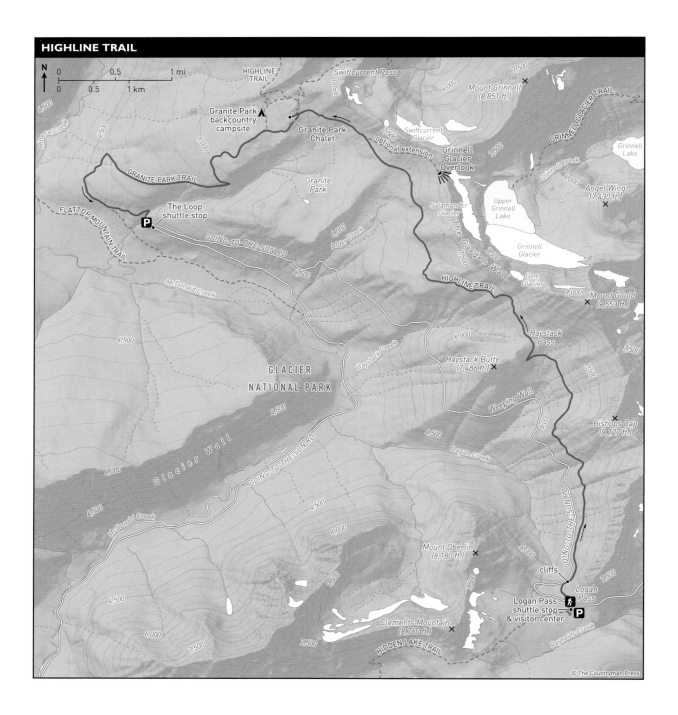

N

0	0.5	1 mi
0	0.5	1 km

HIGHLINE
TRAIL

Swiftcurrent Pass

7,500

6,000

Mount Grinnell
(8,851 ft.)

GRINNELL GLACIER TRAIL

Granite Park
backcountry
campsite

Granite Park
Chalet

optional extension

Swiftcurrent
Glacier

7,500

Grinnell
Glacier
Overlook

Grinnell Creek

6,000

Grinnell
Lake

7,500

Mineral Creek

GRANITE PARK TRAIL

4,500

4,000

Granite
Park

Salamander
Glacier

Angel Wing
(7,430 ft.)

Upper
Grinnell
Lake

FLATTOP MOUNTAIN TRAIL

The Loop
shuttle stop

Alder Creek

The Garden Wall

Grinnell
Glacier

GOING-TO-THE-SUN RD

7,500

Gem
Glacier

HIGHLINE TRAIL

9,000

Mount Gould
(9,553 ft.)

McDonald Creek

4,500

4,500

6,000

Haystack Creek

Haystack
Pass

7,500

7,500

GLACIER
NATIONAL PARK

Haystack Butte
(7,486 ft.)

Weeping Wall

Bishops Cap
(9,127 ft.)

Glacier Wall

4,500

4,500

4,500

Logan Creek

6,000

6,000

6,000

McDonald Creek

Mount Oberlin
(8,180 ft.)

GOING-TO-THE-SUN RD

4,500

6,000

cliffs

Logan
Pass

Logan Pass
shuttle stop
& visitor center

7,500

7,500

7,500

Clements Mountain
(8,760 ft.)

Reynolds Creek

HIDDEN LAKE TRAIL

© The Countryman Press

more adventurous hiker, a short but extremely steep and strenuous side trail heads to the top of the Garden Wall, demonstrating how the wall acts as a boundary between the two halves of the park: on the east side, hikers will glimpse the Grinnell Glacier and a multitude of lakes which require several hours of driving and many hours of hiking to reach from the other side.

Finally, the Highline Trail offers an opportunity to visit the Granite Park Chalet, a unique hiker's hostel at an elevation of nearly 7,000 feet. Although it is reachable only by hiking, guests can nonetheless book a stay at the chalet and use it as a base for additional day hikes and adventures, or simply to watch the sunset from a unique mountain setting without having to pack a tent. The chalet offers a basic kitchen where guests may cook their meals, but it has no running water and no other services besides a backcountry toilet (also accessible for day hikers). Now designated a National Historic Landmark, the chalet was built in 1914 by the Great Northern Railway. Originally one of eight such buildings in the park, only the Granite Park and Sperry Chalets remain today.

TRAIL OVERVIEW

From the Logan Pass parking area, cross the road at the sign for the trailhead, being careful to watch for passing vehicles on this busy road. Continue down the trail as it heads through a small, isolated valley cut off by Going-to-the-Sun Road. Observe Mount Oberlin rising to your left—in spite of the distance you'll be hiking, you will be able to glimpse this peak from a variety of angles for nearly the entirety of your hike.

At 0.3 mile you will venture out onto a steep path along a sheer rock cliff which rises above Going-to-the-Sun Road. A hand cable has been fixed into the rock here to give you something to hold on to—though when passing other hikers, one group will have to take the outside position. Be careful and courteous during this portion of the hike, pausing at sections where the path is wider to allow oncoming traffic to more easily pass. This section of the trail is only a third of a mile in length, so even slow-going hikers moving at a careful, anxious pace will quickly be past this heady portion of trail.

At 1 mile you pass several stream crossings—many streams of snow melt tumble down the Garden Wall here, some turning into the dramatic waterfalls of the Weeping Wall. At 2.2 miles you will hike under more rugged cliffs, though without the steep drop-offs that marked the first

section of the hike. Soon after, the trail will begin to steepen. At 3.2 miles you will pass around a U-shaped valley and begin winding uphill toward Haystack Pass.

At 3.5 miles, if hiking in the first half of summer, you will cross over a snowfield after tackling several switchbacks. At an elevation of 7,024 feet, Haystack Pass forms the saddle between Haystack Butte to your left and the Garden Wall. Here the Garden Wall is in fact the southeastern flank of Mount Gould, the prominent mountain which looms ahead of you for

The Granite Park Chalet at dawn

the duration of the Grinnell Glacier hike. With fantastic views and an option to hike up a short side trail onto Haystack Butte, many hikers pick this spot to stop for lunch, and many who wish to make a shorter day of it simply turn back here for an easy there-and-back hike.

Past Haystack Pass, the trail continues to ascend up the sheer side of the next valley. You will soon reach the trail high point, 7,280 feet, at 4.1 miles, around the bend of a valley. Half a mile later, a view of distant Lake McDonald opens up between the slopes of Mount Cannon and Heavens Peak.

Hike through a few areas of picturesque pines, and at 6.9 miles you will reach an intersection with the side trail to the Grinnell Glacier overlook to your right. This trail offers a different perspective from the Grinnell Glacier hike, which originates on the other side of the Continental Divide and climbs to the glacier from below. This trail, bursting very steeply uphill over less than a mile, looks down on the glacier from above. This dizzying perspective is not for the faint of heart and is a significant challenge after an already long day hike, but the view is staggering, with five of Glacier's pristine lakes visible, in addition to the glaciers.

Past this trail, continue for another half a mile. Here you will reach an intersection where a trail to the left heads downhill, toward The Loop. A short distance straight ahead lies the Granite Park Chalet, a fascinating landmark even if you are not planning to stay the night. Here, hikers may use the pit toilet or purchase snacks and beverages inside the chalet.

At the intersection just before the chalet, the trail (to the left if facing the direction you hiked in from Logan Pass) heading downhill is the Granite Park Trail, commonly referred to as the Loop Trail, which will return you to Going-to-the-Sun Road. A little more than a half mile from the chalet, you will pass a spur trail heading to the Granite Park backcountry campground, which offers four campsites for primitive camping.

Pass through a forested area of pines, where hikers should be on the lookout for bear activity. While much of the Highline Trail traverses steep valley slopes where bears are unlikely to venture, bears are commonly spotted here. Be sure to make noise as you hike to alert bears to your presence, and hike in groups of three or more whenever possible. Here you may also notice lingering signs of the damage done by the 2003 Trapper Creek Fire, which devastated the area.

Continue descending steeply, and at 11.2 miles you will reach the Packers Roost Trail junction. Take the trail to your left and walk another half mile. Cross over a footbridge, and soon you will arrive at the trailhead and Going-to-the-Sun Road. From here, take the shuttle bus back up Going-to-the-Sun Road to Logan Pass and your car.

PLANNING

Glacier National Park is an extremely popular park that has only a narrow season in which visiting is practical. Going-to-the-Sun Road is generally only open from late June to September. As such, the park sees an intense rush of tourism in July and August. Only a few campsites in the park offer advance reservations, and most are first-come, first-served. Campgrounds fill up very early in the day. There is little difference in traffic between a Monday and a Friday in the park—assume that all of the major campgrounds will be full by late morning. The Highline Trail begins at the Logan Pass parking area, which is one of the busiest parking areas in this already extremely busy park.

The Granite Park Chalet allows visitors to stay the night in a rustic mountain lodge

After the lot fills up in the morning, cars will often circle the lot for minutes, waiting for a spot to open.

Snow often persists at higher elevations in the park well into the summer, and hikers attempting the Highline Trail in June and July will most likely encounter snow bridges and potentially difficult snow crossings. Hiking poles can help a great deal with keeping your balance in slick, slippery spots.

Mountain goats and bighorn sheep can often be spotted near the Highline Trail. Hikers should always stay at least 100 feet from all wildlife. Even seemingly harmless animals such as goats and sheep can be dangerous and indeed have resulted in human deaths in the past. Never provoke, pet, or feed animals. An animal that becomes accustomed to humans or begins to associate humans with food can become dangerous. Bears, of course, are extremely dangerous, and they are often seen near the Logan Pass area, as well as by Granite Park Chalet.

GETTING THERE

The trailhead can be found on Google Maps by navigating to "Logan Pass Visitor Center." The parking area is located across the road from the trailhead. Logan Pass is the high point of Going-to-the-Sun Road, located 31 miles east of the west park entrance.

Since this hike relies on a shuttle bus to transport you from one end of the hike to the other—though, optionally, the hike can also be done as a long there-and-back with the Granite Park Chalet as its midpoint—the recommended approach is to leave your vehicle at the Loop Trail parking area, take a shuttle bus to Logan Pass, and then hike from there, ultimately returning to the parking area where you left your vehicle.

BLODGETT CANYON OVERLOOK

Montana: Bitterroot National Forest

DISTANCE: 3 miles

ELEVATION GAIN: 550 feet

TIME COMMITMENT: 1 to 2 hours

FEE: None

DOGS: Permitted

CAMPING ALONG TRAIL: No

DIFFICULTY: Relatively easy climb up a short trail; requires some exertion but no particular challenges.

Left: Looking down upon the massive wilderness of Blodgett Canyon

As an amateur photographer, I've become used to looking at the vistas on hikes from a variety of perspectives. I'm still that same small, humbled human gaping out at the sheer scale of nature, of course. Inevitably, though, I'll also enjoy my landscapes with an eye for composition—attempting to capture the view before me in a way that will translate into a photograph. On some hikes, however, this hobby feels downright futile. Some views are just too breathtakingly massive to ever be captured. The Blodgett Canyon Overlook is one such place: a sudden overview of a space too vast and intricate to come across in a picture. There's nothing to do but stand there and enjoy the scenery in person for as long as you're able to stay. And if that's the only way to really appreciate how grand this vista is, well, then it's all the more reason for recommending this particular hike.

To the west of this overlook, where Blodgett Canyon snakes into the mountains toward the Idaho border, one would have to walk for nearly a hundred miles before coming upon anything resembling a town. However, what makes this hike special is the beauty found on all parts of the trail and its relative accessibility for all levels of hiker. At only around 3 miles round-trip, the Blodgett Canyon Overlook can be tackled confidently even by inexperienced hikers. And the rewards start almost at once, with open meadows and views down into the Bitterroot Valley. Of course, after only a short distance hiking, one reaches the tremendous expanse of the Blodgett Canyon.

While there are no grizzly bears in this area, hikers have reported encountering black bears in the Blodgett Valley below, and it is always a good idea to carry bear spray. While the chances of a bear encounter here may be small, there are plenty of other potentially dangerous animals you might run into. Hikers have also reported moose on the trail—these

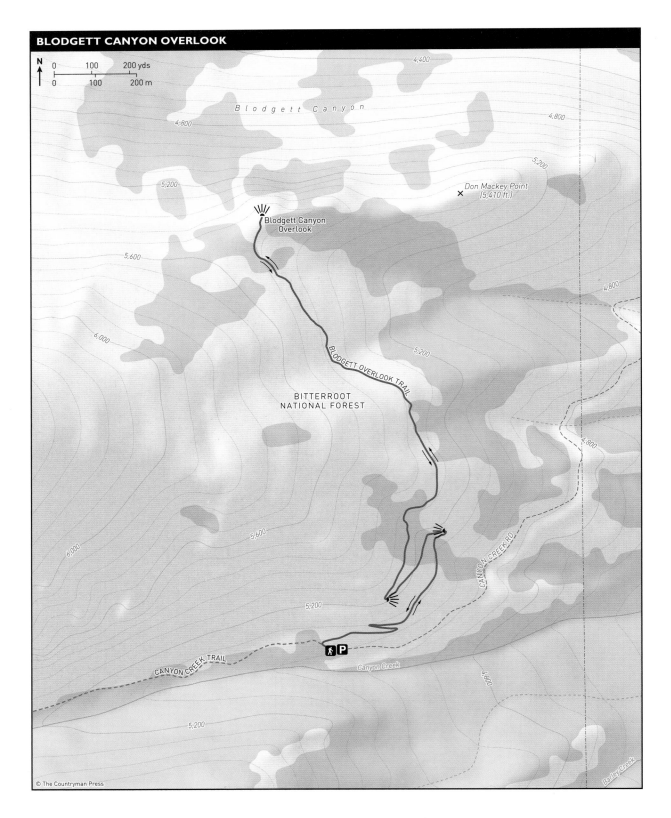

N

| 0 | 100 | 200 yds |
| 0 | 100 | 200 m |

4,400

Blodgett Canyon

4,800

5,200

5,200

Don Mackey Point
(5,410 ft.)
×

Blodgett Canyon
Overlook

5,600

4,800

BLODGETT OVERLOOK TRAIL

6,000

5,200

BITTERROOT
NATIONAL FOREST

4,800

5,600

6,000

CANYON CREEK RD.

5,200

CANYON CREEK TRAIL

Canyon Creek

4,800

5,200

Barley Creek

© The Countryman Press

huge animals can be quite dangerous if they charge, so, as always, keep a safe distance.

TRAIL OVERVIEW

From the parking area, the trail forks immediately. Turn right at the sign as the trail heads uphill. You will begin to ascend through an area of scree, though the trail cuts cleanly through the rock slope, so you will not have to do any scrambling.

The trail switchbacks up a steep slope, and soon you will have views down toward the valley and the town of Hamilton, as well as the distant Sapphire Mountains in the east. At 0.4 mile you will reach a bench overlook that faces Canyon Peak. Continue, and at 0.6 mile you will pass another bench, this one facing east, toward the valley. Along the way, amid the grand ponderosa pines, you will also notice the burnt remains of wildfires from past years.

At 1 mile you will glimpse the Blodgett Canyon opening up ahead. After another half a mile, you will reach the canyon overlook. Here a variety of rocky outcrops offer perches with stunning views into the canyon.

When you are ready to return, retrace your steps back to the parking area.

PLANNING

The trailhead is accessed up a winding, steep dirt service road which might pose issues, depending on the sort of vehicle you drive. Larger vans and RVs may not be able to navigate this nerve-wracking road, cars with low clearance will need to watch out for large rocks on the road, and all vehicles will want to use extreme caution if attempting this route when there may be snow or ice. The parking area is small, and on weekends with nice weather, it may not be possible to find a parking spot. Early mornings or weekdays are best for guaranteed parking. If hiking in the early morning or evening, be especially vigilant for wildlife.

GETTING THERE

The trailhead can be found on Google Maps by navigating to "Blodgett Overlook Trailhead." The parking area is located at the end of Canyon Creek Road North.

MIDWEST

ELK MOUNTAIN

Oklahoma: Charons Garden Wilderness

DISTANCE: 2.3 miles

ELEVATION GAIN: 580 feet

TIME COMMITMENT: 1 to 2 hours

FEE: None

DOGS: Permitted

CAMPING ALONG TRAIL: No

DIFFICULTY: Easy, short trail, though with some rocky areas that require dexterity.

Oklahoma is not a state known for its mountains, and even when you're headed to the Wichita Mountains Wildlife Refuge with every expectation to hike, the first glimpse of these rocky low hills rising above the surrounding flat earth can come as a shock. While perhaps lacking in the height of the mountain ranges of the West or the sense of endlessness that comes with the deep, old, forested mountains of the East Coast, the Wichita Mountains immediately impress with their ruggedness. They may not be big, but in their own craggy way, they bring personality. And, of course, the potential for some very fun hiking.

Fittingly, a summit of Elk Mountain in the Charons Garden Wilderness area of the Wichita Mountains Wildlife Refuge does not necessitate a particularly demanding hike. Though the trail is short it is no less exciting for it, and some hikers may find it more challenging than they anticipated, due to the rocky, rough terrain. There's no true rock scrambling required on this hike, but hikers should nonetheless be prepared for a rough trail. While none of the boulder fields are quite so severe as to warrant real scrambling, you may see why the area is a popular destination for rock climbers: throughout the rest of the refuge there are several large rock faces ideal for the sport. The views from the top are, of course, excellent, as they are almost entirely unobstructed. The low hills of the Wichita Mountains rise around you for many miles, and to the south lies the flat expanse of Oklahoma.

There is much more to see in the rest of the refuge, of course, and the primary draw for many is the wildlife itself. You'll find herds of bison still wandering free, and you may even spot some of the park's elk while on your hike. Deer, longhorn, and prairie dogs make their home here as well. In fact, the park played a vital role in helping to save America's bison at the turn of the 20th century. By 1907, bison had been extinct on the southern Great Plains for several decades. They were reintroduced to the wild here in the Wichita Mountains when the American Bison Society transported 15 bison here by railcar from the Bronx Zoo. Today, the bison herd numbers more than 600.

Left: Prickly pear cactus grows around the summit of Elk Mountain

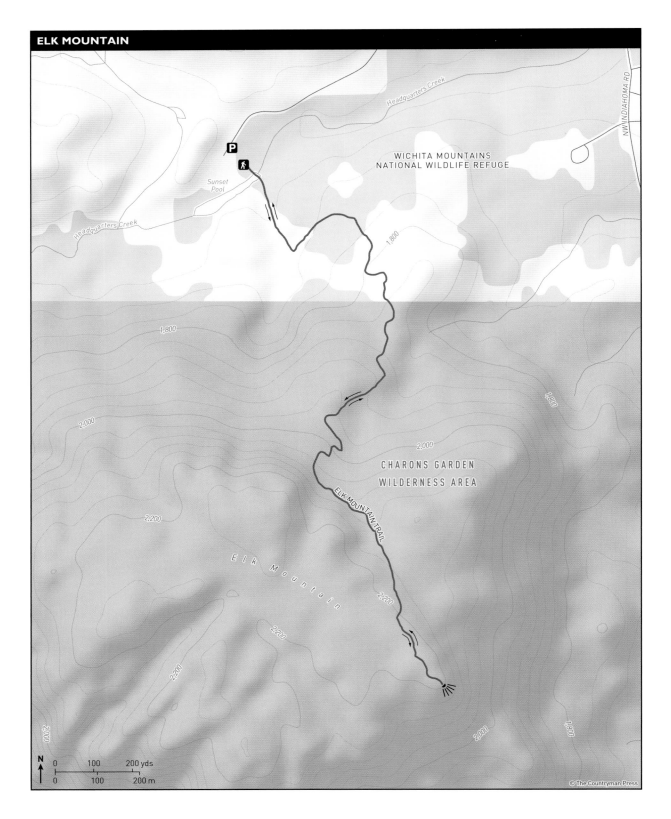

Headquarters Creek

NW INDIAHOMA RD

WICHITA MOUNTAINS
NATIONAL WILDLIFE REFUGE

Sunset
Pool

Headquarters Creek

1,800

1,800

1,800

1,800

2,000

2,000

2,000

CHARONS GARDEN
WILDERNESS AREA

2,200

ELK MOUNTAIN TRAIL

2,200

Elk   Mountain

2,200

2,200

2,200

2,000

1,800

2,000

N

| 0 | 100 | 200 yds |
| 0 | 100 | 200 m |

© The Countryman Press

TRAIL OVERVIEW

The trail begins at the picnic area, though you may have to walk a short distance to find it if you have parked at the first parking area that is just up the road. From the picnic area, a large bridge crosses Headquarters Creek and Sunset Pool. Soon after, you will pass a small falls, then enter a cluster of trees, heading uphill.

In 0.2 mile the trail makes a hard left turn at a large rock. Look for the faint path making its way northeast through high grass. You will begin to make your way around a large boulder field, climbing slowly in elevation. If you wander off trail, it will be difficult to reorient yourself, so pay careful attention during this section. However, for much of this portion of the hike, the path is fairly clearly marked with stone dividers on either side of the trail.

At 0.75 mile you will briefly pass under tree cover. Then, at 1.1 miles, you will arrive at the open rocky summit. This is a large area with many huge boulders to scramble around, nooks and rock fields to explore, and 360-degree views of Oklahoma sprawled around you. One could easily

Elk Mountain offers hikers panoramic views of the rugged Charons Garden Wilderness

spend an hour or more just exploring this expansive summit area. However, be mindful that there are no real trails at this point, and there are several areas where a fall from a rock could cause serious injury. Be careful where you step as well, as the summit is home to many fragile plants, including prickly pear cactus.

When you are ready to return, retrace your steps back to the parking area.

PLANNING

While a short trail, the hike up Elk Mountain offers little shade, and in the summer the heat can be intense. An early morning or late afternoon hike is recommended on hot days. Regardless, plan accordingly—bring plenty of water, a hat, sunglasses, and sunscreen.

While overall this is a relatively easy hike, even easy hikes can pose serious dangers. The trail is rugged, and there are many rocky areas where a fall would cause serious injury. The trail may be dangerous to hike when the rocks might be wet or icy.

GETTING THERE

The trailhead can be found on Google Maps by navigating to "Charon's Garden/Elk Mountain Trail Head." The parking area is located just off OK 49, 7 miles west of the Wichita Mountains Wildlife Refuge Visitor Center.

BLACK ELK PEAK

South Dakota: Black Elk National
Forest/Custer State Park

DISTANCE: 7.4 miles

ELEVATION GAIN: 1,440 feet

TIME COMMITMENT: 4 to 5 hours

FEE: Fee required for entrance
into Custer State Park; see
Planning section for details.
Permit required at self-serve kiosk
halfway up trail.

DOGS: Permitted on leash

CAMPING ALONG TRAIL: No

DIFFICULTY: Moderately
strenuous climb up a
straightforward trail.

Left: The view from the lookout
tower atop Black Elk Peak

Black Elk Peak is not just the high point of South Dakota's marvelous Black Hills but is in fact the tallest mountain east of the Rockies. This prominence is all the more peculiar when one considers the mountain's location—the high point of a state known for being exceptionally flat, in a great region of the country also known for being exceptionally flat. This isn't just a geological trivia point, however, when you are facing Black Elk in person. To truly understand what makes this peak so special, one must first understand how curious South Dakota's Black Hill region is.

The name—*Ȟe Sápa* in the Lakota language—was inspired by the appearance of these mountains from a distance, dark with tree cover, rising stark above endless treeless grassland. Indeed, it is astonishing to approach the region and see mountains rising here, as the world surrounding the Black Hills truly could not be more different. Drive for 200 miles in either direction and you see will nothing but plains. Every time I've visited this area, the experience is strangely powerful, watching this unlikely island of prominence break free of the horizon. Drive into the Black Hills and you will continue to be astonished—its craggy, steep valleys and spires of stone are memorable enough on their own, but the whole time you feel as if you've slipped into some other world, some hidden secret place on the map. In the north, roads wind between sheer, high canyon cliffs. To the south, near Black Elk Peak, stone spires a hundred feet high rise like the fingers of some dead titan. Many of these eroded granite pillars can be found in the area, a number of them visible from Needles Highway, which continues past the parking area for Sylvan Lake. The Needles were in fact the original site proposed for the Mount Rushmore carvings, but the site was moved due to the poor carving properties of the stone.

Naturally, the hiking in this unique area is excellent, and Black Elk Peak is perhaps the most memorable of the region's day hikes. The summit is crowned by a large stone fire tower, now abandoned and open to the

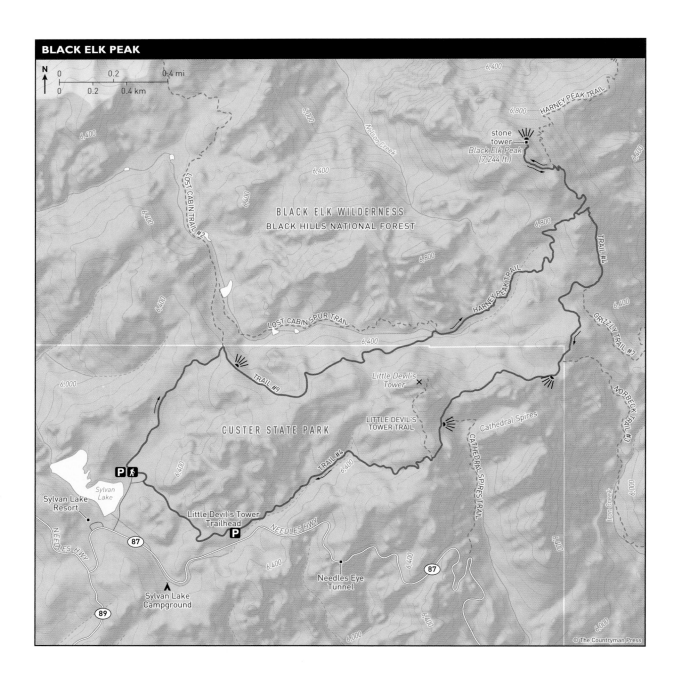

The needles of the Black Hills are some of the most interesting rock formations you will see anywhere in the United States

public. Inside, one can descend into the base of the tower and view the rooms where the volunteers who manned the tower would spend their weeklong shifts. The views from the tower are incredible, and on a clear day one can see four states from this perch: South Dakota, Nebraska, Wyoming, and Montana.

Until 2016 Black Elk Peak was known as Harney Peak, named after US General William S. Harney. The name was controversial for many years, however, due to Harney's massacre of Brulé Sioux warriors, women, and children in the Battle of Blue Water Creek in Nebraska in 1855. In August 2016, the US Board on Geographic Names voted to officially change the mountain's name from Harney Peak to Black Elk Peak. The move was supported by the Lakota Council of the Pine Ridge Reservation, honoring Black Elk, a noted shaman.

TRAIL OVERVIEW

This guide will take you on a clockwise loop, though the hike can be done in either direction. Hiking clockwise saves the dramatic close-up views of Cathedral Spires for the end of the hike.

The trailhead can be found on the north (farther from the entrance) side of the loop road, by the lake. Look for signs indicating the start of trail #9. The trail is an easy, broad, gravel path for the first leg, gently easing you into the hike. Continue for 0.7 mile, and then you will arrive at an intersection. To the left is the Lost Cabin Trail. Turn right.

Soon you will begin to find views up to the peak of Black Elk from the trail. You will even be able to glimpse the fire tower from here and, farther along, views of the hills to the west. Soon the trail veers right and cuts into the woods. At 1.25 miles you will begin to hike below sheer cliffs.

At 1.7 miles you will reach the boundary with the Black Elk Wilderness. Here you must register or risk a steep fine. There is an unmanned registration kiosk here, and it is up to you to fill out the form and keep a tag on you while you hike. Instructions and registration forms are found in the kiosk.

From here you'll cross a stream before reaching a spur trail for the Lost Cabin Trail to your left. Continue straight. At 2.1 miles you will hike past a series of massive boulders that tower above the trail. At 2.8 miles you will come to an intersection with the trail #4, which you will take to complete the loop on your way down. Keep left to continue to the summit of Black Elk Peak.

The trail becomes much rockier and steeper than before. Huge views will begin to open up before you. You will soon come to another intersection—here, turn left and head uphill toward the peak. At 3.25 miles is another intersection where foot traffic and stock traffic are instructed to take different trails. Keep left.

Shortly after, you will reach the fire tower, entering a stone castle–like building grafted onto the mountaintop. Stairs ascend to the summit proper. Here you will find an observation platform as well as stairs heading to the top of the tower. Stunning, unobstructed views can be enjoyed in all directions. Another set of stairs goes down into the base of the tower. Here you can enter empty rooms and imagine how the watchers who monitored the surrounding area for fires must have lived during their shifts.

When you are ready to return, descend back to the intersection with

Black Elk Peak offers views of many unique rock formations

trail #4. Take this trail. In half a mile you will pass the Grizzly Trail #7 to your left. Continue straight, and in another half a mile stay straight again as another trail splits left.

At 5.2 miles you will find yourself facing incredible views of the rocky spires ahead of you. At 5.7 miles gaze up at the Cathedral Spires, stunning rock formations that reach like massive fingers into the sky. Soon after, you will pass a spur trail that leads to Little Devil's Tower. You can explore here if you wish, adding about 0.8 mile to your total mileage. Otherwise, stay straight.

Continue winding your way downhill. At just under 7 miles, you will pass the trailhead and parking area for Little Devil's Tower Trail. Soon after, at the fork, keep right, heading downhill. At 7.4 miles you will reach the parking area at Sylvan Lake.

PLANNING

Summer and early fall are the recommended times to hike Black Elk
Peak. Snow may persist on Black Elk Peak into early summer, and hikers wishing to make their way up the mountain in spring should consult
a trail report to see what conditions are like at the top. Crampons are
recommended when there may be snow or ice on the trail, and only very
experienced hikers with the appropriate gear should attempt hiking here
under winter conditions.

Hikers should, as always, pay special attention to the weather forecast for the day and attempt their ascent on another day if it appears
that a storm is imminent. Nonetheless, even after careful monitoring
of the forecast, storms may roll in out of nowhere. Always carry appropriate gear and assume that there is at least some chance you will get
caught in a storm—even when the skies show nothing but blue and
sunshine at the time you set out. While the lookout tower on Black Elk
Peak is no longer in use, it is of sturdy construction and offers good
protection from the elements in the event that a storm does roll in
unexpectedly.

Custer State Park charges an entrance fee. A park license good for
one week costs $20 per vehicle or $10 per motorcycle. There are several
campgrounds in the area. Most sites can be reserved in advance online
at campsd.com.

GETTING THERE

The trailhead can be found on Google Maps by navigating to "Black Elk
Peak Hiking Trail." The parking area is located by Sylvan Lake, off SD 87.
The parking area is large, but the area is popular and the lot fills quickly.
The trailhead is on the northwest side of the parking area by the lake.

CAPROCK COULEE LOOP

North Dakota: Theodore Roosevelt National Park

DISTANCE: 4.4 miles

ELEVATION GAIN: 1,000 feet

TIME COMMITMENT: 2 to 3 hours

FEE: National Park Pass or entrance fee

DOGS: Not permitted

CAMPING ALONG TRAIL: Yes, with permit

DIFFICULTY: Moderate trail with short climbs and regular ups and downs.

Left: The Little Missouri River winds through Theodore Roosevelt National Park

If there's one thing you'll remember from your time in North Dakota besides the beauty of its parklands, it's the miles and miles of driving through a flat and almost entirely empty landscape required to get to those parks. Fittingly, Theodore Roosevelt National Park is split into three sections, and the northern unit and southern unit are more than an hour's drive from each other. While the southern section of the park houses some unique attractions—petrified forest and numerous prairie dog towns—the northern section is quieter and more peaceful, with miles of beautiful hiking trails.

Caprock Coulee Loop, in the heart of the park's northern section, takes hikers between canyons and across grasslands to a stunning vista over a river valley. On the 4 miles of this loop, with its dramatic and varied terrain, hikers will have a chance to encounter many of the unique geological features the Badlands are known for. Because the Badlands are composed of landforms you won't find in most of the rest of the country, a brief lesson in geology is necessary to fully appreciate what you'll be seeing on this hike. The flat-topped, layered buttes of the Badlands were formed by a unique process of erosion. Often, a butte will have a top layer of harder material protecting the layers beneath, steering its decay into these unique shapes. The top layer is often made of sandstone, limestone, or clinker, a type of rock forged in fire. The harder upper layer of the butte serves as a capstone, slowing erosion from above. Plant life growing on the side of the butte that gets less sun (and thus retains moisture) also helps to prevent erosion, often leading to a lush green side of the butte, and opposite a rocky, sun-scorched side.

The Badlands of Theodore Roosevelt National Park began forming over 65 million years ago, when the western half of North America began heaving under tectonic pressure to shape the Rocky Mountains. As the peaks were birthed, huge amounts of sediment were scraped and washed free of the young mountains. These sediments—mostly sand, silt, and mud—were swept east by ancient rivers and deposited in the location of the present-day park. At the time, there were also volcanoes in South Dakota, Montana, and Idaho, and their eruptions churned out huge quantities of ash, which rained down on the regions to their east. The sediment from this ash would, over time, turn into the siltstone, sandstone, and mudstone layers that would eventually become exposed by erosion, while the ash transformed into layers of bentonite clay.

Incidentally, this clay can make for treacherous footing when the ground is wet. In spring and early summer, the trails along this loop can be quite muddy and much slicker than you might expect of simple mud. While it does not rain often in this area, when it does it typically rains hard, and the trails will be particularly wet for some time afterward.

TRAIL OVERVIEW

A short distance from the parking area, you will come to the trail register and a fork in the trail. Sign in at the register and then keep left, heading down into an area of dense vegetation. The trail here can be very over-

The Badlands of North Dakota showcase buttes and other rock formations created by a unique process of erosion

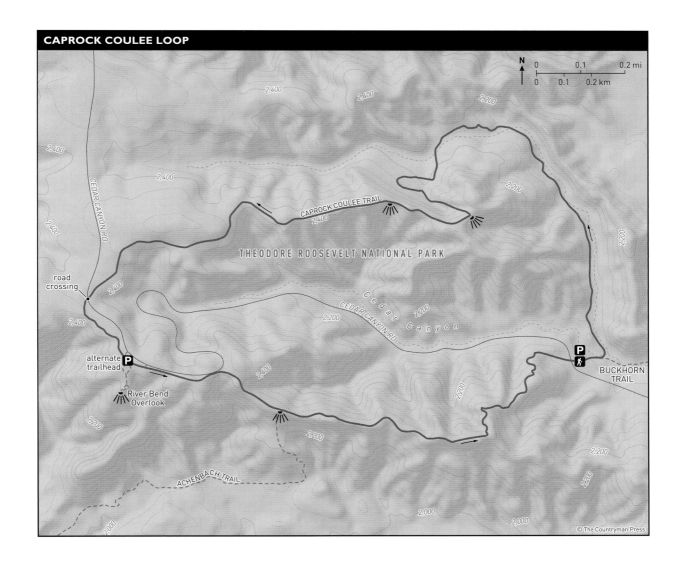

grown in the summer—a sign of trail conditions to come. Continue into open grassland, as the trail winds through a canyon.

At 0.8 mile the self-guided nature trail ends. The trail continues, however, as the Caprock Coulee Trail. Shortly after, you will cross wooden planks over a deep eroded gully, then afterward begin heading uphill. The trail again winds through areas of dense overgrowth, making for a narrow and often muddy path. The trail can be particularly slick in sections after recent rain, especially in early summer.

At 1.4 miles exit from the overgrown forested section of the trail to a

The Caprock Coulee trailhead

hill leading up to the rim of the canyon. Be mindful of the blind spot as you approach the crest of the hill—bison often linger here, and you will not be able to see them as you approach.

Enjoy the new views, then continue. Hike along the ridge before returning to grassland. At 2.6 miles you will cross over the park road and pick up the trail along the canyon at the other side. Soon you will come to the pull-off parking area for the River Bend overlook. A short side trail leads to stunning views of the valley below.

From the pull-off parking area, continue on the trail to the right of the road by the guardrail. At 3 miles the trail leaves the road. At 3.3 miles you will pass an intersection with the Achenbach Trail to your right. Keep left and enjoy more fantastic river valley views.

At 3.4 miles you will approach a formation of the mushroom-like rocks found throughout the park. Look for a sign and hike up this formation.

Be careful to keep to the path to avoid damaging this unique geological anomaly. Hike along a steep drop-off to your left.

At 3.75 miles keep left at the branch, marked by a sign. Heading downhill, you will return to the park road at 4.4 miles and arrive back at the parking area.

PLANNING

On clear, sunny days, be sure to bring sunscreen, protective clothing, and plenty of water, as there is very little shade along this route. In summer, temperatures can be extreme, and hikers should avoid setting out at midday if possible.

Clay in the soil makes for slick footing when the ground is wet, and the trails here are tricky after heavy rain. In spring and early summer, sudden heavy rains can make for a very difficult trail for some time afterward.

Wildlife is abundant in this park, and hikers should be on the watch for both rattlesnakes and bison. While the majestic bison may seem part of the very landscape when viewed in their vast herds from the safety of your car, up close these creatures are in fact deadlier than bears. In recent years, many tourists in national parks have been mauled by bison while attempting to snap a selfie. It's extremely dangerous to get close to these massive animals, which, docile as they may look, are able to charge at 35 mph and often change moods unpredictably. Bison don't pay much mind to trail etiquette, and you may find one squatting, unhurried, right on the trail. Do not attempt to go around the bison unless you have enough space to keep at least 200 feet between you and the animal. Getting too close to a bison may provoke it to charge.

GETTING THERE

The trailhead can be found on Google Maps by navigating to "Caprock Coulee Trail." The parking area is located on Cedar Canyon Road, 6 miles west of the North Unit Visitor Center, off US 85.

DEVIL'S LAKE LOOP

Wisconsin: Devil's Lake State Park

DISTANCE: 5.3 miles

ELEVATION GAIN: 1,030 feet

TIME COMMITMENT: 3 to 4 hours

FEE: A vehicle admission sticker is required; fees for cars with out-of-state plates are $16, or $13 with Wisconsin plates

DOGS: Permitted

CAMPING ALONG TRAIL: Yes

DIFFICULTY: Moderate trail with several sections of steep rugged trail and rock scrambling.

Left: The movement of glaciers during the last ice age left behind many curious rock formations, like Balanced Rock

Jagged cliffs in jumbled, massive configurations rise high above a lake. In places, these configurations look almost intentionally placed: one rock sits balanced like a sentinel; another seems to form a great arch. It is hard to believe that such formations are simply the fluke remnants of random movements of ice and earth, and yet they are: arbitrary patterns born of glaciers and chance.

Driving around America for an entire summer, absorbing the staggering variety of American landscapes one after another after another, my brain began turning to questions I'd never considered before. I began to wonder about simple things like the aesthetics of the outdoors—why certain natural features appeal to us on a purely visual level. After all, mountains were not always even considered beautiful or appealing landmarks: for most of human history they were viewed as no more than an obstacle, or worse, cursed by devils, the domain of monsters. This sort of terrified fascination is still obvious when you consider how many hiking landmarks in America are named "Devil's" something or other. Equal parts curious and terrified, we seem to be innately drawn to a mere jumble of rocks. The more unlikely and intricate the rock formation, the better, and thus we set aside places like Devil's Lake State Park as the finest of hiking destinations. Perhaps it is simply how unlikely these rock formations are, and something in our brain is tickled by the mere novelty. Perhaps what remains of that fearful suspicion in the back of our brain is, even now, subconsciously searching the crags and fissures for devils.

Devil's Lake's quartzite bluffs are part of the Baraboo Range. Scientists believe they were formed around 1.6 billion years ago, making them one of the oldest rock outcrops in North America. Like most hills east of the Rockies, this suggests that the ancient Baraboo Range was likely massive, probably rivaling the Rockies in height and majesty. Devil's Lake itself is much younger, however. Nestled picture-perfect between these

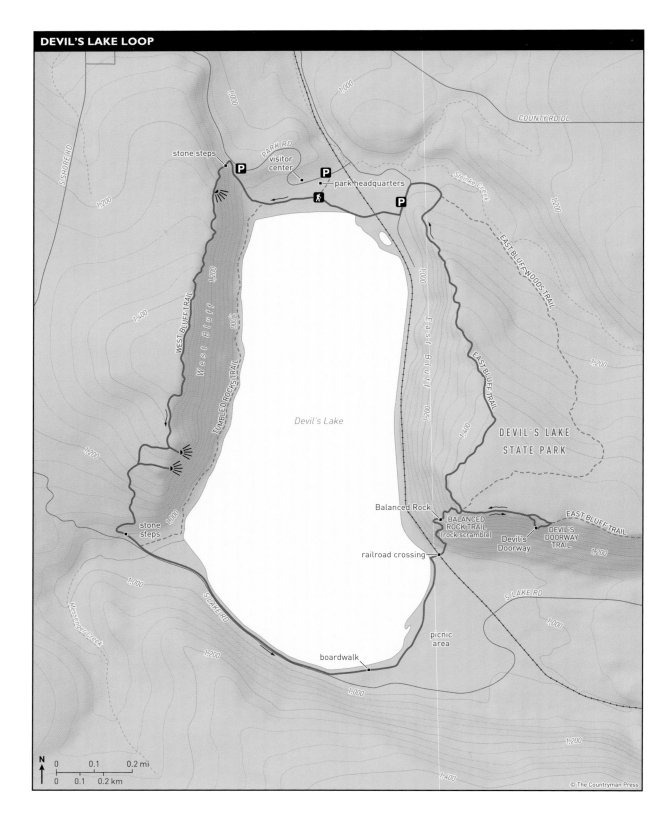

high cliffs, the lake was created during the last ice age by a glacier depositing moraines—masses of sediment—that plugged the north and south ends of the valley between the bluffs.

Not all who visit Devil's Lake State Park do so to scramble around its intense rock piles or teeter at the edge of its cliffs. The park itself is quite modern, and for the most part you will never forget that you are still well within the boundaries of civilization here. Both the north and south shores have food courts and restroom facilities. The lakefront areas are very popular with families and weekend campers during the summer.

TRAIL OVERVIEW

From the picnic area at the north end of the lake, by the visitor center, head toward the woods to your right. At the northwestern edge of the lake, look for the West Bluff Trail at the start of the woods. The trail starts immediately uphill, heading north. After a short distance you will pass another secondary parking area to your right.

Sunset at Devil's Lake

Continue up rough stone stairs, and at 0.25 mile you will already encounter your first views of the lake below. Soon you will pass a series of rocky outcroppings with views of the lake. At 1.5 miles you will reach a side path to your left—take this path a short distance to reach another grand view.

At 1.9 miles you will head down stone steps by Lake Road and soon reach level ground. Upon reaching the road, walk along the shoulder, and soon you will be crossing the southern tip of the lake. Continue along the road, and at 2.7 miles you will reach a boardwalk, which will bring you to a large picnic area.

Continue through the picnic area, following the trail markers as you near the woods once again. At 3.2 miles you will cross over train tracks. Turn left at an intersection, marked by signs, and look for the Balanced Rocks Trail. This trail heads up a boulder field, which you will have

To reach Devil's Lake's most interesting rock formations, hikers will have to tackle a short but challenging rock scramble

glimpsed from a distance. While this massive pile of rocks may look like an intimidating ascent from afar, in reality the path follows an easily navigable, never-technical climb up stone steps. While this ascent is certainly strenuous in terms of the exertion required, there is no real scrambling involved.

At about 3.5 miles, look for Balanced Rock, a unique rock formation precariously perched at the edge of the boulder field, overlooking the campground below. Soon after this you will reach the top of the scramble. Here you will be greeted by a three-way intersection. Turn right onto East Bluff Trail.

About a quarter mile after the intersection you will reach a side trail to the Devil's Doorway on the right. This tumble of rocks forming a rough arch is one of the park's most iconic features.

Retrace your steps back to the three-way intersection at the top of the rock scramble, and this time continue straight, heading back toward the lake. The trail curves right to follow the contour of the cliffs above the lake. At 4.5 miles you will come to an intersection. Stay left.

At around 4.9 miles the trail begins quickly shedding elevation. At 5.3 miles keep left as the East Bluff Woods Trail intersects from the right. Shortly after, you will reach a parking area. To return to the main parking area by the entrance, you will have to continue through this lot and across the train tracks before arriving back at the north end of the lake.

PLANNING

This is a popular park, and on summer and fall weekends you will find the trails to be very busy. If you are looking to avoid the crowds, start very early in the day or plan your hike for a weekday.

The rugged, rocky features of Devil's Lake are both a highlight and a danger of this hike. While this park is very popular with families, parents should be especially cautious with young children. All hikers should be extremely careful if the trails might be wet or icy. A fall on the rocks and cliffs of Devil's Lake would result in serious injury and possibly death.

GETTING THERE

The trailhead can be found on Google Maps by navigating to "Devil's Lake State Park." The parking area is located past the entrance and visitor center, on the north end of the lake.

CHAPEL TRAIL MOSQUITO FALLS LOOP

Michigan: Pictured Rocks National Lakeshore

DISTANCE: 10.5 miles

ELEVATION GAIN: 1,030 feet

TIME COMMITMENT: 4 to 6 hours

FEE: None

DOGS: Not permitted

CAMPING ALONG TRAIL: Yes

DIFFICULTY: Moderate trail with relatively long mileage but no steep climbs. Steep cliffs along the trail in several spots may pose problems for hikers with a strong fear of heights.

Left: Chapel Rock is home to a very tenacious tree

After hours spent driving through the flatness of northern Michigan and the forested wilderness of its Upper Peninsula, the dramatic cliffscapes of Pictured Rocks National Lakeshore, with Lake Superior below, made me feel as if I'd been transported a thousand miles away. Perhaps in a place like Oregon you might expect to encounter towering intricate cliffs backed by deep forest like this, but not in the American Midwest. If no other humans are around, you might even feel as if you've been taken to some primeval alternate world altogether: a calm breeze off the lake, swaying conifers, and the rhythmic lapping of the water have a strangely hypnotic effect. Despite arriving in late June, at the height of mosquito season, I still remember Pictured Rocks as one of the most peaceful places in America I've ever visited. My memory must have erased the unrelenting insects from the experience, because it is just the serene feeling of being there that stays with me now.

The grand sandstone cliffs of Pictured Rocks rise 50 to 200 feet above Lake Superior, forming the dramatic arches and unlikely spires and turrets that make this place so memorable. The name originates from the streaks of minerals that stain the sandstone, adding unique color variance to their already curious shapes. Different minerals "paint" the rocks different colors as groundwater seeps out of cracks: red and orange caused by iron, blue and green from copper, brown and black from manganese, and white due to limonite.

So far removed from any major towns, it's not hard to find solitude along this expansive lakeshore, though this circuit is one of the more popular routes in the area. While the 10-plus miles of this loop make it a relatively significant excursion, there is very little elevation gain, allowing you to maintain a fast pace. For maximum effect (and your best chance of

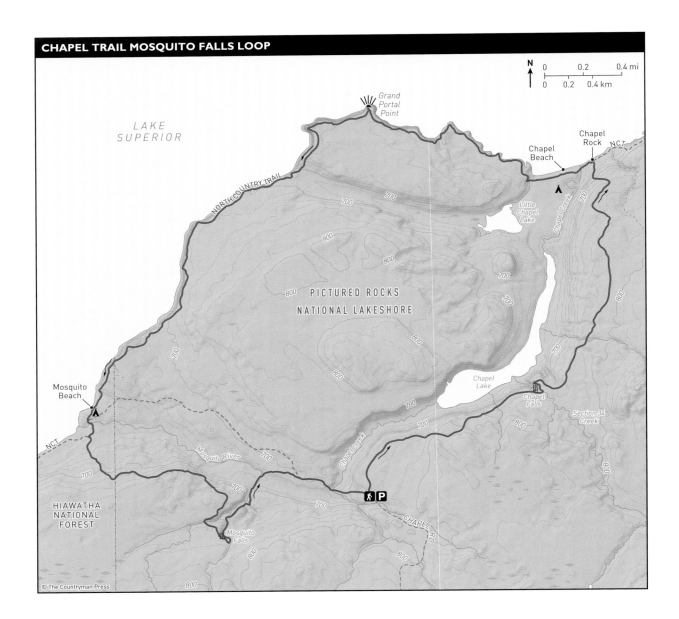

hiking without others around), start out in the early morning, or linger until late afternoon and enjoy the golden hour light painting the cliffs in even deeper colors. While you will still be able to enjoy the tranquility of the setting, hikers should be aware that mosquitoes are both numerous and unrelenting in the summer: bug spray and possibly even a mosquito net hat are advised. Or, consider skipping the beach weather entirely and visiting here in autumn, when the cool lake breezes and vivid colors will both be amplified.

TRAIL OVERVIEW

Start the hike on a flat, well-defined dirt path, making for a pleasant and easy start to the hike. Continue for 0.8 mile, then pass a trail on your left leading to Chapel Lake. At 1.3 miles you will pass Chapel Falls. Take a bridge over the stream, now crossing around to the other side of the waterfall, and you will find a new perspective on the falls from a viewing platform.

Continue, and at 3.2 miles you will arrive at Lake Superior. Here you will be greeted with the incredible sight of Chapel Rock, a pedestal of stone with a tree growing out of the top. Turn left onto the North Country Trail, following the edge of the lake west. For the next few miles you will be able to enjoy regular views of the cliffs from a number of unique perspectives. You will first spot Grand Portal Point, then hike around this massive cliff, coming to an elevated "beach" atop it at 4.6 miles. At several points the trail closely skirts the cliff edges, and these spots may be an issue for anyone with an extreme fear of heights. The cliff edges are sandy and prone to erosion; be especially careful along these sections. A

Arches, boulders, and waterfalls make for dramatic views next to the waters of Lake Superior

AMERICA'S BEST DAY HIKES

fall from the cliffs at any point would be deadly. Go slowly, be mindful of where you step, and don't let the stunning views distract you from paying attention to your footing.

The views will become less frequent after the 6-mile mark, and you will spend more time in the woods, farther from the cliff edges. Still, there are more surprises: you will arrive at another stunning vista at 6.6 miles.

Continue for another mile, then stay straight at the sign for Mosquito Falls. Cross a bridge over the creek, then turn left. As you approach a campground, turn left again at the sign for the falls. Soon you will hike past a toilet close to the campground. After this the trail meanders through gorgeous mossy woods. At 9.2 miles you will cross a bridge and soon come to Mosquito Falls.

Continue past the falls, and at 10 miles you will arrive at an intersection. Stay straight. At the next intersection, at 10.3 miles, turn right. Soon you will return to the parking area.

PLANNING

While few portions of the actual trail pose any significant challenges, this is a fairly long hike for a casual hiker. If you are not used to hiking trails of this length, be sure to budget plenty of time for your hike—the incredible scenery along the hike will certainly slow your pace. In fall, as the days shorten, plan to start your hike in the morning to ensure you have enough time.

The sheer rock cliffs of Pictured Rocks are beautiful but dangerous. The earth at the edge of the cliffs may not be stable, and hikers should stay well back from all cliff edges. Parents should be especially careful with young children. All hikers should be extremely careful if the trails might be wet or icy. A fall from these cliffs could result in serious injury or possibly death.

Spring, later in the summer, or fall are the best times to hike in Pictured Rocks. In early to midsummer, the mosquitoes in this area are extremely aggressive.

GETTING THERE

The trailhead can be found on Google Maps by navigating to "Chapel Basin Parking Lot." The parking area is located off Chapel Road, 5.4 miles north of the town of Melstrand, Michigan.

OLD MAN'S CAVE

Ohio: Hocking Hills State Park

DISTANCE: 5.2 miles

ELEVATION GAIN: 400 feet

TIME COMMITMENT: 3 to 4 hours

FEE: None

DOGS: Permitted on leash

CAMPING ALONG TRAIL: No

DIFFICULTY: Easy trail, with relatively little elevation change, though the section of the trail through the gorge is rocky and can be slick or muddy.

Left: Lower Falls

Ohio is not a mountainous state, but a good hike does not always have to look outward from some epic, prominent viewpoint. Not that the natural beauty found in Hocking Hills State Park is subtle, either: towering, arched cave walls and a half-dozen waterfalls of all shapes and sizes, tucked in a rocky gorge, give this area a unique air of mystery. While the park is very popular on weekends, if you do manage to find solitude here by setting out on a weekday or in the early morning, you may even experience a sort of beauty that feels secret, with an air of things hidden.

The Hocking Hills area is known for a geological oddity called recess caves—not true underground caves, but cliff walls with a distinct concave shape, creating a sheltered area at the base, tucked below a massive wall of rock. Over geological time, the softer layers of sand sediment on the underside of the cliff washed away, leaving the harder stone still looming above. Since this type of cave is open to the air yet sheltered from the elements by the concave cliff wall above, it feels protective, hidden yet accessible. You may be able to imagine how, stumbling upon this quirk in the landscape during centuries past, one might think about simply disappearing here. As it happens, this is exactly how Old Man's Cave got its name: a hermit named Richard Rowe made this cave his home in the late early 1800s, and was even buried in the cave itself.

Old Man's Cave is far from the only appealing feature of this hike. Numerous interesting waterfalls spill from rock ledges and other, smaller recess caves throughout the gorge, some merely a thin spray dancing down to the trail next to you from a dizzying height. The gorge itself, carved out of cliffs of sandstone, makes for fascinating scenery along your walk. This is not a difficult hike, save for a few short rocky stretches in the gorge area. While the easy path and wealth of interesting features do make this a very popular destination for locals on weekends, Old Man's

Cave is found at the very beginning of the hike, and traffic on the trail drops off significantly after Lower Falls, only a half mile into the hike.

TRAIL OVERVIEW

Past the park visitor center, follow the signs toward Old Man's Cave/Lower Falls. At the next signed intersection, keep left at the fork. You will begin descending stone steps toward a dramatic cave overhang: Old Man's Cave. The trail passes through a stone tunnel and then over a bridge.

Turn right after the bridge, following the sign for Lower Falls. You will again descend stone steps and cross over another bridge. The trail continues to head downhill by a waterfall. To view the waterfall up close, cross another bridge to the Lower Falls viewpoint. To continue, cross back over the bridge, then take the trail along the stream into the gorge.

The trail wanders through the gorge, occasionally dipping up and down rocky, tree root–gnarled slopes but without any significant elevation gain. At 1 mile you will hike past large cliffs to your left. At 1.25 miles the Whispering Bridge Trail goes right. Keep left.

At 2 miles pass through a natural stone arch. You will come to a small trickling waterfall splashing down from a rock canopy above. There are several of these unique falls in this area, with another awaiting a quarter mile down the trail. Just past this waterfall, you will have to scramble up a small, moderately steep section of rocks before arriving at another "cave" overhang.

At 2.5 miles turn left at the Cedar Falls Trail intersection. (This intersection offers an extension of 5 miles, round-trip, for hikers who wish to visit Ash Cave.) You will cross over a large, green metal bridge. Just past this you will cross another bridge by Cedar Falls. Climb up the stairs to the right, then turn left onto the trail heading back to Old Man's Cave. Climb up a long staircase, then turn left.

A short distance later you will reach the Cedar Falls parking area. Walk past the road and the small parking area, then over a large metal suspension bridge. Turn left.

From here you will follow an easy, broad trail—this return leg of the loop is significantly easier than the first portion of the hike. At 3.7 miles you will make a short climb uphill. Just past this, you will come to the edge of Rose Lake.

Hike along the lake, then turn left once you have reached the far end. Continue as the trail winds leisurely through the woods. At 5.25 miles

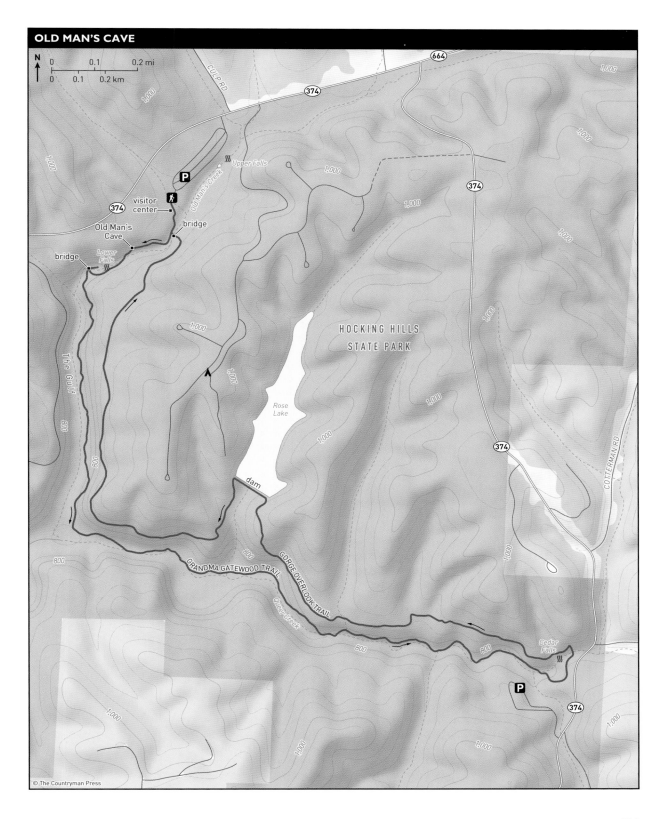

OLD MAN'S CAVE

N

0   0.1   0.2 mi
0   0.1   0.2 km

Culp Rd

664

374

374

374

374

Upper Falls

Old Man's Creek

P

visitor center

Old Man's Cave

bridge

bridge

Lower Falls

The Gulf

800

1,000

1,000

1,000

1,000

HOCKING HILLS STATE PARK

Rose Lake

1,000

1,000

1,000

dam

GRANDMA GATEWOOD TRAIL

GORGE OVERLOOK TRAIL

Queer Creek

800

800

800

800

Cedar Falls

P

374

COTTERMAN RD

1,000

1,000

1,000

1,000

© The Countryman Press

at the intersection, turn left and head down the stairs, following signs for Old Man's Cave. A large bridge crosses over the gorge that you hiked through at the beginning of the hike. Past this you will intersect the trail you originally hiked in on, before descending toward Old Man's Cave. Turn right, and you will soon return to the visitor center. Hike past the visitor center to return to the parking lot.

PLANNING

Old Man's Cave is a popular destination, and the first section of the hike can be very crowded on weekends. Hikers wishing to find solitude should set out in the early morning or on a weekday. However, few visitors choose to continue past Lower Falls, meaning you will find the trails in the rest of the park to be significantly quieter.

The trail in the gorge is often slick and muddy. While this is an easy hike for the most part, there are several sections where you will have to navigate rocky stretches of trail. Use extra caution when the trail may be wet or icy.

Hikers wishing to extend their adventure can hike an additional 5 miles to Ash Cave, another enormous recess cave located in the southern section of Hocking Hills State Park. The extension to Ash Cave begins at Cedar Falls Trail at the midpoint of this loop hike. The trail to Ash Cave is among the quietest in the park, offering more opportunities for solitude. Those who don't wish to cover this extra ground on foot can also reach Ash Cave by car, as it is located a short distance off OH 56, with its own large parking area.

GETTING THERE

The trailhead can be found on Google Maps by navigating to "Old Man's Cave Parking." The parking area is off OH 664, about 13 miles southwest of the town of Logan, Ohio.

SOUTHEAST

WHITAKER POINT (HAWKSBILL CRAG)

Arkansas: Ozarks National Forest

DISTANCE: 2.8 miles

ELEVATION GAIN: 500 feet

TIME COMMITMENT: 2 hours

FEE: None

DOGS: Permitted on leash

CAMPING ALONG TRAIL: Yes

DIFFICULTY: Easy, short trail, though with steep cliffs that pose a serious danger should one fall.

There is much to be said for a scenic trail through the woods, vibrant with greenery, dense foliage, and the static background hum of insect and bird life. But as serene as a trail might be, often it is that one dramatic view, the unusual outcropping or dramatic cliffs, that we remember. These big vistas captivate us in the moment, humbling us with our own smallness, and offer one grand detail for the mind to latch onto. Whitaker Point is home to just such a memorable sight: Hawksbill Crag, a rock formation jutting out from a cliff like the beak of a bird, with a vertigo-inducing drop-off around it into the valley below. The Ozark region surrounding this hike is home to many beautiful trails, quieter woods walks, caves, and small waterfalls, but there's no denying that a dramatic and potentially death-defying cliffside view will almost always grab our attention first. It is said that Hawksbill Crag is the most frequently photographed location in the state of Arkansas.

The Ozark Mountains are a wide expanse of low rolling hills, deeply forested, old, and uniquely appealing. Covering almost 50,000 square miles and encompassing two distinct mountain ranges, the Ozarks are in fact the most extensive highland region between the Appalachians to the east and the Rockies in the west. As with the mountain ranges of the East Coast, the hills of the Ozarks are the remnants of much older mountains that formed hundreds of millions of years ago. Once massive, they eroded over time into these lower hills and crags. While hills like these may lack the towering grandeur of the West Coast's mountains, I appreciate them for their ruggedness, the feeling of ancientness that is worked into every cave and stone. At Hawksbill Crag, you'll find both vistas and atmosphere.

Naturally, extreme caution is required when enjoying the view from the crag, as the drop from the edge would almost certainly be fatal if you fell. There is a sloping lip around the edge of the crag where you could

Left: The dramatic beak-like cliff of Hawksbill Crag

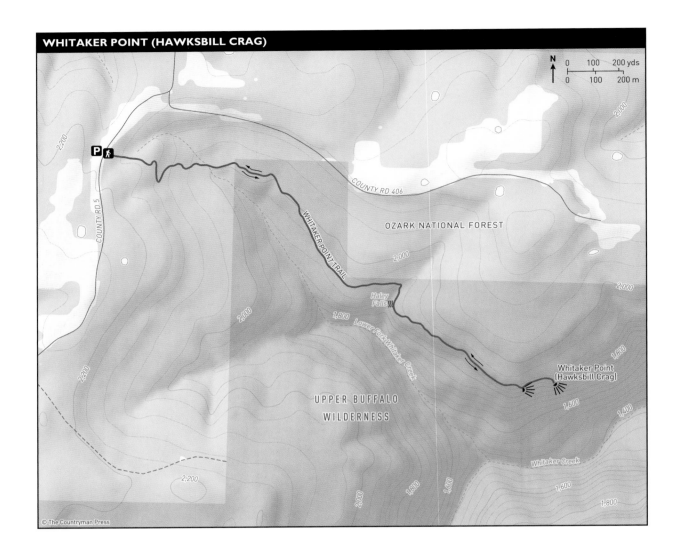

easily lose your balance. Because this hike is often quite busy on week-ends, the crowds congregating around the viewpoint can add an extra layer of danger as people jostle to get the best view. This hike is especially popular on fall weekends, and during peak seasons it may be best to set out early in the day or on a weekday if you wish to avoid the crowds.

TRAIL OVERVIEW

Just in from the trailhead, you will find the trail register. Continue as the trail makes a moderate descent.

At 0.9 mile you will descend a steep bank to a streambed at the lip of the ravine. Turn right, following the streambed for a short distance. The trail curves slightly to the left, heading away from the streambed and now along the edge of a steep rock face. Looking back toward the cliffs behind you, you will be able to see (and hear) water trickling off 12-foot cliffs down into the ravine. This small waterfall is called Haley Falls, named after a six-year-old girl who got separated from her group for three days before being found near here.

The trail begins to wind around large rocks, with the formations increasing in size and drama as you continue. At 1.3 miles you will pass several interesting protrusions and boulders. Views of the canyon will open up to your right.

At 1.4 miles you will reach a small rock protrusion just before Whitaker Point itself. From various spots near here you can enjoy views of the crag itself, jutting out from the cliff. A short distance down the trail you will come to Whitaker Point and Hawksbill Crag. Enjoy the views from the crag, then explore the unique rock formations nearby—there are several other interesting areas to explore beyond the obvious.

When you are ready to return, retrace your steps back to the parking area.

PLANNING

While the easy grade and lack of steep climbs make this an ideal all-season hike, the steep cliffs in the latter portion of the hike make this a dangerous hike to attempt if the rocks are slick or icy. Bring traction devices such as microspikes if hiking here in winter, and if the trail is wet or slick, stay a safe distance back from cliff edges and be extremely careful with your footing.

The road to the parking area is unpaved and somewhat rough, though in general it should pose no problems to sedans and low-clearance vehicles. After heavy rain, however, the road may be muddy enough to make passage difficult for two-wheel-drive vehicles. The parking area is relatively small for such a popular destination and fills quickly on weekends.

GETTING THERE

The trailhead can be found on Google Maps by navigating to "Whitaker Point Trailhead." The parking area is off County Road 5, about a quarter mile south of Cave Mountain Church at the intersection of County Road 406.

GRAY'S ARCH

Kentucky: Daniel Boone National Forest

DISTANCE: 4 miles

ELEVATION GAIN: 960 feet

TIME COMMITMENT: 2 to 3 hours

FEE: Day permit required; $3 fee

DOGS: Permitted on leash

CAMPING ALONG TRAIL: Yes

DIFFICULTY: Easy trail with few climbs, but several creek crossings and areas where you'll need to pay attention to your footing.

Kentucky may always be more famous for its bourbon than its rocks, but maybe that's for the best. The nation's other park known for its dramatic arched stone formations—Utah's Arches National Park—is mobbed with visitors as a result. There are an estimated 150 arches in the Red River Gorge area, second only to Arches in number, though the Kentucky arches have a very different feel, nestled in a lush forest and partially obscured by deep woods. Here the arches are not a horizon-defining landmark but a mystery to be stumbled upon—and to me, this makes them even more intriguing.

Natural rock arches form through the effects of erosion, temperature changes, gravity, and tectonic pressures. The natural arches in the Red River Gorge area form on top of and at the base of narrow sandstone-capped ridges. There are several different types of arches, each created by different processes and materials: shelter arches form on ridgetops, alcove and buttress arches are carved out along the sides of cliffs, and pillar arches form at the bases of cliffs. Gray's Arch is a buttress-type arch spanning 76 feet in length, with a clearance of more than 50 feet between the arch and the ground below.

While Gray's Arch is one of the more popular destinations in the Red River Gorge region, it doesn't receive anywhere near the sort of tourism attention that Utah sees. And at only 4 miles, this loop hike leaves plenty of time in the day to get in a distillery tour at one of the many bourbon producers in the area.

TRAIL OVERVIEW

The best way to hike the Gray's Arch loop is to travel in a counterclockwise direction. This way you save the arch itself for close to the end of the hike. However, the eastern portion of the hike does not begin from the parking area proper but rather enters the woods a short distance down the road. From the parking area, turn left onto the road and walk 0.1 mile east. Just ahead the trail enters the woods, going northeast.

Left: A small waterfall just down the trail from Gray's Arch

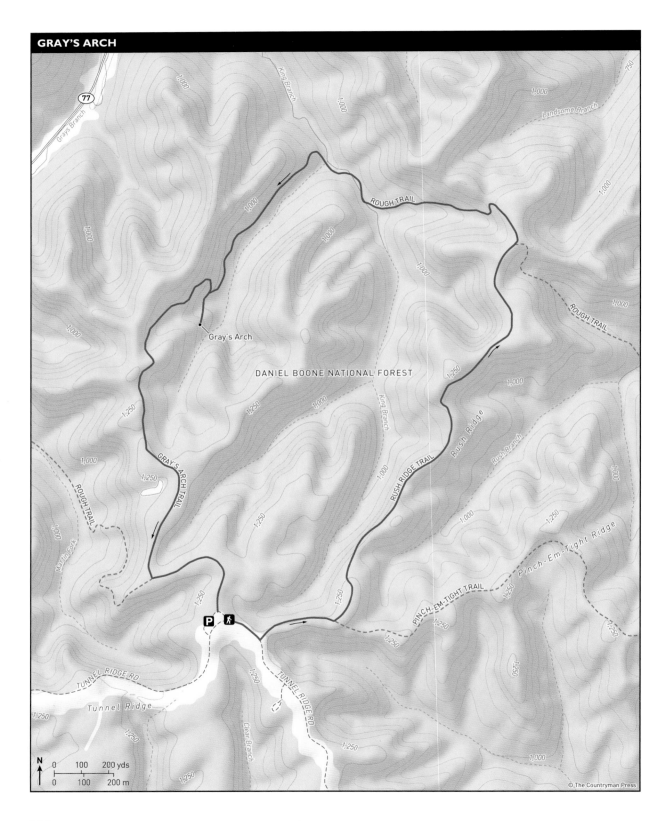

77

Grays Branch

1,000

King Branch

1,000

750

Landsome Branch

1,000

ROUGH TRAIL

1,000

1,000

Gray's Arch

ROUGH TRAIL

1,000

DANIEL BOONE NATIONAL FOREST

1,250

1,000

1,000

1,250

King Branch

Rush Ridge

Rush Branch

1,000

GRAY'S ARCH TRAIL

1,000

1,250

ROUGH TRAIL

1,250

RUSH RIDGE TRAIL

1,000

1,250

1,000

1,250

Pinch-Em-Tight Ridge

1,250

Marcum Fork

1,250

1,250

1,250

P

PINCH-EM-TIGHT TRAIL

1,250

1,250

1,250

1,250

TUNNEL RIDGE RD

TUNNEL RIDGE RD

1,000

Tunnel Ridge

1,250

Clean Branch

1,250

1,250

1,000

N

| 0 | 100 | 200 yds |
| 0 | 100 | 200 m |

© The Countryman Press

At 0.3 mile the Pinch-Em-Tight Trail splits off to your right, veering east. Take the Rush Ridge Trail to the left. Continue along a mellow, easy section of trail. At 1.3 miles, at a signed intersection, keep left to continue toward Gray's Arch. The trail will now veer almost directly west. A short distance later you will descend several sets of steep wooden stairs.

Now hiking through a shallow valley, at 1.8 miles you will pass through a muddy area alongside a creek. A short distance later you will have to make a stream crossing using stepping stones, and then another just after.

At 2.4 miles you will come to an intersection where the trail cuts to your right and ascends a steep set of tall wooden stairs. To the left is a spur trail leading to Gray's Arch. Turn left, and in a short distance you will find a thin waterfall trickling from the high arched rocks above. Just beyond this, the trail climbs for a short distance to reach Gray's Arch.

At the arch, you can explore around the base from both sides. Be careful of your footing on the rocky areas here, which can be slick if it has rained recently. To continue, return to the intersection before the stairs, then ascend the stairs.

After several short bursts of climbing, the trail levels at 3.4 miles. At 3.8 miles you will reach a T-intersection. Turn left. In a short distance you will arrive back at the parking area.

PLANNING

A permit is required to hike here, available from many local retailers. Most gas stations in the area have permits for sale. A one-day pass costs $3, and three-night overnight permits are also available.

While the easy grade and lack of steep, rocky climbs make this an ideal all-season trail, hikers should be mindful of icy conditions in winter and bring traction devices like microspikes if the trail may be icy.

GETTING THERE

The trailhead can be found on Google Maps by navigating to "Gray's Arch Recreation Area." The parking area is off Tunnel Ridge Road, off the Bert T. Combs Mountain Parkway.

ALUM CAVE AND MOUNT LeCONTE

Tennessee: Great Smoky Mountains National Park

DISTANCE: 12 miles

ELEVATION GAIN: 3,080 feet

TIME COMMITMENT: 6 to 8 hours

FEE: None

DOGS: Not permitted

CAMPING ALONG TRAIL: Yes

DIFFICULTY: A strenuous climb plus long mileage combine to create a challenging day hike, but the grade is never particularly steep, making this hike accessible to intermediate hikers who plan appropriately.

Left: Alum Cave Bluff, an 80-foot concave cliff

I admit to being mostly drawn to mountain vistas, but different trails may hold different points of appeal for different hikers. The hike to Mount LeConte in Great Smoky Mountains National Park is a hike that may boast something for everyone—at least if you don't mind the relatively long mileage. At 6,593 feet, Mount LeConte is the third-highest summit in the Smokies and the second highest in Tennessee; though the summit itself is forested, there are several excellent views from ledges around the peak. For those who don't wish to hike all the way to the summit or who are drawn to other natural features besides mountain vistas, Mount LeConte has them covered. There's the first mile of trail, a simply beautiful and serene woods walk next to a stream, with multiple small yet scenic falls. Then there's the massive Alum Cave, a towering concave cliff overhang (and not truly a cave), for many the main destination on this trail. And between Alum Cave and the summit is yet more interesting trail: narrow ledges posing a challenging, rocky traverse with stunning views opening up below you; beyond these ledges, a quiet ridge walk amid aromatic pines and lush forest floors carpeted in green.

I find that hikes such as this need little justification or explanation: if you want to experience the Great Smoky Mountains, this hike will give you a sample of . . . everything. From serene to dramatic and back again, one half mile to the next, this is one of those hikes that will engage you at every step of the way. And while it is somewhat long in mileage, this serves to spread out its elevation gain so that it is never especially strenuous in any one spot.

Mount LeConte boasts one other attraction, or at least curiosity: it is home to the highest elevation lodge on the East Coast. Unlike the Appalachian Mountain Club (AMC) hut system in New Hampshire's White Mountains or Glacier National Park's chalets, LeConte has a distinct look and feel, built in the style of a small camp rather than a single large building. About half a mile from the summit, you will pass this village-like cluster of wooden buildings, their rustic, simple atmosphere almost blending into the woods. The lodge offers the opportunity for hikers to turn this into an overnight, semimodern/semirustic camping experience—though cabins must generally be reserved up to a year in advance.

TRAIL OVERVIEW

Both parking areas offer short access trails into the woods. Just in from the parking areas, you will come to an information sign before a bridge. The trail begins over the bridge.

For the first leg of the hike you will be hiking alongside Alum Cave Creek. There are many small falls along this beautiful, easy section of trail. At 1.2 miles you will make a stream crossing over a one-sided bridge. After another bridge crossing you will come to Arch Rock, a natural tunnel.

At 2 miles views to the west will begin to open up. Soon after you will cross a short, narrow rock ledge, then ascend stairs set into the earth. At 2.3 miles you will reach the Alum Cave Bluff—which is not really a cave at all, but an 80-foot-high cliff overhang.

Continue hiking past Alum Cave. At 2.6 miles you will hike over a slick rock ledge with a cable mounted on the rock face to hold on to. After this is a level, easy stretch of trail until you come to more stairs at 3.1 miles.

At 4.2 miles the trail crosses a narrow rock shelf with a steep drop-off. Be very careful of your footing here. Beyond this, you will traverse a series of winding, narrow ledges. More cables have been fixed to the rock face to help you keep your balance. At 4.8 miles you will reach the ridgetop below the summit, and from here the trail becomes considerably easier.

A short distance later you will come to an intersection with the Bull Head Trail. Keep right. Just beyond, at 5.1 miles, you will see the wooden cabins of the Mount LeConte Lodge to your left. The trail continues straight to reach the summit. The summit is about a quarter mile beyond the campground, along an easy section of trail. However, there are no views from the summit itself.

The primary viewpoint is found on the trail across from the lodge

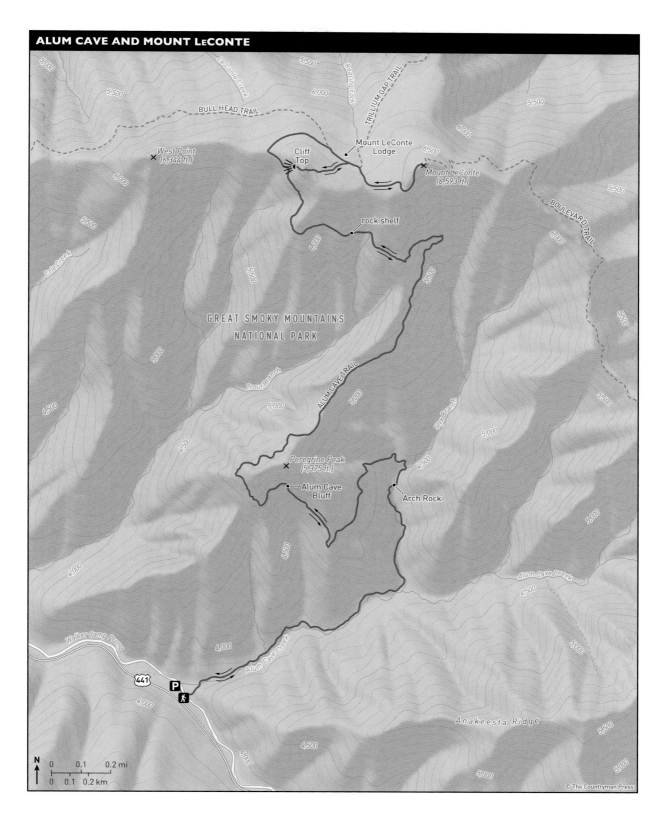

GREAT SMOKY MOUNTAINS
NATIONAL PARK

West Point
(6,344 ft.)

Cliff
Top

Mount LeConte
Lodge

Mount LeConte
(6,593 ft.)

rock shelf

BULL HEAD TRAIL

TRILLIUM GAP TRAIL

BOULEVARD TRAIL

Le Conte Creek

Roaring Fork

Cole Creek

Trout Branch

ALUM CAVE TRAIL

Styx Branch

Peregrine Peak
(5,375 ft.)

Alum Cave
Bluff

Arch Rock

Alum Cave Creek

Walker Camp Prong

Alum Cave Creek

441

P

Anakeesta Ridge

N

| 0 | 0.1 | 0.2 mi |
| 0 | 0.1 | 0.2 km |

© The Countryman Press

camping area. Take this trail uphill to the Cliff Top overlook. The trail is rocky and steep in sections, but the views from the cliff are excellent.

When you are ready, return to the intersection at the campground and head back on the Alum Cave Trail. Retrace your steps back to the parking area.

PLANNING

The parking area for the Alum Cave Trail is large, with ample parking available along the shoulder of the road. However, it must be noted that this trail is one of the most popular trails in the most popular national park in the country. Expect it to be busy. If you are seeking solitude, plan your visit for a weekday or plan to set out in the early morning.

The trail to Mount LeConte has several sections of narrow ledges and cliff walks where wet or icy rocks could pose a serious danger. Practice extra caution if there is a chance the trail may be slick.

LeConte Lodge is a fascinating site, and staying in one of these rustic wooden cabins overnight can make for a wonderful experience. The lodge is popular, however, and cabins must be reserved well in advance—often up to a year. However, day hikers are still welcome to visit the site, and indeed, the lodge sells pack lunches, snacks, and drinks that all hikers are able to purchase.

GETTING THERE

The trailhead can be found on Google Maps by navigating to "Alum Cave Bluffs Trailhead Parking." The parking area is located off US 441, about 12 miles south of Gatlinburg, Tennessee.

Mountains span the horizon across the Great Smoky Mountains National Park

CARVER'S GAP TO GRASSY RIDGE BALD

North Carolina/Tennessee:
Pisgah National Forest

DISTANCE: 5 miles

ELEVATION GAIN: 1,130 feet

TIME COMMITMENT: 2 to 4 hours

FEE: None

DOGS: Permitted

CAMPING ALONG TRAIL: Yes

DIFFICULTY: A moderate hike in almost every respect, with modest climbs and an easily navigable trail.

Left: Carver's Gap provides incredible views of the Blue Ridge Mountains

While the mountains of the East Coast may not boast the staggering height of the West Coast's younger peaks, every mountain chain has its own fascinating features and quirks. One of the most interesting features of the southern Appalachians are the "balds"—treeless summits and ridges found mainly in North Carolina and Tennessee. These highlands offer stunning beauty, a unique atmosphere, and massive unobstructed views, but also something of an ecological mystery: no one knows exactly why they exist. Farther north, mountains of this height—the high peaks of New Hampshire's White Mountains or New York's Adirondack Mountains, for instance—would be home to alpine zones, where the extreme weather conditions for most of the year prohibit tree growth. However, this far south, trees *should* grow on these summits, and indeed do on many neighboring peaks. But the open highlands of the Appalachian balds stand as testament to the fickleness of nature and a reminder that there is still plenty we do not know about the world around us.

Grassy Ridge is part of the eastern flank of Roan Mountain and is the longest stretch of grassy bald in the Appalachians. Roan Mountain is itself a fascinating formation—it is part of the Roan Highlands, a 20-mile massif that straddles the border of Tennessee and North Carolina. The Appalachian Trail runs across the massif, and you will be following the historic trail for most of this hike, save for the final section to the tip of Grassy Ridge Bald. Carver's Gap, the starting point of the hike, actually divides up the two main sections of Roan Mountain. Your hike, over the eastern stretch, will take you over three balds: Round, Jane, and Grassy Ridge. To the west of Carver's Gap are Roan High Bluff and Roan High Knob—also excellent hiking destinations.

255

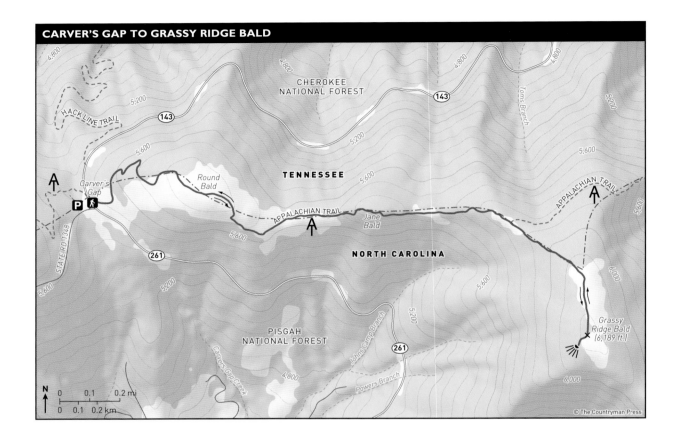

If visiting in summer, you can extend your visit to the area with a drive to the world's largest natural rhododendron garden. The road to the gardens begins next to the Carver's Gap parking area.

TRAIL OVERVIEW

From the parking area, cross the road and head up the steps, through the fence. The trail passes through a strand of spruce-fir forest before climbing several hundred feet to the top of Round Bald.

You will reach the top of Round Bald at 0.6 mile. From here the trail dips about 200 feet, then gains it again before reaching the top of Jane Bald at 1.3 miles.

Continue along the ridge for half a mile, then, at 1.8 miles, veer right at the sign for Grassy Ridge. The trail enters a dark tunnel through shrub before entering the open meadows of the bald.

You will reach the top of Grassy Ridge Bald at 2.3 miles. From here, turn around and retrace your steps to return to the parking area.

PLANNING

Parking at Carver's Gap is limited and fills quickly on weekends.

While not a particularly difficult hike, you should still be careful to plan your hike thoroughly and check the weather before setting out. Weather conditions in this area can change quickly, and the weather itself is often severe, with extremely strong winds whipping across the highlands. Nearly all of this hike is exposed, so there is little shelter available if a storm rolls in.

On clear, sunny days, be sure to bring sunscreen, protective clothing, and plenty of water, as there is very little shade along this route.

GETTING THERE

The trailhead can be found on Google Maps by navigating to "Carver's Gap." The parking area is off NC 261, about 12 miles north of the town of Bakersville, North Carolina.

Round Bald on a foggy, windy fall evening

SHORTOFF MOUNTAIN

North Carolina: Linville Gorge Wilderness

DISTANCE: 5.4 miles

ELEVATION GAIN: 1,280 feet

TIME COMMITMENT: 3 to 4 hours

FEE: None

DOGS: Permitted

CAMPING ALONG TRAIL: Yes

DIFFICULTY: Moderate, with a somewhat strenuous climb in the first mile and a half leveling off to an easy gorge-top walk.

Left: The trail up Shortoff Mountain offers incredible views from the very beginning

For a stretch of 12 miles along the Linville River, towering cliffs, rugged boulder fields, and unique rock formations make Linville Gorge one of the East Coast's most impressive gorges. It is basically inevitable that the largest canyon in any given state will be given the moniker "The Grand Canyon of [state]," but Linville Gorge actually reminds me not so much of the Grand Canyon but of the craggy contours of Yosemite. The curious chimneys and boulder-topped low peaks of Linville give it a memorable geography, a flowing contrast in shapes and colors similar to that of California's much more famous park.

Not that the Linville Gorge Wilderness needs comparison to anything to justify its appeal. North Carolina is one of those states that can boast a bit of everything geography-wise, from towering mountains to beaches, waterfalls, and canyons and everything in between, and a hike around the rim of the gorge offers a nice contrast to the huge open views found in the nearby Appalachian highlands. Shortoff isn't a mountain peak like most of those featured in this guide—you won't be hiking to any clear summit but simply to various rocky outcrops with exceptional views. Despite the rocky cliffs, the trail itself is fairly moderate, and much of the length of this hike traverses the level rim of the gorge.

Shortoff Mountain offers just a brief taste of the sights of the gorge, and there are, of course, many other trails in this area worthy of exploring. The trail you'll be taking continues beyond the end point of this hike—in fact, it's possible to do a loop of the entire gorge through this extensive trail network. This is also an excellent destination for backpacking trips, and indeed, there are several primitive camping areas you'll pass along the way, should you wish to turn this into an overnight excursion.

Linville River

Linville Gorge

2,000

1,600

2,400

2,800

WOLF PIT TRAIL

2,800

2,800

2,400

Shortoff Mountain

2,000

2,400

PISGAH NATIONAL FOREST

LINVILLE GORGE WILDERNESS

2,400

2,000

White Creek

WOLF PIT TRAIL

2,800

2,000

2,400

2,000

1,600

1,400

WOLF PIT RD.

2,000

FAULKNER
FLATS TRAIL

© The Countryman Press

N

| 0 | 0.1 | 0.2 mi |
| 0 | 0.1 | 0.2 km |

TRAIL OVERVIEW

About 0.2 mile from the trailhead, turn right to stay on the Wolf Pit Trail. The Faulkner Flats Trail continues straight. The trail begins to switchback uphill with moderate elevation gain and occasional views, with Lake James visible to the south. At 1.1 miles stay straight to continue on the Wolf Pit Trail. Soon after, you will get your first glimpse of the gorge opening up ahead of you.

At 1.9 miles you will pass a camping area on your left. At 2.4 miles you will pass a rocky area with some of the best views of the hike. Continue on, and in another quarter mile you will reach another open, rocky area with excellent views.

The trail continues past this viewpoint, eventually reaching the Chimneys, the large rock formation visible ahead of you in the distance. However, this area makes for a natural turnaround point for your hike. After exploring, retrace your steps back to the parking area.

PLANNING

The Wolf Pit Trailhead parking area, where the hike begins, is small and has room for only about a dozen cars. The lot can fill quickly on weekends. Wolf Pit Road is unpaved and can be somewhat rough in sections. However, even low-clearance vehicles will be fine on this road if you drive slowly and carefully watch the road ahead for potholes and dips.

GETTING THERE

The trailhead can be found on Google Maps by navigating to "Wolf Pit Trailhead." The parking area is located at the end of Wolf Pit Road, about 4 miles north of the town of Linville, North Carolina.

BEAR ROCKS TO RAVEN RIDGE

West Virginia: Dolly Sods Wilderness

DISTANCE: 6.8 miles

ELEVATION GAIN: 700 feet

TIME COMMITMENT: 3 to 4 hours

FEE: None

DOGS: Permitted on leash

CAMPING ALONG TRAIL: Yes

DIFFICULTY: Moderate, with only short uphill sections.

Sometimes you hit a trail on just the right day, the sort of day bearing the atmosphere, the weather, that just feels ideally suited to the place you're in. Hiking the Bear Rocks to Raven Ridge loop in mid-October, the sky was overcast, the light dim, the temperature crisp and dipping toward frigid. It felt like December rather than October. The highlands of Dolly Sods were wet and windy, each distant cluster of tree cover a muted fence to frame the strangeness of this highland terrain. The atmosphere was almost eerie, even slightly ominous. Based on the landscape around me, had I arrived blindfolded and ignorant of my location, I would have guessed I was somewhere in Maine, possibly Canada.

Dolly Sods may not feel so odd and out of place on a hot summer day, but there's no denying its uniqueness, no matter the weather or the time of year. "Sods" is a regional term, used in the Allegheny Mountains of eastern West Virginia to describe mountaintop meadow or bog in an area that would typically be forested. In the rest of the Appalachian region, these areas are called "balds," and this guide features another of these balds at the Carver's Gap to Grassy Ridge Bald hike. The Dolly Sods Wilderness, however, is not located on a mountain summit, but on a high-altitude plateau some 4,000 feet above sea level. Given that it is a plateau, the views are unusual for this area—you find that you are looking around rather than down or up, with a landscape that seems to swallow you up. Strands of trees cut swatches across vast open meadows and heath barrens, all windswept and warped by the unusually extreme weather found here.

Dolly Sods is very popular as a backpacking destination, as there are many miles of trails to explore, ideal for a two- to four-day excursion and without the strenuous climbing of a more mountainous area. Several primitive campsites are found along the route described here, giving you the option to turn this into an overnight, if desired.

Left: The open highland meets spruce forest

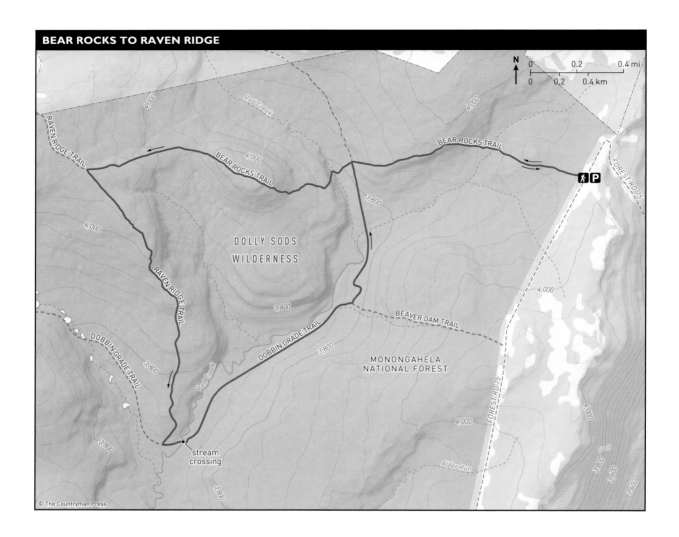

BEAR ROCKS TO RAVEN RIDGE

DOLLY SODS
WILDERNESS

BEAVER DAM TRAIL

MONONGAHELA
NATIONAL FOREST

stream
crossing

© The Countryman Press

While the lack of climbing makes this a relatively easy hike, the unique terrain does pose a few potential challenges. The shallow water table on the plateau, for one: in the spring, or after periods of heavy rain, you should expect the trail to be very muddy. Dolly Sods often accumulates a good bit of snow in the winter, and patches of snow often remain until April. Expect temperatures to be more extreme than in lowland locations—in fall the temperature will begin to dip toward freezing at night, even in October. In summer heat, the open meadows and limited tree cover mean that you will be hiking fully exposed to the sun for much of the time.

TRAIL OVERVIEW

From the trailhead, the trail begins crossing a large meadow, immediately treating you to a quintessential Dolly Sods view. At 0.4 mile the trail enters a forested area. At 1 mile the path dips downhill, and you will arrive at an intersection with the Dobbin Grade Trail. Stay straight. On the return leg of this loop, you will arrive at this intersection again via the Dobbin Grade Trail, currently to your left.

Just beyond the intersection is a bridge, and then you will cross Red Creek and head back into the woods. The trail makes a moderate climb uphill. At 1.4 miles you will hike over a boardwalk. After another quarter mile the trail once again enters an open meadow, with more excellent views of the partially forested highlands.

Turn left at 2.5 miles. The Raven Ridge Trail continues straight. You will return to tree cover in a quarter mile before entering the open highlands again at 3.3 miles.

At 4 miles turn left onto the Dobbin Grade Trail. Just beyond the intersection you will cross Red Creek again. Here the crossing is somewhat more difficult, and in periods of high water you may have to simply ford

Patches of dense forest appear next to open fields at Dolly Sods

AMERICA'S BEST DAY HIKES

across. The trail continues along the course of the creek, and this section of trail can be particularly muddy in wet periods.

The Dobbin Grade Trail continues for a mile before intersecting with the Beaver Dam Trail to the right. If the Dobbin Grade Trail is particularly muddy, the Beaver Dam Trail offers an alternative exit to the hike—it will bring you up through the highlands for 0.7 mile before intersecting with Forest Road 75, along which you parked. Otherwise, continue on the Dobbin Grade Trail for 0.7 mile, until it completes the loop at the intersection with the Bear Rocks Trail. At the Bear Rocks Trail, turn right and retrace your steps from the beginning of the hike back to the parking area.

PLANNING

Dolly Sods is very popular among both day hikers and backpackers, and on weekends the parking area is generally very full. Many cars end up simply parking along Forest Road 75.

To get to the trailhead, you will have to take Forest Road 75 for several miles as the road climbs the escarpment to the plateau. The road is not especially rough, however, and low-clearance vehicles should have no trouble reaching the trailhead.

Both the weather and trail conditions at Dolly Sods can vary wildly depending on the time of year. Trails here will be extremely muddy after periods of heavy rain and for much of the spring. In fall, temperatures can be significantly lower than in the rest of the region, with added windchill. At all times of year, be mindful that much of the hike is exposed, with little shelter from the elements should a storm roll in. Be sure to check the weather before setting out on your hike.

GETTING THERE

The trailhead can be found on Google Maps by navigating to "Bear Rocks Trail Head." The parking area is along Forest Road 75, about 18 miles northwest of Cabins, West Virginia.

OLD RAG

Virginia: Shenandoah National Park

DISTANCE: 9.6 miles

ELEVATION GAIN: 2,450 feet

TIME COMMITMENT: 5 to 8 hours

FEE: National Park Pass or entrance fee

DOGS: Not permitted

CAMPING ALONG TRAIL: No

DIFFICULTY: A strenuous summit climb with the added challenge of a unique, challenging boulder field scramble. Navigating the boulder field requires strong upper body strength and significant dexterity.

Left: Hikers will have to tackle many unique challenges along the trail, including sliding below this boulder wedged into a crevasse

Before I'd hiked here myself, I had always heard Old Rag described as a "rock scramble." Though I'm not a climber, I find rock scramble hikes to be a lot of fun, and several such local scrambles are among my favorite hikes. But in the midst of Old Rag's boulder field, I realized that calling this daunting section of trail a rock scramble is fairly misleading—it's more of a rock squeeze. On a rock scramble, the scrambling is generally over rocks, boulders, chimneys, slopes, and cliffs. Here, you're usually wedging, sliding, crawling, and otherwise hauling yourself between and around and under them. You'll navigate this boulder field in just about every way imaginable.

Old Rag is quite the experience. It is one of those hikes that epitomizes why I wanted to write a book like this—while there are many excellent hikes in Virginia, Old Rag is the sort of hike that demands to be added to your bucket list, the sort of hike you need to experience at least once if you can manage it. While there are certainly similarities to other scramble-style hikes, I can think of no other hike entirely like it. Naturally, this uniqueness has inspired popularity, and on weekends the crowds here become quite intense. Navigating the boulder field creates many natural bottlenecks, so on especially busy weekends you may find that you have to spend a good amount of time literally waiting in line to tackle the next obstacle. It's best to plan your visit for a weekday or plan to arrive early in the morning. And it's best to plan thoroughly for this hike in general—it isn't a trail to be taken lightly. Children and shorter adults may struggle to complete this hike without assistance; strong upper body strength and a good bit of dexterity will also go a long way here. Claustrophobic hikers may wish to avoid this one as well, as there are several moments where you'll need to squeeze yourself through narrow gaps, caves, and rock wedges.

This boulder scramble and squeeze would be attraction enough, even if it were the hike's only real feature. But after navigating the boulder field, you'll be rewarded with exceptional views from the rocky summit as well, the icing on a very intense cake.

269

TRAIL OVERVIEW

Due to the popularity of this hike, Old Rag outgrew its old parking area, and a new, large parking area was opened on Nethers Road. The first mile of this hike simply requires hikers to walk up Nethers Road to the original trailhead. Here the road ends, and you will cross a chain barrier to the information sign at the trailhead. The loop begins and ends here.

Turn left onto the Ridge Trail. The trail begins as a wide, rocky path, and after about half a mile it begins switchbacking uphill. The elevation gain will be steady as you make your way up the shoulder of the mountain.

The trail is relatively uneventful until just after 3 miles. Here you will get your first taste of the scramble ahead. The boulder scramble begins in earnest at 3.3 miles. The first serious challenge is a drop down between large boulders via a narrow gap—look for small footholds below you. Beyond this, there are many obstacles requiring various maneuvers to conquer. Many of these obstacles will be difficult to manage with a full pack on your back—you may have to slide your pack ahead of you, stash it on a rock ledge above you, or hand it off to another hiker.

At 3.4 miles you will pass through a small cave. Shortly beyond this is a unique staircase through a narrow rock crevasse, with a boulder wedged

A hiker enjoys the view from the summit of Old Rag

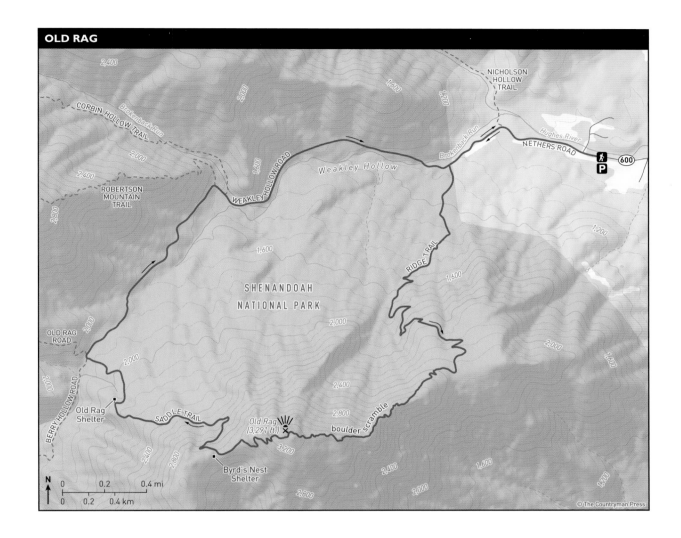

menacingly above the path. At 3.7 miles the trail reaches a crest and the boulder scramble briefly lets up. However, while the most difficult sections are behind you, there is yet more scrambling ahead. Beware of false summits, as your passage through the entire boulder section will be quite slow, and it will likely feel as if you should be reaching the summit "at any moment" for quite some time. There are several spots along this section of trail where it can be easy to lose the trail markers—pay careful attention so you can be sure you are still on the right path.

At 4 miles you will reach the intersection with the Saddle Trail, which you will take for the return leg of your loop. However, to reach the sum-

AMERICA'S BEST DAY HIKES

Massive boulders create a
challenging route to the summit
of Old Rag

mit itself, take the short spur trail from this intersection. The summit itself is home to large boulders, offering fantastic views and the opportunity for more boulder-hopping.

When you are ready to return, head back to the intersection with the Saddle Trail, then take the Saddle Trail downhill. The Saddle Trail is, at this point, a refreshing contrast to the last section of the hike—this trail is quite tame, offering a mercifully relaxed descent after the challenging scramble. You will pass several good viewpoints as you descend.

At 4.8 miles you will pass the Byrd's Nest Shelter, a large stone structure. In another mile you will pass the Old Rag Shelter. Both shelters are for day use only.

Past the Old Rag Shelter, the path becomes a broad road, and your descent will become increasingly easy. At 6.2 miles you will reach Weakley Hollow Road, a broad forest road. Turn right, then take the second right and follow the forest road back. At 8.5 miles you will cross a series of bridges before returning to the start of the loop. From here, walk the final mile back down Nethers Road to the parking area.

PLANNING

Old Rag is an extremely popular hike in a popular national park. While the parking lot is large, it fills very quickly on weekends in the summer and fall. During these times, you may have to wait for a parking spot to open up. Of course, if you do not want to compete with the crowds, the best time to hike Old Rag is on a weekday or early morning on a weekend.

The boulder scramble section of the trail is difficult to manage even in ideal conditions, and is dangerous to attempt if the rocks may be wet or icy. Every year, many search and rescue operations are launched to assist hikers stranded or injured on Old Rag. Make sure you are prepared for this hike, both physically, mentally, and in terms of your equipment and planning. Check the weather forecast before setting out on your hike, and if it looks as if a storm is incoming, turn around. You do not want to be caught in the middle of the boulder scramble when a storm breaks.

GETTING THERE

The trailhead can be found on Google Maps by navigating to "Old Rag Trailhead." The parking area is off VA 600 in the town of Nethers, Virginia.

NORTHEAST

RICKETTS GLEN FALLS LOOP

Pennsylvania: Ricketts Glen State Park

DISTANCE: 6.8 miles

ELEVATION GAIN: 1,010 feet

TIME COMMITMENT: 3 to 4 hours

FEE: None

DOGS: Permitted

CAMPING ALONG TRAIL: No

DIFFICULTY: Mostly easy trail with several sections of moderate uphill climbing. Several portions of the trail may be slick and will require you to pay careful attention to your footing.

Left: Ganoga Falls is the highest in the park, at 94 feet

If you enjoy mountain views, you'll usually base a hike around summiting a mountain peak—more ambitious hikers may even tackle two or three summits in one outing. But waterfall enthusiasts are lucky, with the ability to easily visit many falls along the same stretch of trail, and nowhere are they more spoiled than Ricketts Glen State Park. This loop of 21 named waterfalls—and many more smaller, minor falls—is without a doubt one of the best waterfall hikes in the eastern United States, and one can easily make a strong case that this is among the best waterfall hikes in North America. While other trails bring hikers to taller, more dramatic falls, few trails offer the sheer number and variety of falls found here. These aren't merely small, burbling falls over an unusually rocky stream, either: most of the falls here range in height from 15 to 50 feet, with the highest reaching nearly 100 feet.

Twenty-one major falls is a staggering number of waterfalls to experience in only a few hours' time, and these falls are each unique and beautiful in their own ways. But aside from the obvious appeal of hitting so many waterfalls in such a short span of trail, Ricketts Glen offers a stroll through a lovely stretch of northern Pennsylvania, made richer by the many interesting rock formations and ledges off the trail, as well as old-growth forest that survived in patches throughout these glens thanks to the steep and rocky terrain, which was too rocky for the trees to be logged.

Hikers who are limited for time can still visit most of the major waterfalls by doing just the loop portion of this route, cutting out the initial 2-mile trail from PA 118. For this shorter 3.5-mile loop, hikers will park at the Lake Rose Trailhead parking area and hike a short distance in to begin the loop. Just north of Lake Rose is Lake Jean, a larger lake with beaches, facilities, and campgrounds.

TRAIL OVERVIEW

The trail begins at the west end of the parking area—look for signs for the Falls Trail. The trail crosses several bridges over Kitchen Creek. At 0.2 mile keep right at the service road and cross another bridge. For the first mile, you will hike over an old, mostly level roadway.

At about a mile you'll cross two more bridges before reaching a split in the trail. Here, the Lower Trail to the right follows the bank of the Kitchen Creek, with more difficult footing. If the creek is high, this section of trail may be partially flooded. To your left, the Upper Trail climbs to a slightly higher elevation above the creek, offering an easier (and drier) alternate route. Both paths will converge in a short distance, before the first waterfall.

At 1.3 miles you will arrive at the first waterfall of the hike: Murray Reynolds Falls. The named waterfalls are identified by small wooden signs near each fall. Continue alongside Kitchen Creek, and soon you will pass the 36-foot-high Sheldon Reynolds Falls, and just beyond it the equally dramatic Harrison Wright Falls.

At 1.8 miles you will reach an intersection where the loop portion of the hike begins. The Ganoga Glen Trail heads up the west bank of Kitchen Creek, while the Glen Leigh Trail crosses a bridge to your right. The loop can be done in either direction, but for this guide we will first head up the Ganoga Glen Trail.

The trail passes two nearly 50-foot falls, Erie Falls and Tuscarora Falls, before passing the smaller Conestoga Falls. The path will become steeper and narrower as you climb up the glen, with stone staircases in several sections. Be especially careful on this leg of the hike, as there is often water seeping out from the rock walls and coating the stones, making for slick footing.

After crossing a wooden bridge, you will hike past Mohican Falls, Delaware Falls, then Seneca Falls. At 2.5 miles you will pass a trail on your left, which connects with the Ganoga View Trail and the Old Beaver Dam Road Trail.

Soon you will arrive at Ganoga Falls. At 94 feet, it is not only the highest waterfall in the park, but it towers twice as high as any of the other falls. The trail climbs toward the top of the falls, but to the right, just before the falls, is an unmarked side path. This side trail will bring you to the base of the falls, with fantastic views.

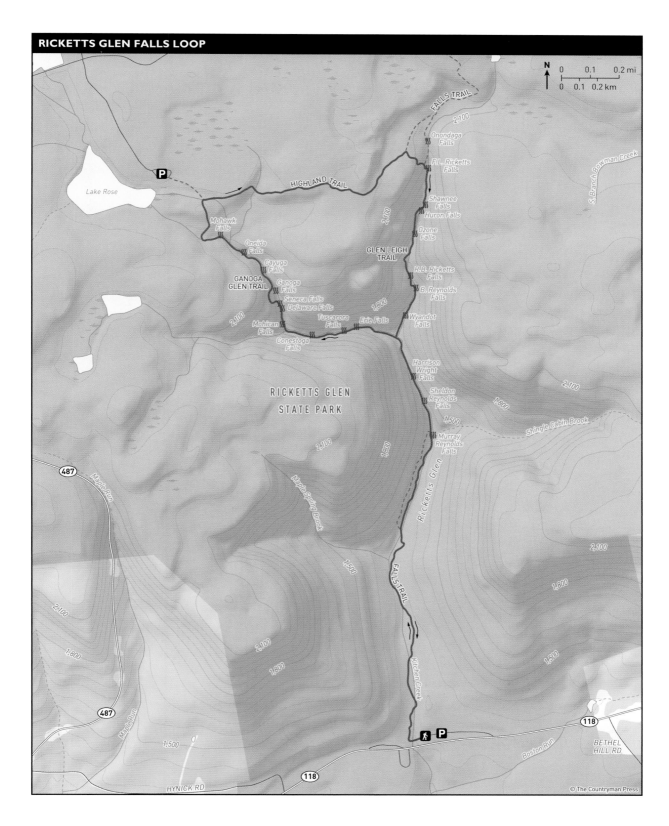

R. B. Ricketts falls

Be careful not to wander off trail above the falls; it would be easy to slip in this area, and serious injury or death could occur. Continuing past Ganoga Falls, you'll pass Cayuga Falls, Oneida Falls, and Mohawk Falls.

At 3.2 miles you will pass another trail junction. The falls trail veers

left, heading toward Lake Rose and an alternate parking area. Turn right onto the Highland Trail. You have reached the high point of the hike—the Highland Trail is relatively level and easy. At 3.5 miles you will pass through the Midway Crevasse, a narrow gap through large boulders of Pocono sandstone.

At 4 miles turn right at the intersection. This short connector trail heads downhill, bringing you back to the Falls Trail, to continue on the final portion of the loop. On this section of the trail you will pass many more waterfalls. From north to south, you will hike past Onondaga, F. L. Ricketts, Shawnee, Huron, Ozone, R. B. Ricketts, B. Reynolds, and Wyandot Falls. Several sections of the trail will require you to descend steep stone steps before returning to relatively level grade at the Waters Meet intersection.

At the end of the loop portion of the hike, turn left. You have now returned to the Falls Trail from the first leg of your hike. From here, retrace your steps for 1.8 miles back to the parking area.

PLANNING

Much of Ricketts Glen is near water, and so the trail can be very slick and muddy at all times of the year. Several sections of the trail require hikers to navigate narrow, steep stone stairs, which may be difficult to traverse when they are wet or icy. Use extra caution after heavy rain or whenever there may be ice on the trail.

The uniqueness of this trail makes it a very popular destination, and the trail can become crowded on weekends. If seeking solitude, you are best off planning your visit for a weekday or starting in the early morning.

GETTING THERE

The trailhead can be found on Google Maps by navigating to "Falls Natural Trail, Ricketts Glen." The parking area is off PA 118, 24 miles west of Wilkes-Barre, Pennsylvania.

BONTICOU CRAG AND TABLE ROCKS LOOP

New York: Mohonk Preserve

DISTANCE: 5.2 miles

ELEVATION GAIN: 1,040 feet

TIME COMMITMENT: 3 to 4 hours

FEE: Entrance fee at Spring Farm Trailhead

DOGS: Permitted

CAMPING ALONG TRAIL: No

DIFFICULTY: This hike features a challenging rock scramble, which requires strong upper body strength, dexterity, and the ability to navigate narrow rock ledges.

Left: A hiker perches on the rocks above Bonticou Crag

It makes sense in retrospect, but going into this project, I didn't expect to have nearly as much difficulty settling on one or two New York hikes that capture the best of hiking in this state. But New York is where I've lived for half my life and thus the place where I've hiked the most. Familiarity, plus the many unique memories I associate with so many of the incredible hikes in my area, make it incredibly challenging to pick favorites, even with other hikers weighing in, their opinions stacking up in favor of one hike over another. As I've mentioned, my goal for the hikes I ultimately selected for this guide was to capture something that felt essential to that area—a hike that I felt could stand in for the essence of a region. Paradoxically, sometimes those hikes ended up being hikes that were drastically different in terrain from the rest of the state around them, hikes that stood out dramatically and therefore stand out as the most memorable. The Shawangunk Ridge in New York's Hudson Valley actually falls into both those categories for me. There's no better spot to appreciate the vastness and diversity of the valley: from the Shawangunk Ridge you can see all the way from the Hudson Highlands to the Catskill Mountains and, of course, trace the path of the Hudson River itself.

But the Shawangunk Ridge is like nothing else in New York. Indeed, it's not quite like anywhere else in America. There are only a handful of ecosystems similar to it in the entire world: a unique world existing on top of a wide, dramatic ridge, home to sheer cliffs of curious white conglomerate rock, huge "sky lakes," craggy boulder fields, deep fissures and chasms, and an ethereal landscape of dwarf pitch pine, warped and

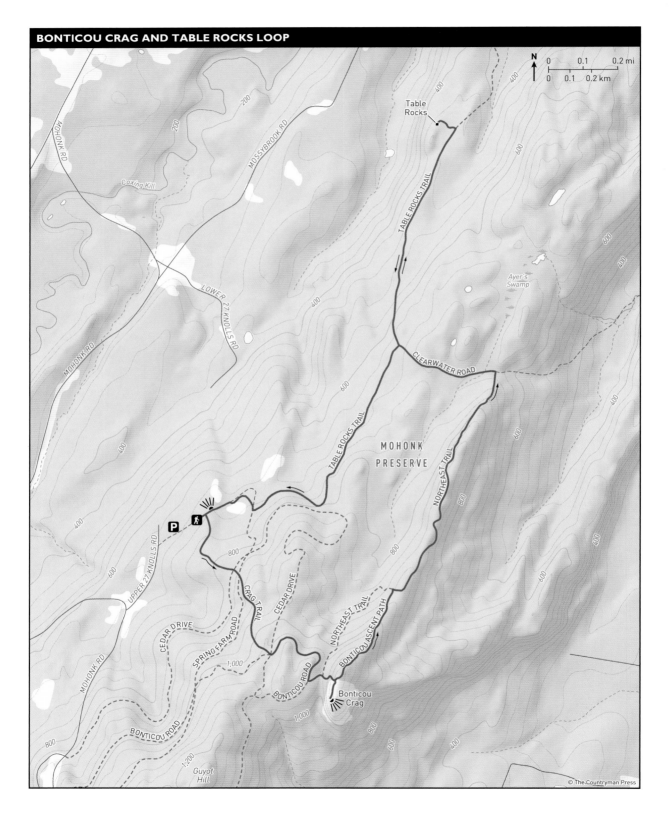

Table
Rocks

MOHONK RD

Coxing Kill

MOSSYBROOK RD

LOWER 27 KNOLLS RD

TABLE ROCKS TRAIL

CLEARWATER ROAD

Ayer's
Swamp

MOHONK
PRESERVE

NORTHEAST TRAIL

P

UPPER 27 KNOLLS RD

CRAG TRAIL

CEDAR DRIVE

CEDAR DRIVE

SPRING FARM ROAD

MOHONK RD

BONTICOU ROAD

BONTICOU ROAD

NORTHEAST TRAIL

BONTICOU ASCENT PATH

Bonticou
Crag

Guyot
Hill

© The Countryman Press

defined by its strange home. I am not the only one to think of this ridge as feeling otherworldly: it was recently used as the film location for a popular Netflix show in a fantasy (as in swords and elves) fantasy (as in, it was all happening in the character's mind) sequence. It is a place I go when I wish to feel like I'm somewhere else, and yet a place I feel is vital to the natural landscape of New York.

There are many excellent hikes to be found along the Shawangunk Ridge, but in the ridge's northeastern end a loop from Bonticou Crag to Table Rocks illustrates how dramatic this landscape can be, offers some of the best views in the Hudson Valley, and, most importantly, is simply an exceptionally fun hike. You'll find excellent views of the Catskill Mountains from right past the trailhead, enjoy a challenging boulder scramble, and hike through serene, pine-scented woods to a massive rock "table" split by huge chasms and rifts. While the scramble is difficult, it does not require ropes or harnesses as a true rock climb would; however, hikers also have the opportunity to circumvent it entirely and still complete the rest of the loop. Beyond the steep scramble, hikers with a fear of heights should be cautious at Table Rocks, where a fall into the deep chasms between the rocks would certainly prove fatal. This is a stunning hike but one that should only be attempted in good weather; if the rocks may be slick or icy, you're better off finding another trail in the area to explore.

TRAIL OVERVIEW

From the parking area, look for the blue-blazed Table Rocks Trail, which heads uphill parallel to Spring Farm Road. Soon the trail will come to the top of a hill, with a large open field to your left. Here you will find one of the best panoramic views of the Catskill Mountains in the region.

Shortly past this viewpoint you will reach an intersection with the Crag Trail. Turn right onto this trail and head uphill. The path continues across a field, near an old stone wall. At 0.4 mile you will come to two parallel carriage roads, one right after the other. The first is Cedar Drive, followed by Spring Farm Road. Continue straight on the Crag Trail, which continues to gain in elevation.

At 0.7 mile you will arrive at a five-way intersection and the start of a loop at a small pond. Cedar Drive makes a hard left, while Bonticou Road makes a slight left. Take Bonticou Road. The trail here is a mostly level carriage road which snakes through the woods before the crag itself comes into sight. At 0.9 mile you will reach an intersection with the yellow-blazed Bonticou Ascent Path. Turn left onto this trail, which heads downhill briefly to reach the rocky base of the crag. From here the intimidating-looking jumble of rocks looms above you, and on most days you will probably see numerous hikers perched at various stages along the climb, enjoying the views from the ridge above.

The Bonticou Ascent Path is not to be underestimated. While short in mileage, this is a challenging section of trail, climbing over 100 feet in elevation via a series of massive boulders and rock wedges. Making your way up the crag, you will climb over giant talus fragments and around narrow ledges. While most of the scramble requires only good balance, several sections may require use of both your arms and legs to find footholds and climb your way up. The yellow blazes painted onto the rocks mark the easiest and safest route of ascent. Pay careful attention and do not veer off course or you may risk losing the yellow blazes.

Near the top of the climb the ridge will begin to level out. Turn right to reach the crest of Bonticou Crag, where you will find excellent views south toward the Hudson and north to the Catskills. While pitch pines grow densely in spots, most of the ridge is exposed rock slabs and boulders, making for one of the most interesting areas of crumbled and jutting Shawangunk conglomerate anywhere on the ridge.

After enjoying the view, follow the yellow-blazed trail as it heads down a rocky, narrow trail along the ridgetop. At 1.5 miles you will reach an intersection with the blue-blazed Northeast Trail. Turn right onto this trail. The path now continues mostly straight along the ridge, dropping slowly in elevation. As you walk north, several excellent views will open up above rock ledges, offering more great views of the Catskill Mountains.

At 2 miles the trail begins to descend several hundred more feet before intersecting with the Clearwater Road at 2.2 miles. The remains of old, decaying structures can be seen in the woods along the trail here. In a quarter mile you will reach an intersection with the Table Rocks Trail, which heads both north toward Table Rocks and south, back to the parking area. To reach Table Rocks, turn right.

The trail continues to descend, steeply at first, before leveling out on the final stretch to Table Rocks. At 3.3 miles you will reach a spur trail on your left that heads to Table Rocks. Take this trail. The path descends past the first of the massive split rocks that form this fascinating geological oddity. After passing several huge stones, the trail winds through the woods up to Table Rocks itself.

Take the Table Rocks Trail back to the intersection where you turned

Right: Deep fissures make a walk around Table Rocks both a fascinating and potentially dangerous experience

AMERICA'S BEST DAY HIKES

onto this trail, off Clearwater Road. Go straight to continue south on the Table Rocks Trail. After a short distance, a parallel trail splits off to the left, but you can ignore this trail and continue straight. Continue through a meadow, and at the tree line head into the woods following the Table Rocks Trail. (To your right, Spring Farm Woods Road offers an easier, more direct pathway back to the parking area, should you wish to speed through this final stretch of the hike.)

PLANNING

The rock scramble section of this hike is a challenge even in ideal conditions and would be dangerous to attempt if the rocks are wet or icy. Between the rock scramble up Bonticou Crag and the dizzying fissures of Table Rocks, this is not a hike for small children or anyone with a fear of heights. Serious injury or death could easily occur on this hike with a slip or a misstep. Make sure you are prepared for the challenges of this route physically, mentally, and with your equipment and planning.

The northeastern section of the Shawangunk Ridge—the most scenic section of the ridge and the most popular for hiking—is managed by three different agencies. Unfortunately, all three agencies charge parking fees, and there is no entrance pass shared among them. The Mohonk Preserve manages most of the area in the far northeastern end of the ridge, including the West Trapps, Coxing, and Spring Farm Trailheads. To the southwest, the Sam's Point and Lake Minnewaska areas are a New York State Park. Between these two is the Mohonk Mountain House, a private resort on one of the ridge's sky lakes, with one parking area accessible to day hikers for a steep fee.

The hiking areas in the Shawangunk Ridge are always very popular, but they become even more so in the fall, when the leaves are changing. The Spring Farm parking area is only large enough for a few dozen cars and will fill quickly on weekends. The Mohonk Preserve parking areas will close when they have reached capacity.

GETTING THERE

The trailhead can be found on Google Maps by navigating to "Spring Farm Trailhead Parking." The parking area is off Mohonk Road, about 5.5 miles west of the town of New Paltz, New York.

Left: Bonticue Crag, looking south down the Hudson Valley

GIANT MOUNTAIN

New York: Adirondack High Peaks Wilderness

DISTANCE: 6 miles

ELEVATION GAIN: 3,040 feet

TIME COMMITMENT: 4 to 6 hours

FEE: None

DOGS: Permitted

CAMPING ALONG TRAIL: No

DIFFICULTY: A strenuous climb up an extremely rocky trail makes this a very challenging hike.

Left: A hiker looks out over Chapel Pond from one of Giant's many viewpoints

Returning to the East Coast, following a summer of hiking around the country, I found myself feeling a bit overconfident about revisiting my favorite New England hiking destinations. Surely after tackling challenging day hikes in the peaks of Colorado, Montana, and California, a hike in the Adirondack Park of upstate New York would feel at least *easier*. Not easy, of course. From a West Coast perspective, it may seem that a 4,000-foot mountain would pose little challenge, compared with 8,000- or 10,000- or 14,000-foot peaks. Yet it's important to remember that few trails start at sea level. Regardless of the ultimate height of the peak, most trails only traverse around 3,000 feet of actual elevation gain. Thus, a hike up a 10,000-foot peak out west or a 4,000-foot peak in the east will usually see the hiker tackling similar amounts of elevation gain.

Still, I figured that at least the experience of hiking for an entire summer would lessen the challenge of these New England mountains. Tackling Giant Mountain on an early fall day, with the trail still slick from recent rain, I quickly realized that I'd simply let my guard down, bolstered by the confidence of widespread travel. What had not occurred to me was that New England trails may actually be *harder* than many trails in the rest of the country—even if these peaks are a third of the height of the Rockies. The main challenge comes from the sheer rockiness of the trails; New England trails are rugged. Really rugged. For much of the hike you won't be walking so much as scrambling around and over boulders or smaller loose stones. If the trail is wet, slick tree roots and rocks further compound the difficulties. Of course, the challenge of these rugged trails is also part of the allure: here, the trails themselves hold your interest, demand your attention. There is a feeling of ancientness among these peaks. After all, the mountains of the East Coast are far older than the Rockies. That is why they are smaller peaks—millions of years of erosion will reduce the stature of even a towering mountain range. But that

erosion does not merely make the upper half of a mountain vanish. Erosion batters the mountain down, year after year, and casts its rocks down its flank. When you are hiking the rocky trails of an eastern peak, you are scrambling around its ancient remains, the missing height of a once towering summit.

The Adirondack High Peaks generate unpredictable weather systems during all seasons

Giant stands out among the Adirondack High Peaks because it stands alone. East of Keene Valley, the 12th-highest peak in the Adirondacks has a striking profile. Besides its prominence, its western face is scarred by steep rock slides. Once referred to as "Giant of the Valley," it is an ideal High Peaks hike due to its relatively shorter trail length. Due to the limited number of trailheads accessing the region, many High Peaks hikes are 12 to 15 miles or more in length. A hike up Giant will give you a taste of the region, the full challenges of a 3,000-foot-elevation-gain hike, and some of the best views in the area—all in only 6 miles.

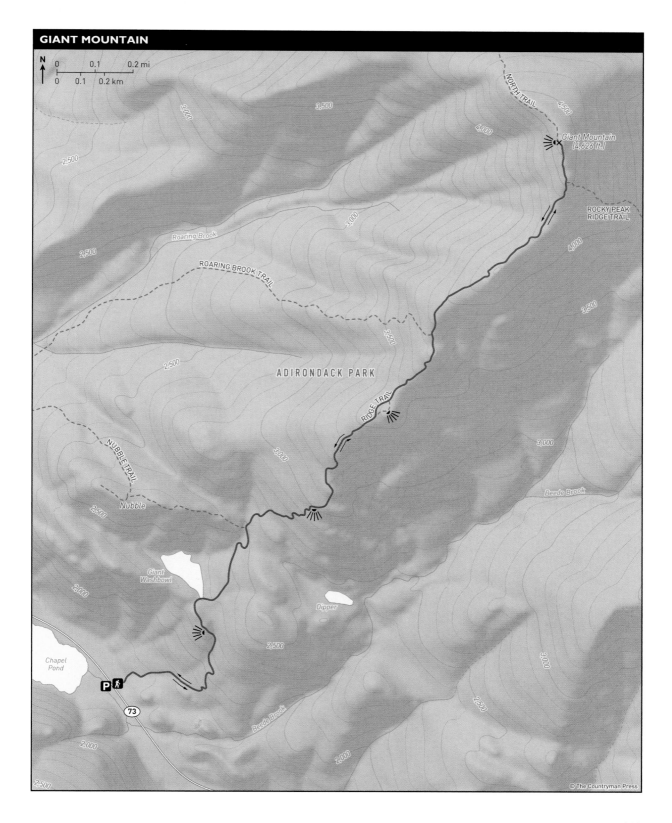

N

0   0.1   0.2 mi

0   0.1   0.2 km

3,500

3,000

4,500

NORTH TRAIL

4,000

✳ Giant Mountain
(4,626 ft.)

2,500

ROCKY PEAK
RIDGE TRAIL

2,500

Roaring Brook

4,000

ROARING BROOK TRAIL

3,000

3,500

3,500

ADIRONDACK PARK

RIDGE TRAIL

3,000

NUBBLE TRAIL

Beede Brook

Nubble

2,500

3,000

Giant
Washbowl

2,000

Dipper

Chapel
Pond

2,500

2,000

P 🚶

73

Beede Brook

2,500

2,000

2,500

© The Countryman Press

TRAIL OVERVIEW

You will find the trail register just in from the road. A short distance later the trail begins to head uphill over crude stone stairs. At 0.25 mile the trail becomes even steeper still, and soon after you will tackle a rocky section that is almost a scramble in its ruggedness.

After this climb the trail levels but remains rocky, and shortly after, you will arrive at the first viewpoint, an excellent west-facing outcrop with views of Hedgehog Mountain and the Wolfjaws. The trail cuts east, and just beyond the viewpoint, at 0.7 mile, you will hike past Giant Wash-bowl, a small pond.

At 1 mile you will arrive at a split. The trail heading straight goes to Giant's Nubble, a viewpoint above the Washbowl that is well worth visiting if you have time. The Nubble is about half a mile beyond this intersection. To continue toward Giant, turn right and head uphill.

Another view opens up at 1.25 miles. This route up Giant will take you

Giant Washbowl in early autumn

on and around many open rock slabs, all of which boast excellent views of the High Peaks.

At 1.7 miles the trail forks, presenting you with the option to go "over the bump" or "around the bump." The bump is merely another viewpoint, with a small amount of climbing required to reach it and again descend. Keep right to climb the bump and enjoy the views, or left to go around the bump. From the bump you will be able to see Rocky Peak Ridge, across the saddle from Giant.

The Roaring Brook Trail intersects at 2.1 miles; keep right and continue to head uphill. At 2.8 miles the Rocky Peak Ridge trail splits right. Just beyond, at 3 miles, you will reach the summit.

PLANNING

Parking in the High Peaks region is limited and fills quickly on weekends in summer and fall. The parking area for Giant Mountain is fairly small. On weekends, you might have to park at one of several other parking areas just down the road.

The trail up Giant Mountain is extremely rocky and rugged. Much of the trail more closely resembles a rock scramble than a gentle walk in the woods. Shoes with good traction are a must here, and hiking poles help significantly. If the trail is wet, slick tree roots and rocks further compound the difficulties. If the trail is icy, traction devices like microspikes or crampons are a must. Due to the ruggedness of the trails, winter hiking in the Adirondacks is only recommended for those with experience and the proper gear.

GETTING THERE

The trailhead can be found on Google Maps by navigating to "Whitaker Point Trailhead." The parking area is off County Road 5 at the intersection of County Road 406, about a quarter mile south of Cave Mountain Church.

MOUNT MANSFIELD

Vermont: Underhill State Park

DISTANCE: 6 miles

ELEVATION GAIN: 2,600 feet

TIME COMMITMENT: 4 to 6 hours

FEE: $4 entrance fee at Underhill State Park

DOGS: Permitted

CAMPING ALONG TRAIL: Yes

DIFFICULTY: A very strenuous climb made more challenging by the volatile and potentially dangerous weather conditions found on the ridgetop portion of the hike. Hikers must be prepared for a wide range of weather extremes in any season.

Left: A hiker descends the Sunset Ridge trail

We humans love to anthropomorphize just about anything we can. Especially out in the uncertain wilds, it seems to give us a sense of familiarity to help soften (in our minds) the raw power of nature. Mount Mansfield, from a distance and with a great deal of imagination, might be said to resemble a human head, and so certain features of the mountain have been labeled the Chin, the Upper Lip, the Nose, and the Forehead. Most telling of this hike's challenges, however, might be the path to the summit dubbed "Profanity Trail."

While there are multiple routes to the summit of Mount Mansfield—the highest mountain in Vermont, at 4,393 feet—this particular route avoids the profanity (or at least the trail by that name) for a still-challenging loop that crosses Mansfield's scenic ridgeline. A toll road from the Stowe Mountain resorts takes drivers to within a mile of the summit, so despite the challenges, Mansfield's easy access and prominent station within Vermont make this a popular peak to tackle. Of course, popular does not mean easy, and many hikers may decide to go for an abridged version of this hike, turning around somewhere in the alpine zone before the summit. Mansfield generates erratic weather conditions similar to the White Mountains of New Hampshire, and with challenging terrain along the exposed portions of the Sunset Ridge Trail, hikers should certainly wait for the right day to bag this peak. Be prepared for anything: once you are up on the ridge, the weather can change rapidly, winds can grow extreme, and hikers will find very little shelter for some distance in either direction. As always, exercise caution and turn around if weather above the tree line seems to be turning hazardous.

On a clear day, you'll enjoy unrivaled views from the summit: the Green Mountain state stretches all around you, with Lake Champlain to the west, the Adirondack Mountains farther west still, and New Hampshire's White Mountains visible in the east. To the south, the distinct profile

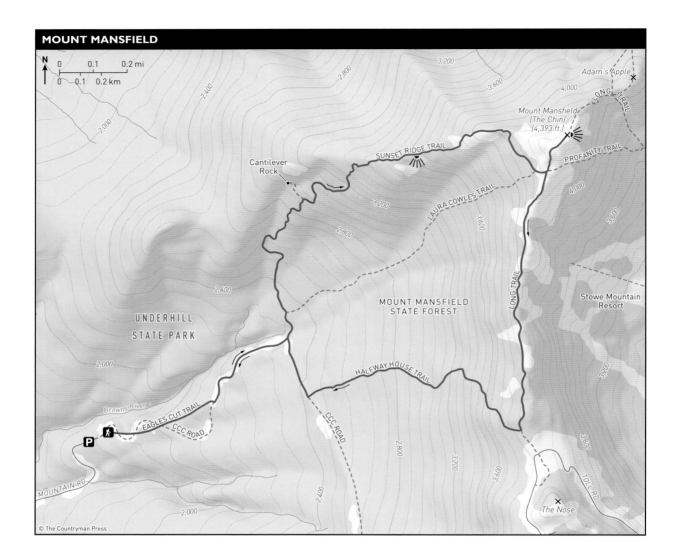

of Camel's Hump rises from the jumble of green hills. Mansfield's summit is an alpine zone and thus home to numerous rare plants. Dispensia flowers and mossy lichen grow here, as well as creeping snowberry and old-man's beard. During your ascent and at the summit, you will notice string trails—these guidelines are meant to steer you away from fragile alpine plants and keep you on the designated trail. Always stay within the boundaries of the strings to avoid harming the extremely delicate ecosystem that exists within the mountain's alpine zone. These plants have only 90 days each year to thrive, and if you catch the mountain on a day of its frequent weather extremes, you'll be able to understand just what a fight it is to survive up here.

TRAIL OVERVIEW

The trail begins at Underhill State Park, where Eagle Cut Trail offers a shortcut from taking the switchbacks of the CCC woods road. You will tackle a mild climb for 0.3 mile. Upon reaching the woods road, turn left and take CCC Road another 0.3 mile. Here you will finally reach the trail register. Sign in, then take the Sunset Ridge Trail to the left of the trail register, crossing over a bridge.

Soon you will pass an intersection with the Laura Cowles Trail—an alternate, steeper route to the summit—to your right. Continue on the Sunset Ridge Trail. The climb soon will begin to grow more intense. In 0.7 mile a spur trail to the left veers off the main trail for 0.2 mile to reach Cantilever Rock, a unique geological anomaly. Cantilever Rock resembles a thin stone tongue jutting from the mountain around it, and it is worth the short detour to visit.

Following the Sunset Ridge Trail, you will continue up a moderate climb through beautiful, craggy woods. Before long you will reach the open expanse of Sunset Ridge, with stunning views west toward Lake Champlain and the Adirondacks, and south toward Camel's Hump.

Continue, being mindful from here on out to follow the path carefully, both so that you do not lose sight of the trail markers and to preserve the fragile alpine ecosystem. The climb becomes relatively steep, but the trail over large rocks offers sure footing if one is careful. Nearing the summit, the trail cuts right and again passes Laura Cowles Trail. Turn left and hike for a short distance to reach the true summit at 4,393 feet.

From the summit, turn back and continue south. Follow the Long Trail over the ridge for 1 mile, crossing the Lower and Upper Lips as you hike toward the Nose. The views here will continue to astonish, but as dramatic as this ridge looks, there is little opportunity for hikers to "fall off," such as on the traverse of other ridgeline hikes, such as Mount Katahdin's Knife Edge. However, much of this traverse is rocky, with light scrambling in some sections. Hikers should be especially careful of their footing in these sections.

On either side of the ridge, the Canyon Notch Trail and Subway Trail offer alternative routes with ledges and caves for more experienced and daring hikers. These trails are significantly more difficult, however, and should not be taken lightly. Hikers who are prepared for the challenges of these routes will find the intersection for these trails at 3.1 miles.

At 3.7 miles you will see structures and radio towers ahead of you and the Nose jutting prominently up from the ridge. After a large cairn, look for the Halfway House Trail to your right. This trail descends steeply from the ridge, heading back down below the tree line. After about a mile you will rejoin CCC Road. Turn right. Soon you will reach the trail register and the intersection with the Sunset Ridge Trail. Turn left to follow your original route back down to Underhill State Park and the parking area.

Mount Mansfield in late autumn

PLANNING

Trailhead parking is found within Underhill State Park, a popular state campground located on the western flank of Mansfield. The main lot fills up quickly on weekends, and you may have to park along the side of Mountain Road, just before the campground.

Hiking off-season can help to dodge the summer crowds, but hikers should be wary of hiking Mansfield if conditions look questionable. In winter you will face the typical snow and ice that is an ever-present concern on the great New England peaks. If you wish to tackle a mountain like Mansfield under winter conditions—which may extend from fall until late spring—it's best to start with a lesser peak first, to better know what you'll be in for. Once atop Mansfield's exposed ridge, you do not want to discover that you are unprepared or underdressed. Conditions can turn life threatening quickly, even in warmer months.

GETTING THERE

The trailhead can be found on Google Maps by navigating to "Underhill State Park." The parking area is located off Mountain Road, about 6 miles east of Underhill, Vermont.

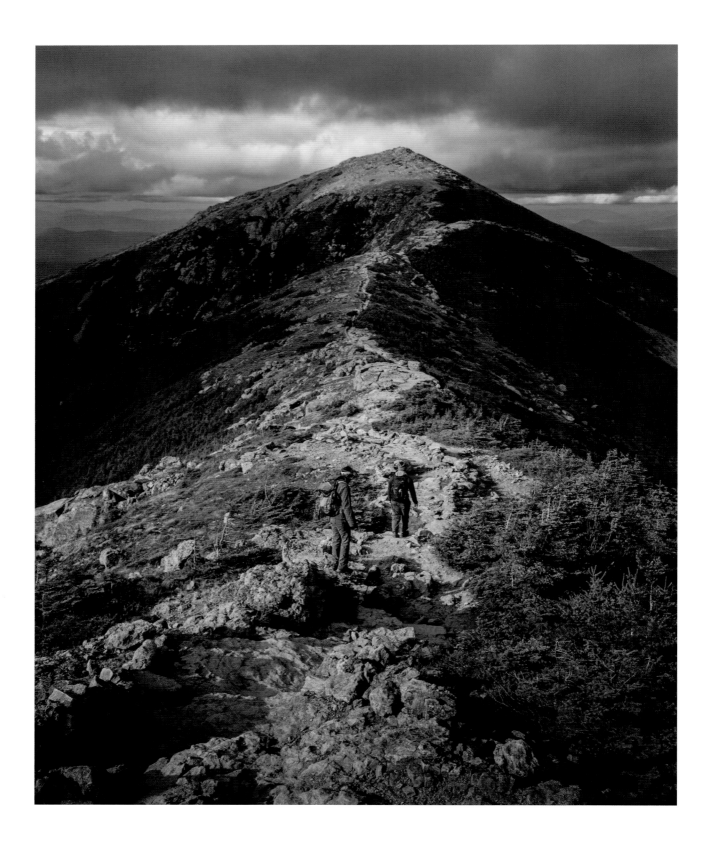

FRANCONIA RIDGE LOOP

New Hampshire: Franconia Notch State Park

DISTANCE: 8.8 miles

ELEVATION GAIN: 3,830 feet

TIME COMMITMENT: 6 to 8 hours

FEE: None

DOGS: Permitted

CAMPING ALONG TRAIL: Yes

DIFFICULTY: A very strenuous climb made more challenging by the volatile and potentially dangerous weather conditions found on the ridgetop portion of the hike. Hikers must be prepared for a wide range of weather extremes in any season.

Left: Hikers wind their way across the Franconia Ridge

Few sights in New England are as memorable as the crest of Franconia Ridge. Hiking through the alpine zone of a rugged mountain is always a riveting experience, an up-close glimpse of the brutal extremes found atop such high peaks. Often, however, such rugged summits sport only a narrow cap hosting an alpine ecosystem; usually the summits of such mountains are crowned with scree and boulder fields, difficult to climb, dangerously harsh even to the briefly visiting hiker. Not that Franconia Ridge isn't both dangerous and harsh—it certainly is both—but the bald, narrow ridge that runs between Mount Lafayette (5,260 feet), Little Haystack (4,760 feet), and Lincoln (5,089 feet) offers something rare on such summits: the opportunity to venture across miles of alpine zone while barely changing elevation. Here, the ridge connecting the peaks allows hikers to easily stroll (well, easy on at least the few days when the weather is mild) along 2 miles of high alpine terrain. This 2-mile ridge is like few other places on earth you will ever visit; it is certainly one of my all-time favorite hikes in the country, let alone the Northeast. It is a popular hike, but I can't think of anywhere better to enjoy the exceptional views and rugged environment of the White Mountains.

Other knife-edge alpine hikes similar to Franconia Ridge are usually far more difficult and dizzying—I enjoy that this ridge walk doesn't stimulate vertigo the way that, say, Maine's Mount Katahdin does. The trail follows a well-defined path, wide enough that there's no real need to fear falling, though it is certainly a long way down. You will enjoy open, incredible views of the White Mountains and Vermont—on a clear day, distant Camel's Hump and Mount Mansfield are visible to the west. Only a few modest sections of rock scrambling add challenge to this section of trail; the real difficulty is simply the strenuous hike up, and the unpredictability of the weather once there. With almost 4,000 feet of elevation change over the course of this hike, it's easily one of the more strenuous hikes covered by this guide.

While walking the Franconia Ridge on a good day may not pose nearly the challenge of other knife-edge ridge hikes, it's important to note that there are only so many good days on the high peaks of the White Mountains. On a less-than-good day, the ridge can quickly turn quite dangerous. With the entire ridge portion of the hike above the tree line, there's little opportunity for shelter if the weather turns foul. This is not the hike to attempt if there is any chance of a thunderstorm that day, and even experienced winter hikers should use extra caution when attempting this hike in the cold months of the year. The White Mountains in winter host some of the most extreme weather ever recorded in the world. No matter the season, continuously monitor the weather forecast before beginning your hike, and be prepared to turn back if a storm approaches.

The ridge is not the only attraction of this loop: Falling Waters Trail is home to numerous waterfalls and babbling streams and, for many hikers, is destination enough. Off the Old Bridle Path, on the other side of the loop, you'll also hike past AMC's Greenleaf Hut. The White Mountains boast some of the only high-elevation backcountry huts on the East Coast, and hikers can opt to turn their hike into an overnight by booking a stay at the hut in advance through AMC's website. Even if you're simply hiking by, the hut is a unique attraction where hikers from all over congregate to share stories of alpine adventure.

TRAIL OVERVIEW

The trail begins just in from the parking area, by the bathrooms. After a short distance, Old Bridle Path and Falling Waters Trail split. Keep right to take Falling Waters Trail, crossing the bridge over Walker Brook.

At 0.6 mile you will cross a wide stream. In late summer and fall, this crossing can easily be made by rock hopping, but in spring and early summer you might have to wade through the water. Shortly after, you will have to make another stream crossing between two waterfalls, Stairs Falls and Swiftwater Falls.

You will arrive at Cloudland Falls at 1.3 miles. This 80-foot fall is a "fan-type" waterfall, with the top width only about 2 feet, but the bottom of the falls spreading out to around 25 feet in periods of high water. The trail scrambles uphill to the left of the waterfall, passing above the fall itself.

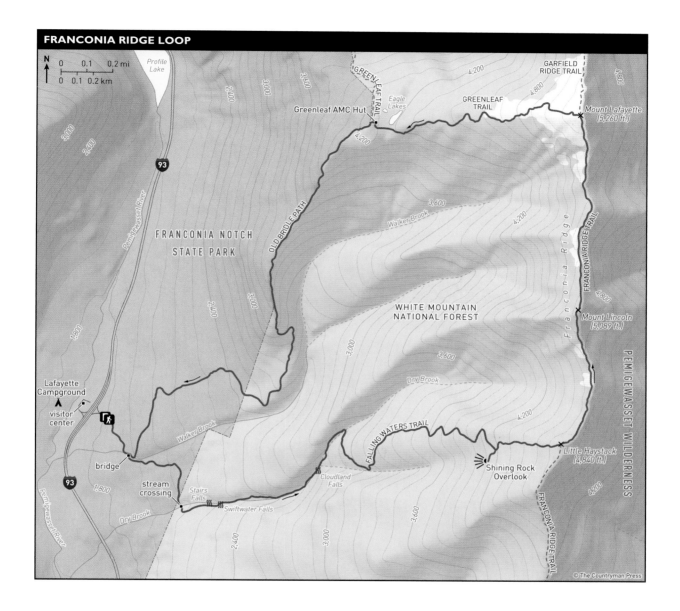

From here the trail leaves Dry Brook Creek and begins to climb steadily uphill, soon beginning a series of short switchbacks. At 2.7 miles a small side trail to your right leads downhill to an overlook of Shining Rock, a steep, sheer rock face with a stream trickling down over it from above, creating a unique reflective surface. The trail to Shining Rock is short, a little more than 0.1 mile, but it necessitates a relatively steep climb downhill and then back up. The mileage indicators from this point on do not include the additional 0.2 mile to reach Shining Rock.

You will pass the tree line at 2.9 miles, reaching the ridgetop a short distance after. At the sign, turn left to begin crossing the ridge toward Mount Lafayette. The trail to the right heads along the ridge to Mount Liberty, a smaller summit to the south.

Though dramatic, the ridge walk is not a difficult traverse. The trail is broad, and there is no real risk of "falling off." In fact, the trail is flat and well defined by rocks. Be sure to stay on trail—this is a fragile alpine ecosystem, and wandering off trail will harm the flora clinging to a delicate existence here.

At 3.7 miles you will arrive at the summit of Mount Lincoln. The trail continues to wind along the ridge, with short sections of climbing. The final uphill push toward Mount Lafayette begins around 4.5 miles, and soon after you will reach the summit—the highest peak in New Hampshire outside of the Presidential Range.

From the summit, the ridge trail becomes the Garfield Ridge Trail and continues north, toward Mount Garfield. You will turn left, descending the west side of the mountain. In a mile you will arrive at the Greenleaf Hut. At the hut, the Greenleaf Trail continues straight, heading north. Turn left to continue hiking west, down the Old Bridle Path.

The shoulder of the mountain soon extends south, forming a long ridge from which you will enjoy several excellent views back up to the Franconia Ridge.

At 8.6 miles the Old Bridle Path intersects with the Falling Waters Trail, completing the loop portion of the hike. Turn right and hike the short distance back to the trailhead.

PLANNING

This route ascends via the Falling Waters Trail and descends via the Old Bridle Path. If you are hiking in the afternoon, this is ideal for enjoying the best views; there are a number of excellent viewpoints along the Old Bridle Path. The setting sun in the west will catch on the ridge during sunset's golden hour, and these viewpoints are perfectly positioned to enjoy the sight of the ridge during this time of day. In addition, the Falling Waters Trail is often wet and slick, and climbing up rocks is generally easier, and safer, than descending them. However, many hikers choose to hike this loop in the alternate direction. You

Looking south along the Franconia Ridge

may choose to reverse the route in this guide if you wish; the route is easily navigable either way.

This trail is not easily navigable in cloudy or stormy weather, however, and hikers should use extreme caution if setting out on such a day. Even in summer, the temperature differential between the base of the mountain and the summit of the mountain can be drastic; in spring, fall, and winter, this temperature differential can easily prove deadly if you are not prepared.

GETTING THERE

The trailhead can be found on Google Maps by navigating to "Old Bridle Path Trailhead." The parking area is off I-93 N, about 8 miles north of Lincoln, New Hampshire.

PRECIPICE TRAIL

Maine: Acadia National Park

DISTANCE: 2.6 miles

ELEVATION GAIN: 950 feet

TIME COMMITMENT: 3 to 4 hours

FEE: National Park Pass or entrance fee

DOGS: Not permitted

CAMPING ALONG TRAIL: No

DIFFICULTY: A via ferrata-style climb involving sheer cliffs and steep drops, with metal ladders, handrails, and bridges to guide you. Despite the short length of the trail, this is a challenging hike that is not for those with a strong fear of heights.

Left: The view of Bar Harbor from Champlain Mountain

Maine's Acadia National Park, encompassing the rocky headlands of Mount Desert Island, feels like no other hiking destination in the eastern United States. Its rocky cliffs are more rugged, its oceanside forests deep and shadowed with spruce and pine. On a foggy morning in Acadia, one could be forgiven for imagining they'd been transported to the shores of the Pacific Northwest, though Acadia's atmosphere is ultimately distinct from anywhere else you'll visit in the country.

Part of this atmosphere may be attributed to Acadia's mountains. While they may be low in elevation compared to the peaks of inland Maine, Acadia's craggy peaks offer a commanding view of the Atlantic. It's said that Cadillac Mountain sees the first sunrise light in the United States during the fall and winter, making it an immensely popular destination for extremely early risers. However, no hiking destination in Acadia is as memorable or challenging as Champlain Mountain, home of the Precipice Trail. Ascending nearly 1,000 feet up the east face of Champlain Mountain, this trail resembles a European via ferrata route, using steel rungs and poles to aid hikers in their scramble up this daunting cliffside. While no sections of the trail reach the difficulty level of a technical climb, expect to use hands and feet equally here: this climb is a full-body workout.

While the hike's overall length and elevation gain are fairly minimal compared to others in this guide, it is the sheer intensity of the trails along this route that earn it a high difficulty rating. The Precipice Trail should not be attempted by those with a serious fear of heights or anyone unsure of their balance and footing. For the same reason, this route should never be undertaken when the trail may be wet or icy—it can be very easy to lose your footing when conditions are treacherous. Indeed, accidents have claimed the lives of several hikers here in the past. Only tackle this hike if you are confident in your abilities and certain of weather conditions. If possible, avoid hiking this trail alone.

For those prepared for the challenge, however, the scramble up steel ladder rungs and skirting sheer cliff drops make for an exhilarating, unforgettable adventure. Once you finally reach the summit of Cham-

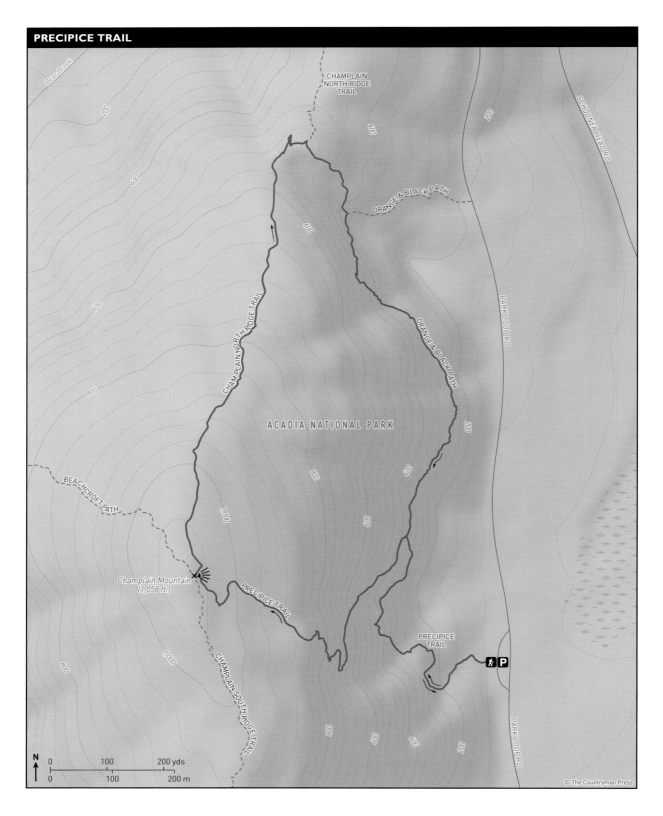

CHAMPLAIN
NORTH RIDGE
TRAIL

Bear Brook

200

400

400

600

800

ORANGE & BLACK PATH

CHAMPLAIN NORTH RIDGE TRAIL

ORANGE & BLACK PATH

200

400

SCHOONER HEAD RD

PARK LOOP RD

ACADIA NATIONAL PARK

BEACHCROFT PATH

1,000

800

600

400

600

400

800

PRECIPICE TRAIL

Champlain Mountain
(1,058 ft.)

CHAMPLAIN SOUTH RIDGE TRAIL

1,000

800

PRECIPICE
TRAIL

800

400

400

200

PARK LOOP RD

N

| 0 | 100 | 200 yds |
| 0 | 100 | 200 m |

© The Countryman Press

plain Mountain, after nearly a thousand feet of climbing, you will be rewarded with sprawling views looking out over Acadia, Frenchman Bay, and the Mount Desert Narrows to the Atlantic. The town of Bar Harbor nestles up against the base of the mountain.

Adding to the challenge of conquering the Precipice Trail is the brief window of time each year that the trail is open. The cliffs of Champlain Mountain are home to endangered peregrine falcons, and to protect these rare birds, the trail is generally closed from late spring through mid-August. Because this route would be dangerous to hike in the winter and early spring, when ice and snowmelt render the rocks and ladder rungs slick, this leaves only a few months at the end of the year when the Precipice may be attempted. Of course, the perks of visiting Acadia in autumn should be obvious—the views from the trail are only enhanced by the colors of fall foliage.

TRAIL OVERVIEW

Setting out on the trail—which may appear tame at first—you will soon arrive at the first sign of the challenges to come. A short distance into the trail, you will reach a boulder outcropping that can be climbed via two iron rungs. Use this first obstacle as a test: if you have any trouble here, you may want to reconsider venturing farther.

From here the trail continues to gain ground, with more rungs here and there to aid in your ascent. You will soon cross a large boulder field and afterward begin working your way over a series of ledges and up the cliff itself. Here the trail employs guardrails to keep you from falling as you navigate the steep cliff ledges and cross wooden bridges.

After a brief section of boulder scrambling, you will arrive at the first section requiring a serious ascent via the iron rungs. Practice caution, go slow, and don't let yourself become too distracted by the scenery—it's at this point that the astonishing views begin.

Soon after navigating this dizzying obstacle course, you will be atop the cliffs and ready to make your final ascent to the summit of Champlain Mountain. From the top you'll find incredible views out to all of Mount Desert Island.

From the summit, to avoid a dangerous descent down the Precipice Trail, take the Champlain North Ridge Trail, which heads north as it descends, overlooking the town of Bar Harbor. This section of trail follows a much more typical grade than the Precipice Trail.

Although it is possible to descend the Precipice Trail, it is not recommended, so a simple loop hike down the Champlain North Ridge Trail (previously known as the Bear Brook Trail) to the Orange & Black Path (previously known as the Champlain East Face Trail) will return you to the Precipice Trail parking lot. Hiking down the Champlain North Ridge Trail is a breeze compared to the hike up Precipice, but the Orange & Black Path requires a fair amount of work, as the trail goes up and down several sets of granite steps as it makes its way back south. Soon enough you will be back at the junction with the start of the Precipice Trail, hiking familiar territory back to the parking lot.

Right: Looking down the Precipice Trail

PLANNING

The Precipice Trail is generally closed for peregrine falcon nesting between March 15 and August 15. Prior to March 15, the trail will most likely be too icy and slick to attempt a hike. Winter hiking on the Precipice Trail is not advised. As such, you should plan your visit to Acadia to hike the Precipice between late August and late October. Even in mid- to late autumn, or any time the forecast is calling for rain, storms may render this hike too dangerous to attempt. Before setting out, check the trail status with the National Park Service.

While most steep trails are made easier with the use of hiking poles, you'll want to leave them at home for this trek. Since much of the hike is a scramble up ladder rungs and narrow climbing paths, poles will only get in the way. If you do choose to pack them, leave them in your pack until summiting Champlain Mountain and use them only while descending the north face and beginning the easier half of this loop.

Acadia is a popular national park, and the parking area for Champlain Mountain can fill up quickly during the busy summer and fall months. Parking is also allowed along the shoulder of the road.

GETTING THERE

The trailhead can be found on Google Maps by navigating to "Precipice Trail." The Precipice Trail parking lot is located along Park Loop Road, about 2 miles from the Sieur de Monts entrance.

KATAHDIN KNIFE EDGE LOOP

Maine: Baxter State Park

DISTANCE: 10.1 miles

ELEVATION GAIN: 3,970 feet

TIME COMMITMENT: 8 to 10 hours

FEE: Yes (see Planning section)

DOGS: Not permitted

CAMPING ALONG TRAIL: Yes

DIFFICULTY: An extremely challenging hike with both long mileage and considerable elevation gain, Mount Katahdin should only be undertaken by experienced hikers confident in their abilities. The Knife Edge section of this hike is among the most intimidating sections of trail in America.

Left: A hiker looks down from the Knife's Edge

I can't imagine a more fitting final hike in this bucket list of America's best day hikes than Maine's Mount Katahdin. For one thing, the mountain has been allotted plenty of significance already: it's the northern terminus of the famed Appalachian Trail and therefore one of the most significant summits in American hiking. But even without that designation, Katahdin would be an unmissable peak for any ambitious hiker. It is a trail as challenging as any day hike in America: indeed, for anything approaching the difficulty of Katahdin, one would have to tackle a mountain four times its height out west. Simply put, this is as challenging as a hike can get before it ceases to be a hike at all and enters the realm of mountaineering.

What makes this trail so difficult? First, there's the sheer amount of elevation gain: just under 4,000 feet, with 10 miles of hiking, would be strenuous under any circumstances. Then, typical of New England mountains, there's the rockiness of the trail, though Katahdin goes above and beyond in this way too. This is one of the rockiest trails I have ever hiked, constantly boulder-hopping and scrambling, slowing my pace to a crawl for good portions of the hike, and that's before I even reached the main attraction: the Knife Edge.

About a mile in length, the Knife Edge is one of the most exposed, vertigo-inducing stretches of trail in America. To find a stretch of trail more intimidating, one would have to advance to actual mountaineering. This route is designed strategically to summit Katahdin before tackling the Knife Edge itself, giving hikers the option to turn back if they find the Knife Edge too intimidating, while still being able to enjoy the summit of this famous and historic mountain. Therefore, the most challenging portion of the Knife Edge on this route will arrive at the end. This section is called "the Chimney": a nearly vertical climb up and down a prominent notch in the Knife Edge so distinct it is clearly visible from the summit.

Navigating the Chimney from either direction requires several maneuvers that approach Class 4 free climbing. Patience, willpower, and strong upper-body strength are necessary for this section. Tall hikers will find these spots relatively manageable on their own; shorter hikers may need assistance from others to safely complete these maneuvers.

Much of the Knife Edge before the Chimney should be easily accomplished by most experienced hikers, assuming there is good weather and good traction. As daunting as it looks from a distance, the trail is mostly wide enough that there's little danger of falling off—with a few exceptions. As one heads east toward the Chimney, the trail begins to narrow, and there are several sections where you will have to cross a narrow platform of rock only a few feet wide, with dizzying drops on one or both sides. This is, to reiterate, not a hike for those with a strong fear of heights, or for anyone if the weather is threatening or good traction cannot be assured. Other hikes in this guide include stretches that are reminiscent of Katahdin's Knife Edge in one way or another, but none pose challenges on this level. Utah's Angels Landing also forces hikers over a narrow, dizzying "knife edge" of rock, but it's less than half a mile in length and offers cables for hikers to hold on to. In New England, Franconia Ridge is an even longer exposed ridge walk, but it's wide enough and level enough that there's no real danger of falling off—the true danger is getting caught at such elevation exposed to the elements. Here too, of course, any inclement weather would quickly shift the Knife Edge from daunting challenge to deadly.

There are other hikes I have found more exhausting than Katahdin—a few high-elevation hikes out west that simply caught me on a low-energy day or where the elevation affected me more than I expected. But all things considered, Mount Katahdin is perhaps the most challenging, intense day hike I have ever done. It is, of course, also one of the most memorable hikes I have ever done; staggeringly rugged, incredibly dramatic, beautiful, threatening—a truly appropriate symbol of American hiking.

TRAIL OVERVIEW

A number of trails begin at the Roaring Brook Campground area. Past the ranger station, keep left at the Russell Pond Trail junction. The trail heads west, following the course of Roaring Brook, and in 0.1 mile the Helon Taylor Trail (which you will take on the return portion of the loop) intersects from the left. Continue straight on the Chimney Pond Trail.

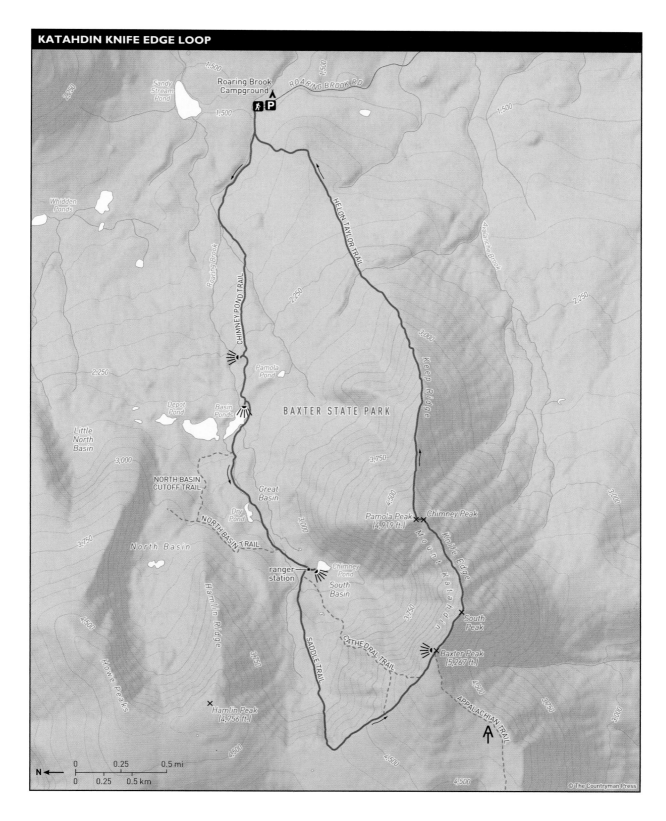

Sandy Stream Pond

Roaring Brook Campground

ROARING BROOK RD

1,500

1,500

2,250

1,500

Whidden Ponds

HELON TAYLOR TRAIL

Roaring Brook

CHIMNEY POND TRAIL

2,250

Pamola Pond

BAXTER STATE PARK

Keep Ridge

3,000

2,250

Depot Pond

Basin Ponds

Little North Basin

3,000

Great Basin

3,750

NORTH BASIN CUTOFF TRAIL

Dry Pond

NORTH BASIN TRAIL

3,000

3,750

North Basin

Pamola Peak (4,919 ft.)

Chimney Peak

4,500

3,750

Hamlin Ridge

ranger station

Chimney Pond

South Basin

Mount Katahdin

Knife Edge

South Peak

3,750

SADDLE TRAIL

CATHEDRAL TRAIL

Baxter Peak (5,267 ft.)

4,500

Howe Peaks

4,500

Hamlin Peak (4,756 ft.)

APPALACHIAN TRAIL

3,750

3,000

4,500

4,500

N

0   0.25   0.5 mi

0   0.25   0.5 km

© The Countryman Press

There are many bridges on this portion of the trail, crossing small streams and swampy areas. At 1.7 miles you will pass a viewpoint looking north, and at 2 miles you will skirt the southern end of Basin Pond. The views from the pond are excellent.

Shortly after the pond, you will cross a very long, wooden bridge-boardwalk. Just after this, the North Basin Cutoff Trail intersects from the right. Continue straight. You will make several more bridge crossings in the next half mile.

At 3.1 miles the North Basin Trail intersects to your right. Keep straight. At 3.3 miles you will arrive at the Chimney Pond area. Hike past the camping and picnic areas. The trail turns right just before the ranger station. However, to enjoy the view from the pond itself, continue past the ranger station. Chimney Pond is a short distance beyond and offers excellent views of Katahdin.

From the ranger station, take the Saddle Trail, heading west. A short

Katahdin's Knife Edge, seen from the summit

distance later the Cathedral Trail splits left, with a side trail heading back toward the campground to the right. Stay straight.

The ascent is gradual at first, but it begins to grow steep around 4.4 miles. Soon you will be making a steep scramble toward the saddle. This strenuous section is a good test for the harder portions of trail to come. If conditions are bad here, they will likely be worse on the Knife Edge itself.

You will reach the top of the saddle at 4.8 miles. From here the grade is significantly easier to the summit, as you cross the gentle incline of the tablelands. The Saddle Trail turns south, toward the summit. You are now above the tree line, with only periodic cairns to navigate you, so pay careful attention to stay on the trail. This is a fragile alpine ecosystem, and wandering off trail will harm the flora clinging to a delicate existence here.

At 5.2 miles the Cathedral Cutoff Trail intersects to the left. Continue straight. A short distance later the Cathedral Trail itself intersects from the left. This trail makes a steeper, more difficult climb from Chimney Pond. At 5.7 miles you will reach the summit. The views from here are stunning—on a clear day you will be able to see a significant portion of the state of Maine and into Canada. Ahead of you now looms the Knife Edge, its crags and contours clearly visible.

When you are ready, if conditions are good, set out over the Knife Edge. Only attempt to hike this portion of the trail if the weather is clear and the ground is dry. In fog, rain, snow, or simply when the rocks are slick and wet, the Knife Edge portion of this hike could be very dangerous.

Hiking the Knife Edge from the west heading east, you will tackle the easy portion of the trail first, saving the most difficult sections for the end. If you feel uncomfortable with the first section of the Knife Edge or if conditions prove more hazardous than expected, this is the time to turn back. The first half mile is a relatively broad ridge walk. While rocky, the "edge" is generally quite wide. And while the drop-offs are steep, there is plenty of room to spare even hikers with a fear of heights from a bout of vertigo. However, this section of the hike is very rocky, and you will have to watch out for loose stones. The greatest danger during this stretch is simply twisting your ankle.

After about half a mile the ridge reaches a crest that is only about 15 feet lower in elevation than the summit of Katahdin itself. From here the ridge begins to descend and becomes much more difficult to navigate. The trail occasionally narrows, and at times you will have to cross sections of rock that are only about 4 feet wide, with dizzying drop-offs on either side. Many sections of trail here will require you to move forward on all fours, using handholds either for balance or leverage. During the final section of the Knife Edge, the way forward begins to resemble a climb more than a hike. Taller hikers will find this portion more manageable than shorter hikers; there are several maneuvers that necessitate pulling yourself up by your hands, with feet loosely braced against the rock face for leverage. The final challenge on the Knife Edge trail is the Chimney, a notch in the ridge that will send you down a 40-foot vertical scramble, then right back up again.

After the Chimney you have conquered the most challenging portion of the trail—indeed, you have completed one of the most challenging sections of trail in America. Above the Chimney, at 6.9 miles, you will come to Pamola Peak at 4,919 feet elevation. From here you will take the Helon Taylor Trail to your right. Look for the cairns marking the path downhill.

While the narrow ridge walk is over, the trail down from Pamola Peak navigates the exposed, rocky flank of the mountain, and the trail still requires careful concentration. This portion of the hike also involves rock hopping and light scrambling. After about a mile you will return to the tree line.

Below the tree line the trail remains rocky, with difficult footing, especially when wet. At 9.8 miles your path will intersect with the Chimney Pond Trail once again. Turn right and hike the short distance back to the ranger station and the parking area.

PLANNING

If you're hiking for the day and not staying at the park overnight, there are multiple trailheads at which to park and begin the hike, all of which require online reservations (parking areas are capped at a certain number of vehicles). Maine residents can reserve a spot anytime after April 1, nonresidents up to two weeks before the hike. Reservations must be presented at the entrance gate on the morning of your hike. They are held until only 7 a.m., so plan on arriving early and waiting in a line of cars during peak season.

Due to the park's remote location, the duration and intensity of this hike, and the reservation system used for day hikers, most visitors to Baxter State Park will likely find it easier to simply camp in the park for several days. This is recommended not only for purposes of practicality:

Chimney Pond in autumn

Baxter is a gorgeous park, offering many more trails and stunning views than just Katahdin itself. In addition, given the unpredictable weather that often descends upon Katahdin's summit, it is best to have several options for days to make your ascent.

The entrance fee to Baxter State Park is $15. A variety of camping options are available, from tent sites to lean-to's to cabins, at reasonable rates.

GETTING THERE

The trailhead can be found on Google Maps by navigating to "Roaring Brook Campground." The parking area is at the end of Roaring Brook Road, about 8 miles northeast of the Togue Pond Gatehouse park entrance.

The author at Oregon's Mount Hood

ACKNOWLEDGMENTS

Countryman has now seen me through three hiking guides, and each one has been a wonderful experience, both in the research (getting to hike and writing a book about it!) and editing phases. Many thanks to Róisín Cameron, Michael Tizzano, and the rest of the wonderful Countryman team for their incredible work on the whole 50 Hikes series as well as this adventurous new book. I have wanted to be a writer my entire life, but never did I consider that any book project would be as exciting in the making as *America's Best Day Hikes*.

Of course, without knowledgeable and passionate people fighting to preserve our wilderness areas, the rest of us wouldn't be able to casually enjoy hiking trails like these at all. As always, utmost thanks to those who work tirelessly to preserve and protect our parks and wild lands.

I certainly do not claim to have authoritative knowledge of every hiking trail in America, and so a great deal of research was required in assembling this book. While in the research phase of this project, I reached out to a number of other hikers and landscape photographers to gather a variety of opinions on the most notable day hikes in the country. Below is a list of those who were kind enough to provide suggestions, feedback, and even companionship on the trail. Some are friends and family, but most are simply passionate hikers kind enough to take the time out of their day to respond to a random email from a stranger. Many, many thanks to the following individuals for their assistance in making this book possible: Mitchell Andrew, John-Anthony Gargiulo, Keriann Bartley, Chris Bennett, Zach Bright, Chris Carver, Matthew Cathcart, Andrea Ebur, Dan Elis, Christian DeBenedetti, Lena DeLeo, Garth Dellinger, Graham Dellinger, Lorrie Dellinger, Becky Fajardo, Ashley Farlow, Bonny Fleming, Ben Ganon, Alex Gwin, James Hardman, Brandon Hayes, Hutch Kugeman, Eva Larson, Jeff Makuta, Max McClaskie, Merritt McKinney, Corey McMullen, Melanie Miller, Katie Moon, Andrew Pinnella, Justin Potter, Jack Roberts, Josh Robert, Ben Smith, Dana Marion Smith, Will Swann, Alex Samson-Rickert, Chaney Swiney, Emily Tarr, Gillian Turcotte, and Christian Weber.

Island Lake, Colorado

INDEX